The
Oral-Style
South African Short
in English

Cross / Cultures

Readings in the Post/Colonial Literatures in English

37

Series Editors:

Gordon
Collier
(Giessen)

Hena
Maes-Jelinek
(Liège)

Geoffrey
Davis
(Aachen)

Amsterdam - Atlanta, GA 1999

The
Oral-Style
South African Short Story
in English

A.W. Drayson to H.C. Bosman

Craig MacKenzie

∞ The paper on which this book is printed meets the requirements of "ISO 9706:1994, Information and documentation - Paper for documents - Requirements for permanence".

ISBN: 90-420-0527-0 (bound)
©Editions Rodopi B.V., Amsterdam - Atlanta, GA 1999
Printed in The Netherlands

Table of Contents

Preface

ɢ ──────────

THIS STUDY IS CONCERNED WITH a certain tradition or sub-genre of South African short story – what I have termed the 'oral-style story.' The introduction explores the defining characteristics of this kind of story in some detail; suffice it to say here that the oral-style story evinces in its narrative structure and general ambience an affinity with oral narrative modes. Some of the other terms which are used to describe this kind of story are fireside tale, tall tale, yarn, *skaz* narrative, and frame narrative. As can be gauged by the range of this terminology, the kind of story with which this study is concerned can take many forms: it can be merely a short anecdote recounted by an internal narrator[1] and reported by a frame narrator; it can also be a lengthy and complex story-form employing many narrators; even more advanced varieties can include layers of irony and ironic interplay between the various narrators in the story.

The oral-style story constitutes a small part of the very extensive body of South African short stories, but it is significant: the nineteenth century was in fact dominated by this kind of story. It has received very little attention, however, and this alone warrants the present study.

This investigation is primarily concerned with the period from the 1860s to the 1950s, and explores the development of the oral-style story from A.W. Drayson's fireside tales in 1862 to Bosman's bushveld stories of the 1930s, 1940s and 1950s. As will be pointed out, the oral-style

---

[1] Throughout this study the term 'internal narrator' will be used to describe a narrator who tells a story within an 'outer' narrative frame. This outer narrative frame is usually established by a frame narrator who 'reports' the internal narrator's tale. Other terms which are occasionally used here to describe the internal narrator are 'intradiegetic narrator,' 'fictional narrator,' or 'storyteller figure.' In the sense in which it is used here, the internal narrator is not to be confused with a narrator whose internal monologue (or 'interior' style of narration) is employed by an author. This latter style of narration is not of concern to this study.

story in South Africa – indeed, the short story as a genre – goes back a lot further than is generally acknowledged. Examples of this style of story appeared in Cape periodicals as early as 1848. The first collection of such stories to appear in print, however, was A.W. Drayson's *Tales at the Outspan* (1862); this collection of fireside tales is therefore used here as a point of departure. Stories by Frederick Boyle and Joseph Forsyth Ingram are also looked at briefly before the more recognized short-story writers of the late nineteenth century are examined.

The first of these is William Charles Scully, many of whose stories reflect his interest in, and his attempts to capture, aspects of Nguni oral culture. Stories from his three collections, *Kafir Stories* (1895), *The White Hecatomb* (1897) and *By Veldt and Kopje* (1907), will be looked at and one story in particular discussed in detail. Sir Percy FitzPatrick's collection of stories, *The Outspan* (1897), also receives attention here, as the title-story employs a fictional narrator and evokes the fireside ambience of the oral tale.

Ernest Glanville's *Tales from the Veld* (1897) is the first example in South African literature of a sequence of stories employing a fictional narrator – the memorable old yarnster "Uncle Abe Pike." It will be argued that, despite the weight of influence from the American yarn tradition (which manifests itself chiefly in the style and humour employed by Glanville), this writer nonetheless plays a significant role in the development of the South African oral-style story.

Perceval Gibbon raised the fireside-tale genre to new heights in his collection of stories *The Vrouw Grobelaar's Leading Cases* (1905). In comparison with Scully and FitzPatrick, Gibbon demonstrates a far greater skill with literary artifice and the art of storytelling, and this technical skill is accompanied by a more complex social vision. Gibbon also uses his storyteller figure – the redoubtable Vrouw Grobelaar – in a sustained manner, and this suggests that he had found a successful formula that he could use repeatedly. In this, Gibbon anticipates Bosman's *Mafeking Road* (first published in 1947), the latter representing the peak in the popularity of the story cast in the oral style and there-fore forming the centrepiece of this study.

Stories by Francis Carey Slater, Pauline Smith, and Aegidius Jean Blignaut will also be examined as precursors to Bosman. Each of these writers anticipates Bosman in different ways and they all thus possess significance for this study.

The last chapter, dealing with the period from the 1950s to the present, briefly explores the use of various aspects of oral culture in short stories by black writers. Writers examined include R.R.R. Dhlomo, A.C. Jordan, Bessie Head, Mtutuzeli Matshoba, and Njabulo Ndebele.

No full-length general work on the South African short story has yet been published, and it is perhaps the sheer volume and diversity of South African short stories that has discouraged such a project. The heterogeneity of this corpus of work threatens to reduce a survey study to superficial and symptomatic readings of works, where discontinuities prevail over the tracing of connections and trends. As the outline above indicates, this study has therefore concerned itself with a certain style of story – that which reveals in its narrative structure and content some relation to oral narrative modes.

Clearly, the criteria of selection applied mean that at least two-thirds of South African short stories fall outside the purview of this book. No attempt will be made, in other words, to cover a representative range of South African short-story writers. There will be scant mention of Paton, Gordimer, Mphahlele, Wilhelm, Roberts, Jacobson, Hope, Essop – to name but a few. The discussion will be confined to those writers who style themselves "storytellers," who claim (implicitly or overtly) some relationship or affinity with oral storytelling.

My grateful thanks are due to Malvern van Wyk Smith for his expert advice and guidance and to Stephen Gray for inspiring me with his work on Bosman and South African literary historiography. To my wife, Sue, and children, Daniel, Matthew and Jessica, I owe an enormous debt of gratitude for enduring my absence in the years it took to complete this study.

1 Introduction
The Oral-Style Story

✎ ──────────────────────────────

T HE POINT OF DEPARTURE TAKEN HERE is the notion that, in the diachronic view of human history, writing (hence written literature) was preceded by many thousands of years of cultural life rooted in oral discourse. By way of preliminary definition, 'oral discourse,' or 'orality,' may be taken here to mean the kind of social exchange uttered in spoken words, a mode of cultural interaction transacted by word of mouth in which one generation hands on to the next a body of lore – tales, proverbs and maxims – without the intervention of the technology of writing. This kind of cultural interaction takes place preeminently in what Walter J. Ong refers to as "primary oral cultures," which he defines as "cultures with no knowledge at all of writing" (1982: 1), but it may coexist alongside new, literary forms of cultural expression. It may also – and this is the area of particular interest in this study – exist as a trope within literary works.

Ong argues that the "psychodynamics of writing matured very slowly in narrative" (1982: 103). By this he is alluding to the obstinacy of what he calls "oral residue," the elements of orality rooted so deeply in the human unconscious that they continue to influence patterns of thought and expression long after the advent of literacy. Literature itself has been witness to the resilience of residual orality. Ong cites the dialogues of Socrates and his listeners as an example from classical times of an oral setting being rendered in written literature. Later, Boccaccio and Chaucer provided the reader with literature framed as storytelling events so that, says Ong, "the reader can pretend to be one of the listening company" (103). The point here is that, even among fully literate people, oral modes of thought and expression continued to exert an influence. Oral storytelling settings were frequently re-created in written literature, and Boccaccio and Chaucer are but two examples of this.

What, then, is the purpose of invoking an oral milieu in relation to the stories I shall discuss in this study? To return to the point above: modes of cultural interaction which have their origin in a social context in which oral discourse prevails may come to exist as tropes within written discourse. One of the most important of these elements is that referred to by Ong in relation to Chaucer and Boccaccio: the re-creation, within a literary context, of an oral storytelling setting. The principal manner in which this is achieved is by the introduction of a storyteller figure (fictional narrator) who narrates the story. This device has, of course, become an established literary convention (two famous examples of this in modern literature are Mark Twain's seminal 1865 story "The Celebrated Jumping Frog of Calaveras County" and Joseph Conrad's novella *Heart of Darkness*, first published in 1902). Its use in stories by the writers examined here probably testifies as much to the weight of literary influence as to the predominance of oral milieux in nineteenth-century and early-twentieth-century South Africa. (Bosman, for example, was possibly indebted for his bushveld stories as much to the American yarnster tradition of Mark Twain and Bret Harte as to the immediate social context of the Marico.) Nonetheless, it is not simply fortuitous that nearly all of the stories examined in this study employ fictional narrators who 'tell' their stories to an implied audience; or, if they do not overtly employ such a figure, contain elements which evoke in other ways forms of oral discourse.

This prompts the question that is at the centre of this study: why did this kind of story have such currency in South Africa for nearly a hundred years from the middle of the nineteenth century? Other questions arise: what are the various ways in which oral forms have been appropriated and deployed in written stories? Are there continuities ('traditions') to be traced in the oral-style story? Were there periods in which this kind of story was popular and others in which it was in decline? Are there crucial differences in the ways in which black and white South African writers have used oral forms? And what has been the fate of this kind of story?

A question which frequently arises in this context – and which needs to be dispensed with immediately – is whether it is appropriate to subject 'oral-derived' texts to the same techniques of analysis as those used to interpret works of literature. It is not my purpose here to interrogate this old chestnut of orality–literacy studies. Since this study deals explicitly with written literature (as opposed to oral art), the whole debate about the appropriateness of critical approach is simply not relevant. Works which may take the form of the written word but which are oral-derived in the sense that they were first performed and only later captured in writing are not my concern here. It is probably more accurate to speak of a spectrum or continuum ranging from oral performances to written works, with many texts poised in-between in varying degrees of indeterminacy; but it would be an error for me to assign anything but (written) literary status to the works examined here.

— Ω —

My focus, then, is on a selection of South African short stories in English: principally, works by A.W. Drayson, W.C. Scully, Percy Fitz-Patrick, Ernest Glanville, Perceval Gibbon, Francis Carey Slater, Pauline Smith, Aegidius Jean Blignaut and, most important of all, Herman Charles Bosman. Although a mere fraction of the corpus of South African short stories in English, the stories of these writers exemplify a significant – and largely unexplored – narrational tendency: they all adopt, in various ways and in varying degrees, an 'oral style.'

As it is the burden of this study to examine examples of this style of story in detail, a preliminary definition will have to suffice here. In this context, the word 'style' refers to a certain manner or mode of expression that characterizes a body of writing, while 'oral' implies that this mode of expression has some sort of kinship with cultural interaction transacted by word of mouth. Taken as a whole, then, the term refers to the kind of story that simulates the dynamics of the spoken word on the printed page.

In a sense, virtually all stories (all narratives, for that matter) can claim kinship with oral forms. There are very few stories that do not employ dialogue, for example; and surely dialogue can be understood as an attempt to represent the spoken word on the printed page?

Clearly, I intend more than this with the term 'oral style.' Perhaps another way of approaching the issue is to ask how the stories I have selected are to be distinguished from others in the larger corpus of South African short stories.

The key lies in the second term of the phrase ('style'). The principal manner or mode of expression of the 'oral-style' story turns on the presence of a fictional narrator and his or her speaking voice in the story. Again, most stories contain characters who 'narrate,' to a greater or lesser extent, their lives, those of others, and certain incidents and events central to the story. What distinguishes the oral-style story narratologically, however, is the central status assigned to such a character. The fictional narrator in the oral-style story is the pivotal narrative and narrational device; he or she is the 'voice' through which the story is mediated.

Other important implications of using the fictional narrator will be discussed below; for the moment, however, I wish to address just one of these – the introduction of simulated 'speech,' or the 'voice' of the narrator, into the written story. A useful way of discussing this deploy-ment of oral discourse within written literature is provided by the Russian term *skaz*.

The Russian Formalist Boris Eichenbaum used the term *skaz* to describe literature which has "an orientation toward the oral form of narration" (quoted in Bakhtin 1984: 191). Elsewhere he discusses *skaz* in the following terms:

> By *skaz* I mean that form of narrative prose which, in its lexicon, syntax and selection of intonations, reveals an orientation toward the oral speech of a narrator [...] a form which fundamentally departs from written discourse and makes the narrator as such a real personage [...] It signalizes, on the one hand, a shift of centre of gravity from the fable to the verbal fabric (and by that same token, from the 'hero' to the telling of this or that happening, incident, etc.) and, on the other, liberation from the traditions connected with the culture of the printed word and a return to oral living language. (Eichenbaum 1994: 87–88)[1]

---

[1] This quotation comes from one of the translator's notes in Eichenbaum's "O. Henry and the Theory of the Short Story," in Charles E. May's *The New Short Story Theories* (see Eichenbaum 1994). The original article in which it appeared and from

The *skaz* narrative, Eichenbaum is arguing, employs a special vocabulary, word ordering, and set of verbal inflections that textually represent the presence of a narrator. As I remarked above, there must be very few stories indeed which do not employ such techniques to some degree. The implication in Eichenbaum's formulation, however, is that in the *skaz* narrative such techniques are the actual mode in which the story is presented and are therefore central to the way the story is constituted.

Eichenbaum's additional remarks about the distinctions between the *skaz* story and other narrative forms are both illuminating and problematic, hence invite closer scrutiny here. The *skaz* narrative, he says above, "fundamentally departs from written discourse and makes the narrator as such a real personage." In a sense, this statement is totally unhelpful. The *skaz* narrative does not depart at all from written discourse: it is one convention among many others which make up the range of written discourse. The *illusion* is created that we are hearing rather than reading a story, but the *skaz* narrative is as 'literary' as any other narrative mode to be found in written literature.

More helpful is his statement that the form "signalizes [...] a shift of centre of gravity from the fable to the verbal fabric" – that the *events* of the story, in other words, surrender pride of place to the *recounting* of such events. It is worthwhile recalling here Tony Bennett's very useful formulation of the conventions employed in what he calls the "classical canons of novelistic realism." These latter, he argues, "convey the illusion that they are literal transcriptions of reality, forms in which, as it were, reality writes itself" (1979: 24). By contrast, in the *skaz* narrative the *telling* of the events in the story is foregrounded, allowing very little sustenance for the illusion that reality is somehow being presented in an unmediated way. As we shall see with some of Bosman's later stories, this feature of *skaz* narratives makes them inherently predisposed to metafictional play, to the literary selfconsciousness more commonly associated with modernist and postmodernist texts.

Eichenbaum's last point above: namely, that *skaz* narratives "signalize" a "liberation from the traditions connected with the culture of the printed word and a return to oral living language," is only partly

---

which it is translated here is Eichenbaum's "Leskov and Contemporary Prose," first published in Russian in 1926.

accurate. In the sense that such narratives revitalize and bring alive the cadences of spoken language within the written form, Eichenbaum is surely correct in identifying some sort of stylized "return to oral living language." However, certainly in the case of Leskov (whom Eichenbaum clearly has in mind here), the *skaz* narrative form is employed as a variant of written discourse – one that bears the traces of its oral provenance, to be sure, but one that is nonetheless merely a *convention* within written literature. Some of Leskov's stories are over a hundred pages in length, and the illusion that "oral living language" rather than written discourse is being employed is difficult to sustain.

Anne Banfield has offered a useful interpretation of the Formalist use of the term. She argues that for the Russian Formalists a tale in *skaz* was not accurately to be labelled 'oral' but was, rather, to be considered a "written, literary imitation of a discourse" (1982: 171–72). She herself defines *skaz* as "a kind of first person narrative which takes the form of discourse and is distinct from classic first person narratives like *David Copperfield* or *A la Recherche du temps perdu*" (171). In conventional first-person narratives, "a narrator narrates, but addresses the story to no one," whereas in *skaz*, according to Banfield, "the first person addresses a second and the story is told formally as a communication" (171). This has important implications for the structure of the narrative: the fictional narrator in *skaz* narratives, says Banfield, "addresses the tale to some audience, whose presence is linguistically reflected in the tale itself" (172); the "I–you" relationship, in other words, bestows its "communicative structure" on the narrative (177).

Two important points emerge from Banfield's discussion. The first is the notion that the *skaz* narrative is not, strictly speaking, 'oral,' but rather a "written, literary imitation of a discourse." Here Banfield rightly emphasizes the distinction that should be maintained between oral and written narrative forms. Written stories which make extensive structural use of oral discourse remain, indisputably, written works. They merely attempt to *imitate* – or, more accurately, *transpose* – elements of oral discourse in print. And, as I shall argue at greater length later, those stories in which oral discourse is the least slavishly reproduced – which, in other words, merely *stylize* oral discourse in a literary framework – are invariably those which are most successful on the printed page.

The second point is the notion of 'audience' in *skaz* narratives. Frequently, there is a 'fictional audience' to accompany the 'fictional narrator' of the story. This audience is usually composed of persons like the fictional narrator – fellow travellers around the evening camp-fire or in the country inn for the night, fellow farmers congregated on a farm stoep or at the village post office – and storyteller and audience often exchange roles. The audience, however, is also often constituted by a single person, a frame narrator who encounters someone with an interesting story to tell, and who then 'embeds' the story he hears in the circumstances in which he came to hear it. In yet another variant of 'audience,' characters are sometimes not explicitly identified as composing such an entity, yet the narrator tells the story as if he had an audience gathered around him (a good example of this is Conrad's *Lord Jim*).

This range of storyteller–audience relationships can be demonstrated by a brief look at the narrative structure of some of the stories that will be discussed in subsequent chapters of this study. In the stories by Drayson, Boyle, Ingram, Scully, and FitzPatrick, for example, a clearly identifiable audience and/or frame narrator is present, and the relationship between it and the fictional narrator is fairly simple and transparent. This is not the case in the stories of Gibbon and Bosman. In Gibbon's stories the first-person narrator is introduced in a gradual fashion as the story-cycle unfolds. However, having established the setting – the Vrouw herself, her extended family, and the social milieu – this persona withdraws and allows the storyteller to take centre-stage. In Bosman's case, the frame has almost disappeared altogether. Someone, of course, 'relays' Oom Schalk's stories to the reader, but this is to be deduced only from the narrative structure of the stories. Oom Schalk's manner of telling implies a listener or, more probably, a group of listeners, yet these listeners are not always textually represented. The opening passage of "The Love Potion" is a good example of this: "You mention the juba-plant (Oom Schalk Lourens said). Oh, yes, everybody in the Marico knows about the juba-plant" (1949: 57). This is an example of Banfield's "I–you" relationship set up by the narrative structure of the story. The "you" mentioned by Oom Schalk is an implied interlocutor (not the reader) who exists on the same ontological plane as the fictional narrator.

This issue will be taken up in greater detail later. The purpose of briefly addressing it here is to indicate something of the importance of the notion of 'audience' in discussions of oral-style narratives. I wish now to return to the debate about *skaz* narratives.

Mikhail Bakhtin took issue with Eichenbaum's definition of *skaz*, claiming that he missed the most important dimension of the literary device. For Bakhtin, an important distinction in *skaz* is to be drawn between the type which displays "an orientation toward the oral form of narration" (Eichenbaum's formulation) and the type which displays "an orientation toward another person's discourse" (1984: 192). The first case Bakhtin called "simple *skaz*," the second "parodistic *skaz*."

In simple *skaz*, no attempt is made to stylize another person's individual manner of speech for the sake of that 'foreign' discourse, the narrative is monologic in nature (in other words, direct authorial discourse prevails), and the narrative, according to Bakhtin, therefore "directly expresses the intention of the author" (191). He uses Turgenev's story "Andrei Kolosov" as an example of simple *skaz*: the story is narrated by an intelligent and literary man of Turgenev's own circle, and the implication is that Turgenev would have told the story in the same way himself.

Parodistic *skaz*, on the other hand, introduces a storyteller figure precisely because of the individual attributes, attitudes, and intonation that he or she brings to the story. These are distinct from the author's own voice and attitudes, and a dialogic structure is therefore set up in which the author's intention is 'refracted' through the storyteller's act of narration. Bakhtin uses the example of Nikolai Leskov to illustrate this form of *skaz*. Leskov, he argues, resorted to a narrator "largely for the sake of a socially foreign discourse and socially foreign worldview, and only secondarily for the sake of oral *skaz*" (192).

The importance for Bakhtin of his refinement of Eichenbaum's original formulation is that he is able to distinguish between monologic (single-voiced) and dialogic (double-voiced) narrative forms. Dialogic narratives are inherently more complex and introduce the possibility of irony and parody, qualities that Bakhtin valorizes.

As we shall see in this study, the Bakhtinian deployment of the original Formalist notion of *skaz* provides a useful way of analyzing stories which adopt an oral style. Very briefly, the argument that will be advanced later is that the potential for irony and parody is more fully realized in the stories of Gibbon and Bosman than in those of the earlier writers, and their stories are well-developed examples of, in Bakhtin's terms, "parodistic *skaz*." There are competing voices in the stories of Gibbon and Bosman, and the relationship in each case between the fictional narrator, the frame narrator and/or audience, and the implied author is mediated by layers of irony. This represents a more advanced use of the *skaz* narrative mode and indicates that both Gibbon and Bosman adopted a narrative form more suited to a critique of the communities they portray.

— Ω —

One of the principal arguments that will be developed in this study is that the South African short story in the period 1860–1950 was dominated by the oral-style tale, which typically took the form of the oral anecdote or frame narrative, and that this kind of story grew in sophistication with the passing years until it became 'artful' – at which point layers of irony and greater narrational complexity were introduced to the oral-style story. The 'artful' tale, best exemplified by Perceval Gibbon and Herman Charles Bosman, was itself gradually displaced by what may for the moment simply be called the 'modern short story,' which typically employed third-person narration, turned inwards on the psychological world of a central protagonist, and – in South Africa – most frequently explored, in graphic and realistic detail, the pain and anguish caused by iniquitous social and political policies.

There are actually two arguments here. The first (to be explored in detail in this study) pertains to the internal shift in the oral-style story itself – the shift from the 'artless' to the 'artful' oral-style story. An outline of this argument – using the notion of *skaz* – has been presented above. The second argument concerns the broader transition from oral tale to modern short story, which, in historical terms, occurs after the rise to prominence of the 'artful' oral-style story. As this study is not concerned with the South African short story *per se*, but rather with the sub-genre of the oral-style story, the modern South African short story, as exemplified by Plomer, Paton, Gordimer, Jacobson, Rive and others will not receive attention here. My chief concern in invoking the category of 'modern short story' is to distinguish this from what I have called the oral-style story, and to account for the decline of the latter.

In his entry on the short story in the *Companion to South African English Literature* (1986a), Ernest Pereira notes that the "transition from 'tale' or 'anecdote' to 'short story' in SA English fiction is a gradual one, and the pioneering origins of the orally transmitted 'tale' remain prominent in the titles, or persist in the story and the manner of its telling, well into the present century" (182). His necessarily brief entry does not pursue the reasons for, and the implications of, this transition, but he returns to this point in his longer article "Tall Tellers of Tales: Some Fictional Narrators and their Function in the South African Short Story in English" (1986b). Here he observes that the postwar generation of writers has produced no works employing fictional narrators of note, and that the contemporary period is dominated by the realist mode and the voice of protest. He then appeals for "a wider perspective, for a glance at a fictional world not easily accessible to the present-day reader, and at a literary tradition (or fictional strategy) which the present-day writer should at least be cognisant of" (106).

Pereira contrasts the 'tall tales' which are the primary focus of his article with the kind of story that came to dominate South African literature in the hands of Nadine Gordimer, Jack Cope, James Matthews, Sheila Roberts and others in the postwar period, and goes on to remark:

> That the post-war generation of writers has produced no such fictional narrators or settings worthy of their talents is indicative of a significant socio-economic change: what could be seen as the challenging diversity of South African society has become mere fragmentation, whereby communities – and even families – are divided and driven apart. The resources of satire and fantasy can seem pitifully inadequate, if not irrelevant, in a world where the absurd and unthinkable have become painful realities. (1986b: 106)

It is clear here that Pereira is tracing the same kind of social shift discussed by Walter Benjamin[2] in relation to nineteenth- and early-twentieth-century Europe: the drift from rural areas to the cities, the shift from labour-intensive to capital-intensive industry, and all of the

---

2 Walter Benjamin's influential essay, "The Storyteller: Reflections on the Works of Nikolai Leskov" (1973 [1936]), is discussed in the conclusion to this study.

social and psychological changes wrought in the human subject by this large-scale, irreversible historical transition.

As the title of his article indicates, Pereira is concerned primarily with the fictional narrator in South African literature, having taken his cue from two other critics whom he acknowledges. The first of these is Stephen Gray, who, in what is perhaps the earliest reference to a literary lineage in the oral-style story, notes that Oom Schalk Lourens "succeeds Gibbon's Vrouw Grobelaar and C.R. Prance's Tante Rebella as the backveld Boer humorist" (1979: 193). Here Gray is alluding to an entire tradition of storytelling in South African literature, a delineation which Pereira fleshes out in greater detail. A little later, in his Introduction to Aegidius Jean Blignaut's *Dead End Road* (1980), Lionel Abrahams – citing Gray's argument – explores the mutual influence of Blignaut and Herman Charles Bosman. Abrahams argues that Bosman, recently released from prison and embarking on a literary career with the memory of his spell in the Marico still fresh in his mind, was ripe for the influence of Blignaut's fictional narrator, Hottentot Ruiter. Abrahams's argument will be taken up in more detail later; I wish for the moment to stay with Pereira's work on the South African short story, as it is the only substantial attempt to explore aspects of what I have termed the 'oral-style' story.

In his article, Pereira begins by drawing a distinction between the "fictional narrator" and "[r]eal or reputed author–narrators" (1986b: 103). The latter, exemplified by Aesop and "blind Homer," merely provide a "traditionally accepted framework of reference, enabling the reader to identify the 'type' of story he is dealing with and relate it to its appropriate context" (103). There are also fictional narrators like Sinbad the Sailor or Uncle Remus who, remarks Pereira, "neither intrude upon nor challenge the supremacy of the stories they tell" (103).

By contrast, the use of the fictional narrator in literary (as opposed to oral or folkloristic) tradition introduces a more complex relationship between teller and tale. The literary use of a fictional narrator, says Pereira, "serves both as a 'masking device' – enabling the author to distance himself from the narrative – and as a means of recreating the situation and recapturing the ambience of the story-teller's direct and intimate contact with his audience" (103).

Pereira thus distinguishes the oral from the literary use of the storyteller and imputes a greater degree of complexity to the latter. In oral tradition there are only two principal narratological elements: the teller and the tale. In literary tradition, on the other hand, there are three: the author (or implied author), the fictional narrator, and the tale. Pereira uses Conrad's Marlow to demonstrate this greater complexity: "as narrator Marlow's own personality cannot be identified with that of the author, cannot be regarded merely as a 'framing device' for the story, and cannot be separated from the narrative which he not only presents, but is usually personally involved in" (103). He concludes:

> What we have here is a shift from a fairly straightforward and inarguable distinction between teller and tale [...] to an equally pronounced distinction between the author on the one hand and, on the the other, the fictional narrator through whom the story is mediated. (103)

Pereira then sketches the development of the South African short story from the 1890s to the present. Identifying verisimilitude, coherence, and immediacy of impact as the distinguishing features of the orally transmitted tale or personal anecdote, he notes that these can "conveniently be achieved by the introduction of a fictional narrator, and the pioneering short story in particular is characterized by the 'teller of tales' – whether grizzled prospector or backveld Boer, country midwife or dorp magistrate, tribal grandmother or transport rider" (105–106). The remainder of his essay is devoted to tracing some of the literary antecedents to Bosman's Oom Schalk Lourens noted in his entry in the *Companion*; his commentaries will be taken up in later chapters of this study.

Pereira's well-researched and perceptive article provides much of the groundwork for the present study. He outlines the broad tendency of the South African short story from 'tale' to 'modern short story' and points out some of the complexities in the literary use of the fictional narrator. He also identifies some of the hallmarks of the orally transmitted tale and discusses some key examples of written South African stories which redeploy these features in literary form. Finally, he identifies some important milestones in the development of the fictional narrator in South African literature which culminated in Bosman's Oom Schalk Lourens.

In which ways, then, does the present study build on the skeleton provided by Pereira? In the first place, the origins of the oral-style South African short story are traced back to the 1840s – some fifty years earlier than Pereira's earliest dates. Secondly, a theoretical model (based largely on the work of Bakhtin) is provided to analyze the intricacies in the development of this genre of story. In the third place, authors not discussed by Pereira are looked at and those he does discuss receive more detailed attention. Fourthly, an attempt is made in the last part of this study to chart some of the developments in the black short story which draws on oral art forms.

This last section will thus be dealing briefly with the 'post-Bosman' era and the rise of the black short story, and will trace tendencies that to some extent run contrary to those featuring in the main discussion. The development of the (overwhelmingly white) South African short story from its beginnings in the middle of the nineteenth century to the stage it has reached in the present day I have characterized very broadly as a progression from fireside tale to modern crafted short story. The tale, yarn, or anecdote that was spawned by the frontier lifestyle of the descendants of European settlers in Africa in the nineteenth century has, in other words, gradually given way to the modern short story in the received tradition as it evolved in America and Europe under Poe, Hawthorne, Gogol, and Chekhov.

When one turns to the black short story, however, this progression from fireside yarn to modern short story (which brings with it the decline of oral influence) is to some extent reversed: after an initial reliance on Western literary models in emergent black South African fiction in the late 1920s, many black writers sought increasingly to throw off Western influence and adopt African (and largely oral) cultural modes. As I shall argue later, however, the 'oral style' adopted by black short story writers is not, formally speaking, the same as that adopted by the white writers examined in the body of this study. The discussion of the intersection of oral and literary modes in the black South African short story is therefore not an integral part of my main argument, and instead takes the form of a Postscript.

The major focus of this study, then, is the South African oral-style story from its beginnings in the mid-nineteenth century to its most sophisticated and celebrated form in Bosman's Schalk Lourens stories of the 1930s through the 1950s. Bosman's oral-style stories are probably the best known in South African literature, but – apart from the (for the most part) cursory work done by a few critics (alluded to above) – very little attention has been paid to the literary antecedents of Oom Schalk Lourens. It is to address this lack that this study has chiefly been undertaken. Following identification and discussion of some of Schalk Lourens's progenitors, attention will be devoted to the internal shift in this style of story from its 'artless' form (Bakhtin's "simple *skaz*") to its more complex, 'artful' form ("parodistic *skaz*"). The study will conclude by examining some of the reasons for the decline of a style of story that dominated the South African short story for nearly a century.

—————   ℘ ℘   —————

2 The '*Ur*-South African' Oral-Style Story

A.W. Drayson, Frederick Boyle and J. Forsyth Ingram

༄ ────────────────────────────────

THE PURPOSE OF THIS CHAPTER IS TWOFOLD. First, a brief survey of the early South African short story will be undertaken in order to establish a larger literary context for the discussion to follow. This discussion constitutes the second (much longer) part of the chapter and will focus on writers whose work can be taken to represent the beginnings of the oral-style story in South African literature.

The writers whose work has been selected for discussion here – Drayson, Boyle, and Ingram – are also among a group of early short-story writers about whom very little is known, and this in itself warrants attention. The stories of Scully, FitzPatrick, Glanville, Gibbon, and Schreiner are frequently taken to represent the early South African short story, and it is surely important to give some cognizance to writers who precede them.

The Early South African Short Story

The earliest manifestations of the South African short story have not been fully acknowledged. In his pioneering survey of South African literature, Manfred Nathan actually remarks: "During the first three-quarters of the nineteenth century there was little, if any, production of fictional literature relating to South Africa" (1925: 200). Nathan then goes on to cite *Tales Written in Ladybrand* (1885) by Marguerite de

Fenton (Marguerite Mostyn Cleaver) as the earliest collection of South African tales.

Surveys of the South African short story typically commence with collections published in the 1880s. In her brief overview (1973: 74–78), Mary Morison Webster, noting that many of the early short-story writers were women, also lists *Tales Written in Ladybrand* as the earliest published collection of short stories about South Africa, followed by Mary Anne Carey–Hobson's *South African Stories* (1886) and Olive Schreiner's *Dreams* (1891). Webster does not make reference to collections which predate 1885. And in his entry on the short story in the *Companion to South African English Literature* (1986a: 181–82), Ernest Pereira's earliest listings are Schreiner's *Dreams*, Scully's *Kafir Stories* (1895), and Bryden's *Tales of South Africa* (1896).

Malvern van Wyk Smith's *Grounds of Contest* (1990) is more reliable. He lists R. Hodges's *The Settler in South Africa and Other Tales* (1860) and A.W. Drayson's *Tales at the Outspan, or Adventures in the Wild Regions of Southern Africa* (1862) as two of the earliest examples of collections of South African tales. Van Wyk Smith might also have added Frederick Boyle's *The Savage Life: A Second Series of Camp Notes* (1876) and his *On the Borderland* (1884) – two further examples of early collections not mentioned by either Webster or Pereira.

However, stories which appeared singly in early Cape periodicals occur still earlier than any of these collections.[1] One of the earliest of all

---

[1] It is worth noting here that Harriet Ward (*Five Years in Kaffirland*) and Jasper Lyle, authors of works published in the 1840s and 1850s, also published short prose reminiscences in this period. Most of these pieces appeared in *Bentley's Miscellany* and the *United Service Magazine*. One of them, "Emma, the Sailor Girl" (1850) – as is typical of the prose narratives of the period – purports to tell the tale of a real incident: "The following story is not merely 'founded' on fact – the chief incidents are literally true, and the scene is from nature" (Ward 1850: 384). However, no internal narrator is employed to tell the tale. Mrs Ward speaks in her 'own' voice, as the conclusion to the tale attests: "During the latter part of the Kafir war, in 1847, a little party, of which I was one, was brought into circumstances of difficulty [...]" (392).

Although many of the pieces are subtitled "A Tale of [...]," the narrator is recognizably an authorial one recounting 'sketches from life,' and in none of them is a frame-narrative structure employed. Ward's narratives therefore fall outside of the concerns of this study, although they do secure her place as one of the earliest woman writers of South Africa. (I am indebted to Valerie Letcher for providing me with information on this writer.)

South African stories is "Dirk van Splinter, a Legend of the Devil's Peak," which appeared in *The Cape of Good Hope Literary Magazine* in February 1848. The tale is prefaced by a note in which the author, "H. van Plaaks" (C.A. Fairbridge is the attribution made by the librarian at the South African Library), claims that the story was found in the journal of the Reverend Barendz Weiland, private chaplain to Jan van Riebeeck. The journal in question covers the period 1652–1659, so the date of the 'original' story (whether apocryphal or not) ostensibly falls into this period.

Another story which appeared in the same journal in April 1848 is the anonymously penned "My Uncle's Tale," a story remarkable for the times in its gentle debunking of the arrogance and jingoism that accompanied the British efforts in the Frontier Wars of the 1840s. The story takes the form of a cautionary anecdote told by an uncle to his naive nephew, who has enthusiastically enlisted in a volunteer force destined for the frontier.

R. Hodges's *The Settler in South Africa and Other Tales* (1860) can probably claim to be the first published collection of short stories about South Africa. However, it is remarkable only for its curiously bland, inconsequential descriptions of settler life at the Cape. It also employs a highly conventional narrative style and is therefore of no real interest to this study.

A.W. Drayson's *Tales at the Outspan, or Adventures in the Wild Regions of Southern Africa* (1862) is another early example of a prose work employing a recognizable short-story form and using local settings, characters, and themes in a sustained manner, but its narrative style is utterly unlike that employed by Hodges. The stories which make up the bulk of the text are fireside tales, and the text is therefore given central attention in this chapter, as it represents a story form – what I have called the 'oral-style' story – which is taken up and developed in the work of later, better-known writers.

Frederick Boyle's *The Savage Life* (1876) – aptly characterized by its subtitle ("Camp Notes") – typifies the generic indeterminacy of many nineteenth-century collections, which were frequently a miscellany of folk-history, frontier lore, autobiographical anecdotes, sketches, tales and legends, manifesting in their heterogeneity the unsettled tenor of the times. Only a third of the twenty-one pieces in *The Savage Life* deal with South Africa, while the others recount adventures in Borneo, Costa Rica, Nicaragua, the Gold Coast, and elsewhere. The story "My Kaffir Chawles" has been selected for discussion below, as it takes the form of a frame narrative and is therefore central to the question of the interpenetration of oral and literary forms.

The most significant feature of the stories produced by the woman writers of the period is – with one exception, noted below – their divergence in nature from the tales told by their male counterparts.

As noted in the various surveys already cited, Marguerite de Fenton's *Tales Written in Ladybrand* (1885) was perhaps the earliest collection of tales by a South African woman writer. The volume was also possibly the earliest collection of short stories to have found a local publisher (C. Borckenhagen in Bloemfontein). However, *pace* Manfred Nathan's remark that the period after the first Anglo-Boer War "belongs" to this work (1925: 201), de Fenton's sentimental fantasies have virtually nothing to do with South Africa, either in theme or setting, and it is entirely understandable why they have been consigned to literary oblivion.[2]

---

[2] De Fenton's "Faithful unto Death," for example, concerns the blind loyalty and selfless service that successive generations of members of the Jacobini family offer to Napoleon I and his successors. The story has a double narrative frame. An anonymous frame narrator recounts the narrative "found in the pocket of the young soldier, who wrote it and who died in Africa" (1885: 3). During "the Zulu war" (3), this nameless young soldier briefly encounters a fellow soldier by the name of Louis Joseph Jacobini, who, it transpires, has secretly devoted his life to the service of the "Prince Imperial" (Louis Napoleon's son). The anonymous young soldier reports that the Prince Imperial dies in Africa at the hands of the "black devils" (3), and, like his father and grandfather before him, the Prince's faithful and unacknowledged guardian, Louis Jacobini, dies brokenhearted, his life now meaningless.

As can perhaps be gauged from this synopsis, Africa has a very minor and inglorious role to play in this sentimentalized history. The greater part of the story concerns Napoleon I's campaigns in Europe and the life of Louis Napoleon, both of these figures shadowed "faithfully unto death" by members of the Jacobini family. With one exception, the other stories in this small collection – "The Old Harmonium," "The Daisy and the Butterfly," and "The Congress of the Winds" – have even less to do with South Africa, and take the form of facile allegories.

"Excelsior," the only other story that has some bearing on Africa, tells the story of a high-minded young clergyman who resolves to join the British troops fighting the Anglo-Zulu War with the words: "If I cannot fight I can at least exhort the fighting, and comfort the dying" (39). Seizing the British flag in the midst of a

Mary Ann Carey–Hobson's *South African Stories* (1886) is a more noteworthy early collection. In her Preface, Carey–Hobson classifies her collection as a "boy's book"[3] and as "'traveller's tales'" (5). She then goes on to express the hope that her tales "may interest those for whom they are intended, for it is my earnest desire that the rising generation may be attracted towards that country in which I have spent so much of my life" (5–6). And, indeed, the tales attempt to cover the spectrum of experience in South Africa: adventure, encounters with "Kaffirs" and Boers, animal stories, and other miscellanea typical of colonial South Africa. In their attempt to deal with the social texture of life in the Colony, albeit at a juvenile level, Carey–Hobson's tales are more rooted in the reality of nineteenth-century South African life than are those of her female contemporaries. This can perhaps be partly explained by her desire to "offer this little work to 'our boys,' knowing that they will at least find in it some true pictures of South African life" (5). The first story in the collection, entitled "How Piet the Bugler was Cured of Brandy Drinking," is worth mentioning here, as it takes the form of a frame narrative and employs an internal narrator.[4]

---

desperate encounter, he urges the outnumbered British soldiers on until they all succumb to "the savage foe" (40).

[3] The South African Library has actually catalogued *South African Stories* under juvenile literature.

[4] "How Piet the Bugler was Cured of Brandy Drinking" recounts the story of a Hottentot bugler attached to the Cape Mounted Rifles. Initially diligent and punctilious, Piet the bugler becomes very fond of brandy and falls asleep in a drunken stupor when out one day with a party collecting firewood. He awakes to find himself being carried off by a lion and only manages to escape by blowing his bugle and frightening off the beast. This incident, he later claims, cured him of his drinking problems: "'[T]he good Lord delivered me out of the lion's mouth, and the devil himself shan't tempt me to taste Cape smoke again!'" (17).

The story is told by an old Hottentot woman who periodically came to Fort Beaufort to visit the narrator's family: "Charlie, our big boy, liked the old woman, and always came to beg a long stick of 'Boer tobacco' for her; and then, after regaling her under the verandah at the back of the house with coffee and other comestibles, would make her tell him all sorts of wonderful stories about lions and tigers, etc." (10). Thus the familiar elements of the oral-style story are present here: an old and wise narrator, a congenial setting in which time is not of the essence, a receptive audience, and, of course, a 'tall tale' to tell.

Carey–Hobson's tale also conforms to the characteristics of the early oral-style story in two other respects: her tale is told principally to convey the atmosphere of Africa (an intention already spelled out in her Preface), and there is no sense that

Olive Schreiner's *Dreams* (1891) and *Dream Life and Real Life* (1893) are, unsurprisingly, infinitely more substantial and memorable than the narratives of her female contemporaries. However, despite their indubitably superior quality, Schreiner's stories maintain some continuity with those of de Fenton. Dreams, fantasies, and allegories play a significant role in her stories, in sharp contrast to the realism that is the dominant mode of the stories by male writers of the period.[5]

Another notable early collection is J. Forsyth Ingram's *The Story of a Gold Concession, and Other African Tales and Legends* (1893) which, along with de Fenton's work, is perhaps the only pre-1900 collection to have found a local publisher (W.H. Griffin of Pietermaritzburg), although it was printed in London. Ingram's book is discussed in some detail below because, in its concern to translate the oral lore of Africa into written form, it is a good example of a text positioned at the oral–literary interface.

In 1895, W.C. Scully published his first collection, *Kafir Stories*, and this was soon followed by another collection by him and also by works from the pen of FitzPatrick, Glanville, Gibbon and others. The South African short story had come of age, and the work of these writers is the subject of later chapters.

This very brief survey of some of the earliest South African short stories demonstrates the point that notions of linear continuity in

---

the two voices that are heard (those of the first-person frame narrator and her informant) are pulling in different directions. Indeed, the frame narrator concludes the story with the remark that although she has "not been able to tell the story in the old woman's words, as she spoke in the Hottentot–Dutch [...] I have given the substance of it, and I believe it to be a true story" (17). It is interesting to observe, then, that this tale conforms to the early oral-style tales of Drayson, Boyle, and Ingram, in that it deals with a highly improbable incident but nonetheless claims to be "a true story."

[5] In Schreiner's "Three Dreams in a Desert," for example, the narrator falls asleep under a mimosa tree and has three allegorical dreams about the subjugation of women and the path they must tread in order to achieve liberation from male domination. The 'real world' of the Karoo – the African plain, hot sun, and parched bushes briefly alluded to in the opening lines – is abandoned for the world of fantasy, where ideas triumph over the quotidian materiality of everyday life, a life the more attractive aspects of which would in any event be denied a woman growing up in the late nineteenth century. Dreaming presents the woman writer with the opportunity to transcend the stultifying, gender-defined roles assigned to her, and this informs the narrative style of the writing by de Fenton and Schreiner.

literary history, of evolution and steady development, are fictions constructed by critics who have the advantage of hindsight. The early South African short story is characterized by divergence and discontinuity, fragmentation and incongruity: fireside tale (Drayson) develops alongside allegorical fantasy (Schreiner), oral anecdote (Boyle) alongside introspective memoir (de Fenton).

It is with due caution, therefore, that I attempt to identify certain examples of 'oral-style' stories in the larger corpus of South African fiction. As should become clear, discontinuity often prevails over continuity in the South African short story, with pioneers of the form not always being aware of each other, and often drawing inspiration from literary sources beyond South Africa. From our present vantage-point it is possible to discern patterns and contours in South African literary history; however, I proceed with the awareness that the perception of such formations does not emerge from the body of literary works itself, but from critical constructs imposed after the event.

The Beginnings of the Oral-Style Story

As should be clear by now, stories by Drayson, Boyle, and Ingram have been selected for discussion here because – unlike the stories by their contemporaries Hodges, de Fenton, and Schreiner, for example – they all attempt to negotiate the interstices between oral and written narrative modes. The stories by Drayson, Boyle, and Ingram take the form of frame narratives in which are embedded tales told by various internal narrators. This feature of the writing is, of course, typical of the period, as Pereira (1986a: 182) and others have noted. However, no thoroughgoing attempt has been made to trace the fireside-tale genre to its earliest manifestations in South African literature – the chief purpose of this chapter.

It should be stressed at the outset that, strictly speaking, the stories by Drayson, Boyle, and Ingram are more accurately described as 'ur-South African' oral-style tales rather than as oral-style stories proper. They contain all of the principal constituents of the sub-genre – they employ an internal narrator (or set of narrators), are 'reported' by a frame narrator, and are set in an oral milieu (usually a campfire setting) – but they also possess some features which mark them off from what I have characterized as the 'artful' oral-style story, which really begins with Gibbon at the turn of the century. The oral-style story, as the word 'style' suggests, really comes into its own when the constitutive elements of the sub-genre are used merely as a conventional foil for the operation of destabilizing devices – when, in other words, the fireside-tale 'style' is affected in order to exploit in an ironic manner its conventional claims of 'authenticity.'

It should also immediately be pointed out, though, that frequently no clear dividing-line exists between what purports to be 'authentic' oral testimony and what is, on the other hand, clearly a fictional and conventional use of the oral narrative mode. Indeed, as we shall see in this chapter, part of the convention of the nineteenth-century oral-style tale is precisely the author's claim that he is being entirely truthful and accurate in his relaying of the 'original' oral narrative. Nevertheless, there is one clear textual signal that can alert the reader to the form of oral narrative he or she is dealing with: the presence of irony. This usually reveals itself as ironic interplay between the various levels in the narrative structure of the tale. There are at least three such levels in the oral-style story: the embedded tale itself; the frame containing it; and the (usually implied) attitude of the authorial persona. When the frame narrator 'reports' the internal narrator's story in a manner which implies that there is a discrepancy in their respective attitudes to the embedded tale, a degree of irony is present. Conversely, when the embedded tale is reported in a manner which does not set up such a dissonance between the narrative levels of the story, the oral-style tale is being used ingenuously rather than ironically.

The stories of the three writers discussed below belong to the 'ingenuous' category of oral-style tale. They employ the constitutive elements of the genre without exploiting their potential for irony. And this is why these stories provide an ideal point of departure for this study. In them can be seen the 'ur-elements' of the oral-style story, the early, incipient features providing the matrix for such stories.

A distinguishing feature of the 'ur-' or 'originative' nature of the tales by Drayson, Boyle, and Ingram is their generic indeterminacy. As the discussion will show, the stories of these writers are poised uncertainly between what are now considered to be distinct modes of writing: travelogue, oral testimony, history, anthropology – as well as fictional modes of writing. Drayson's collection is a kind of 'fabular travelogue,' with the tales told by various narrators being interspersed with notes and observations about travel and hunting. The tale by Boyle which has been selected for discussion below is a semi-fictionalized piece of oral testimony, while Ingram's stories are a blend of folkloristic research and fabulation. This generic indeterminacy is also a sign of the immaturity of these precursors to the oral-style tale proper. In its rough and indeterminate shape, the early oral-style story ranged over a spectrum of generic modes – chiefly those listed above – before settling into a more conventional form in the hands of Glanville and Gibbon at the turn of the century.

While the stories by Drayson, Boyle, and Ingram display different facets of the generic indeterminacy of writing in the period, they will also be shown to display certain common characteristics. The most conspicuous of these is their stock claim of 'authenticity.' They all claim to present "the plain truth," and to eschew fabulation and fictionality – even when these qualities are palpably present in the tales. Accordingly, the tales of the putative internal narrators (the 'authentic' oral informants) are relayed in an ingenuous fashion. In none of the stories selected for discussion here is there any attempt to create any distance between the frame narrator and the various internal narrators whose stories are relayed. Irony and subversion, it will be argued, were clearly not the purpose of stories of this period.

What the stories share, instead, is a fairly straightforward desire to impart something of the redolence and texture of African life to a largely metropolitan audience. The voices of the various narrators are therefore used to 'speak Africa,' and the complicating factors of mediation, translation, and transposition are barely addressed. What is posited instead (either implicitly or explicitly) is the notion that what is carried over from oral anecdote or testimony to the written form and a literary audience is the 'truth,' although this may often be more the larger 'truth of life' than the narrow literal truth. Hence the fictional dimension of the stories (and they are often fictional to the point of being incredible) is suppressed in favour of what the writers in their various ways all claim to be the plain telling of events as they encountered them, or the faithful re-telling of such by their informants. Clearly, the early oral-style story shared a great deal with the early travel literature of Africa: its primary purpose was not so much to construct artful, elaborate fictions, replete with fully rounded characters, as to convey something of the authentic 'spirit of Africa.'

A.W. Drayson

A.W. Drayson's *Tales at the Outspan, or Adventures in the Wild Regions of Southern Africa* (1862) is probably South Africa's first collection of fireside tales.[6] However, the book has received little or no critical attention and, unlike the later nineteenth-century writers Percy FitzPatrick and W.C. Scully, selections of whose stories have been reissued in recent years,[7] Drayson's tales have long been out of print and have dropped from view entirely.

It is not difficult to see why. *Tales at the Outspan* is in many ways unmemorable: the themes with which it deals are unexceptional, its pace is ponderous, its subject-matter predictable. Of course, this is interesting in itself: as an archetypal colonial text, treating an encounter with Africa in a way entirely consonant with the age, its very typicality commends the text to the attention of the modern critic. It is possible, in other words, to measure the distance the South African short story has travelled in ideological terms when one uses an early text like *Tales at the Outspan* as a point of departure.

However, the main area of interest here is the narrative structure of *Tales at the Outspan*: in its use of a frame narrator and a set of internal

---

[6] One would need immediately to qualify such a statement. Captain Alfred Wilks Drayson (1827–1901) was an English sojourner in South Africa, and the author of many travelogues about the region (see his *Sporting Scenes amongst the Kaffirs of South Africa* [1858]; *Among the Zulus; the Adventures of Hans Sterk, South African Hunter and Pioneer* [1879]; and *The Diamond Hunters of South Africa* [1889]). He was by no means a "South African writer" in the contemporary sense of someone who is a South African by nationality or domicile. However, his numerous books about South Africa reveal his knowledge of the region, and in *Tales at the Outspan* he sets most of his tales in South Africa and employs South African themes and characters.

[7] A selection of Scully's tales, *Transkei Stories*, edited by Jean Marquard, was released by David Philip in 1984. FitzPatrick's *The Outspan*, which originally appeared in 1897, was re-issued by Lowry in 1987. The title-story of FitzPatrick's collection is another example of the outspan genre in South African literature. Earlier examples are provided in the poems "The Bechuana Boy" and "The Forester of the Neutral Ground" by Thomas Pringle (Pereira & Chapman 1989: 3–7; 58–61). However, Drayson's tales are among the earliest fictional examples of the genre.

narrators who 'tell' the stories, it is a prototypical example of a collection of what I have called 'oral-style' stories.

The stories which make up the bulk of *Tales at the Outspan* are framed by a narrative in the form of a travelogue in which details of the journey from London to the Cape and observations about life in the colony are provided. The opening passages of the text are worth quoting in full, as they express very clearly attitudes and orientations which are typical of the literature of the period, but which one seldom encounters in so compressed a form:

> The regions amidst which the events occurred related in some of the following tales [sic], lie far away in the other hemisphere. They are many thousand miles distant from our own civilized land, and are rarely visited by any traveller who, whilst capable of attuning himself to the life in the desert, is at the same time able to appreciate the advantages, and to perceive the drawbacks, which attend the progress of civilization.
>
> There is usually a great gulf between the natural resident of the wild plains or forests, and the inhabitant of the city and town; there are scarcely any ideas in common between them, and the amusements or occupations of each would be distasteful to the other. There is, however, usually considerable curiosity to hear or read of the habits and manners of each other. Whilst the civilized man is lost in amazement when he hears that there are beings apparently formed like himself, to whom war against dangerous wild beasts is the most interesting occupation of life, the denizen of the wilderness is no less puzzled when he learns that there are men whose sole enjoyment consists in accumulating money amidst the foul, smoky atmosphere of some crowded thoroughfare, or in passing their days and greater part of their nights lounging or talking in crammed and heated saloons. (1862: 1–2)

Drayson's unselfconscious use of the notion of "the other hemisphere" which is "many thousand miles distant from our own civilized land" immediately identifies a centre and a periphery, as well as an implied audience. Civilization is then readily invoked to characterize the metropolitan centre, and savagery or barbarism will soon follow as descriptions of "the other hemisphere" – also called the "desert."[8]

---

[8] "Desert" is clearly used here in the sense of a wilderness, an uninhabited and uncultivated tract of country, rather than in the sense of a barren, treeless and waterless region, which is the more common modern usage.

Despite setting up these oppositions, the passage quoted above appears also to propose the idea of cultural relativity and thus suggests a sense of balance, of detachment, on Drayson's part. Civilized man's amazement when he hears about the life-style of "the natural resident of the wild plains" is balanced by the latter's puzzlement when he learns about men living in "the foul, smoky atmosphere of some crowded thoroughfare," or about their activities in "crammed and heated saloons." As we shall see, however, this posture of cultural relativity will soon be undermined by Drayson's derogatory descriptions of the local inhabitants of South Africa.

Drayson extends an invitation to any interested party – lovers of nature, or those curious about the activities of other Europeans in exotic regions, or "brother travellers" wishing to rekindle old memories – to "journey with us" to a "far distant country" (2). Thus the convention established is that of a party of kindred spirits journeying into unknown territories. Accordingly, the story is told in the present tense, as if the members of the party were witnessing events as they unfold:

> Let us now step on board one of those beautiful fabrics which we may daily and hourly see passing down the muddy waters of the Thames and being conducted to the more open sea, where it is capable of showing its power in combating the elements. (2)

Thus, as in Conrad's *Heart of Darkness*, the Thames is the origin of this journey, and its metaphorical dimensions are also explicitly evoked.[9] It has trapped – "crowded upon" (3) – the ship, the latter being but "an emblem of many a man whose true value has never yet been known" (2). The "wider ocean of life" (3), then, offers the space required for man to explore his unrealized potential. By implication, Africa, which lies beyond the wider ocean, represents still greater possibilities for exploring this potential. Significantly, the ship (metaphorically denoting unfulfilled man) strains towards Africa "like a fresh, highly-bred hunter" (3).

The rest of the opening narrative describes the journey to Africa, the arrival at the Cape, and the trek into the hinterland. At the Cape the

---

[9] Conrad's use of the Thames as a fictional motif is very unlikely to have had anything to do with Drayson's work, but this coincidence does raise the interesting issue – too substantial to go into here – of the origins of the motif and its popularity in this period.

ship is exchanged for the ox-wagon, and the first of the "natural residents" of Africa is encountered and unflatteringly described:

> The captain of this craft is the pigmy Hottentot, whose small deep-set eyes are nearly concealed by his high cheek-bones, whose nose is but two openings in his face, and whose protruding lips indicate that he is, as some believe, very closely allied to the "origin of our species." (10)[10]

Shortly afterward, the teeming game of Africa is sighted, and it is not accidental that the human and animal species of Africa are brought into close juxtaposition. Hunting the large game, we read, provides "many a narrow escape or thrilling adventure" (13); likewise, the "forays of the Kaffirs and Bushmen" have yielded "many exciting incidents well worthy of record" (13).

It is worth noting here that when the Hottentot driver sights the first game seen on the expedition, Drayson quotes: "'Tis 'The Zebra wantonly tossing his mane, / In fields seldom freshen'd by moisture or rain'" (11). Drayson is quoting from the first version of Pringle's "Afar in the Desert," which appeared in this form in the *South African Journal* in 1824 and in the *Wesleyan Methodist Magazine* in 1825.[11] It is significant that he draws upon a literary source to give expression to his first sighting of African game. It is also interesting to note that in his later descriptions of Africa's teeming game, Drayson again appears to draw on Pringle's lyrical descriptions in "Afar in the Desert." Several of the animals (eland, hartebeest, oribi, rhinoceros, antelope) reappear, and where Pringle's rhinoceros "wallows at will" (Pereira & Chapman 1989: 81), Drayson's hippopotamus "wallows in his still pool" (12). Pringle

---

[10] The reference to Darwin is, of course, a contemporary one, Darwin's *The Origin of Species* having appeared in 1859 – a mere three years before *Tales at the Outspan*. Drayson's comment reveals his adherence to the tenets of what became known as "Social Darwinism," the chief feature of which was the notion that only the fittest species would prevail. In their useful survey of Social Darwinism, Leroy Vail and Landeg White argue that this notion "was especially welcome to the energetic racists of the later nineteenth century, for it justified the imperial expansion upon which they were then embarked, and it soon came to be one of the key intellectual assumptions of educated Westerners both in Europe and in America" (1991: 3–4). Drayson's cast of mind as manifested in *Tales at the Outspan* is an excellent early example of this tendency abroad in Africa.

[11] This information is drawn from Pereira & Chapman's *African Poems of Thomas Pringle* (1989).

has an elephant browsing near "grey forests o'ergrown with wild vine" (81), and Drayson also describes a forest which has "graceful festoons of wild vine" (35), in which elephants are hidden. These intertextual details suggest that Drayson may be describing a southern Africa which has already been constituted in literary discourse.

This is ironic in view of Drayson's later claims of eschewing literary sources in favour of 'authentic,' first-hand ones. The opening section ends with the observation that the "narrow escapes," the "thrilling adventure" and the "forays of the Kaffirs and Bushmen" (13) alluded to have become so vague with the passage of time, so removed from the context in which they occurred, that "the far-off land of the Cape is even now almost a *terra incognita* to the lover of tales of adventure, or to the devotee of light reading" (13). Having established the unreliability of such sources of information, Drayson concludes by making a case for "a few years' residence" in the country, where the writer of "tales of adventure" will find no need to "draw on his imagination, nor invent characters to enable him to fill volumes, but need merely relate those anecdotes which have been communicated to him over the bivouac fire" (13). (This remark, of course, forms a perfect prelude to the remainder of the book, which is largely composed of such tales.)

Having thus established the 'authority' of his own literary venture, Drayson offers a general description of the purpose of an outspan,[12] how hunters find their way to it after a day's hunting, and a detailed description of the ox-wagon. What then follows is a description of the "human attendants at the outspan" (18). The "Fingoes," "Kaffirs," "Hottentots," Dutch Boers and, finally, the Englishmen are described in turn. In the process, the reader is left in no doubt that Drayson's sympathies lie with the white men in the party.

An elephant hunt is then described. The elephants are tracked through a forest, and this provides an occasion for the author to indulge some of his fantasies about the dark, unknown qualities of the continent:

> As we look upon the graceful festoons of wild vine, the trunks upon
> which the brown and green masses grow, and the dark and gloomy

---

[12] The *uitspan* or "place of rest, where the oxen are unyoked and turned out to graze" (*OED*, second edition, *outspan*, sb[2], quotation from *Colburn's United Service Magazine*, 23 May 1844); cf also "inspan" (a verb meaning to harness or yoke).

character which the interior of this jungle presents, our imagination conjures up the idea that animals hitherto considered as antediluvians, or fabulous, may still exist amongst the solitary depths of this glen. Mammoths and dragons may still live in this world, and where but here could they be found? (35)[13]

Nothing more exotic than a herd of elephants emerges from this jungle, however, and the hunters soon set about ambushing and shooting them.

The next section of the narrative describes an evening at the outspan. Supper is cooked and served in one of the tents, where "Dutch Boers, English sportsmen, and settlers all meet on an equality" (47) – an equality, it need hardly be remarked, that does not extend to the "Totties" and "Kaffirs." Thereafter smoking and drinking ensue, the day's battles are fought again, and silence descends.

This, of course, is the occasion for the telling of tales, a process which is prompted by a chance remark about a hyena:

> [...] the hyena would have been forgotten had not a Boer remarked that this creature was a great friend of his, whom he would be happy to treat. So strange a remark required an explanation, and the Boer was at once called upon to tell why he liked a rascally thief like a hyena. Not unwillingly, the hunter complied, and gave the following account of an adventure. (48)

The Boer's tale, entitled "A Strange Friend," then proceeds. It is the first of eighteen stories, all told around the campfire after the day's hunting. Like Chaucer's pilgrims (and this hunt is a secular pilgrimage of a sort), the hunters take turns in telling tales, many of which are loosely connected by theme.[14] The first two, for example, concern man's relation-

---

[13] The reference to the "fabulous" nature of the animals that the continent of Africa may contain strongly suggests that, despite Drayson's attempts to characterize his writings as 'authentic' (as drawn from 'real-life' experience), his perceptions of Africa are coloured by literary myths and legends about animals like dragons. (Incidentally, in the same passage the use of the term "glen" – a word of Gaelic origin – would also now be considered inappropriate as a description of an African forest, and here Drayson may again be following the Scotsman Pringle in his description in "Afar in the Desert" of "the buffalo's glen" [Pereira & Chapman 1989: 81].)

[14] Drayson's tales resemble Chaucer's *Canterbury Tales* in that they employ a series of narrators who are travelling together and tell stories to while away the

ship with wild animals (a hyena and a leopard). The first tale – about a narrow escape from a pit into which the Boer had fallen, and from which a point of exit is identified by a hyena that also falls into the pit – prompts another Boer's recollection of an incident with a leopard. He prefaces his tale ("The Crafty Leopard") with the following remark: "I never see a leopard now but what I take a good look at him, to see if I can recognize my old friend; but here goes for my tale" (67).[15]

At the conclusion of his tale he asks one of the travelling hunters, a captain, to relate some adventures which "happened to him in Europe," and which would "be interesting to us African men" (79). To complete the cultural symmetry, the captain's tale, about the underhand practices of lawyers, is followed by a tale by another Englishman, the subaltern. (Incidentally, there is no hierarchical pattern in the sequence of the stories. The captain's tale is followed by the subaltern's in this instance, but thereafter the tales generally follow an alternating pattern, with a tale or pair of tales told by the travelling Englishmen being followed by one or two told by the Dutch settlers.)

The campfire, then, provides the meeting-point for the different cultures, clearly identified as European (the travelling group of adventurers), on the one hand, and African (the Boers, the "settlers"), on the other. Significantly, the polarity 'European'/'African' does not include the native inhabitants of Africa, who are therefore effectively denied a full human subjectivity by the author. (I shall return to this point later.)

The sequence of stories is broken by an account of another excursion into the wilds, this time in search of a variety of large game. Thereafter, the focus once again falls on the campfire at the evening's outspan:

> Once more assembled at the outspan, the brilliant moon lighting the plains around, the smoke of the bivouac fire gracefully curling upwards above the waggon-tilts, and the red light from the flame illuminating the dark visages of the savages around, we will again listen to the tales told by various hunters, uninterrupted by any noises save the voices of distant hyenas and jackals, which creatures are now searching for prey, or feasting on the offals of the slain. (124–25)

evening hours. An important distinction to be made here, however, is that while Chaucer manipulates his various narrators for ironic effect (and his tales therefore bear a greater structural resemblance to those of Gibbon and Bosman), Drayson's narrative strategy is far simpler and more ingenuous.

[15] This story will be examined in greater detail in the chapter on Bosman.

What then follows is a sequence of fourteen stories told by the various members of the hunting party. These are uninterrupted by further descriptions of excursions undertaken by the party, and they bring the text to a close. By far the greater part of the text is thus made up of these framed narratives, usually linked by comments prompted by a particular tale. These comments in turn preface – or elicit – another tale which often thematically resembles the foregoing one. The convention adopted is that the tales are told on successive nights at the outspan.

Following this description of *Tales at the Outspan*, I wish now to return to some of the more engaging aspects of the text.

The first of these is the idea of a 'passage to Africa' starting in the restrictive confines of the Thames and extending into the open ocean and the even more open continent of Africa. Drayson's use of this topos predates Conrad's by forty years, but his achievement ends there. Whereas Conrad reveals a "heart of darkness" to lie as much at the origin of Marlow's journey as at its destination, Drayson has no difficulty in locating the respective centres of civilization and savagery. Indeed, to the modern reader, Drayson's book is characterized throughout by breathtaking complacency.

This can be seen in the naked racism of the narratives. The issue of a human commonality between European and "Tottie"/Bushman/ "Kaffir" is adumbrated by *Tales at the Outspan*, but denied by the ideological thrust of the text, which assigns centrality to the white settlers and travelling hunters and consigns the other races to the periphery. This function is enacted by the narrative structure itself: in *Tales at the Outspan*, European meets African, but the latter term refers to the white settlers only, and the native of Africa is utterly silent, a mere "dark visage" around the campfire. So, in a quite fundamental sense, African voices are excluded from participating in the cultural communion that the campfire represents.

If one looks at the narrative structure more closely, it can be seen that this complacency is reflected in the relationship between the various narrators whose voices *are* heard: the frame narrator (the author himself – whose comments on the journey precede and contain the tales told around the campfire) merely reports the tales he hears at the evening outspan. There is nothing in the narrative to suggest that he attempts to create any distance between the tales themselves and his reporting of them. No irony is discernible, and a relationship of simple felicity exists between the various raconteurs and the frame narrator.

Tales at the Outspan is a curious, artless text. The balance struck between framing narrative (the journey and hunting expeditions) and the embedded tales is awkward. Indeed, it is not strictly correct to speak of a 'narrative frame' in the case of *Tales at the Outspan*. The term suggests (following the artwork analogy) that there is a 'frame' which contains, focuses attention upon, and is therefore subordinate in interest to, the artwork itself – in this case the embedded series of tales. But this is by no means how *Tales at the Outspan* works. For one thing, the 'frame' is incomplete, and the text ends abruptly with the last tale told. No encompassing narrative structure, which would enclose the tales, is attempted. Another area of indeterminacy is the focal point of the narrative: is the reader meant to be engaged primarily by the description of the journey and that of the hunting adventures in the interior, or are the tales themselves the principal area of interest?[16]

Is *Tales at the Outspan*, in other words, a collection of tales prefaced by a description of the circumstances in which they were encountered, or is it a travelogue embellished by tales which merely serve to add texture to the exotic setting? The artlessness of the stories themselves – the absence of ironic interplay between the various narrators – would suggest that the latter is a more apt description of the text as a whole. On this reading, the tales become mere decorative features superadded to enhance the descriptions of travel in Africa. However, the tales take up four-fifths of the text, a disproportionate amount of space for mere decorative details, and the text as a whole therefore becomes something of a clumsy anomaly.

Its anomalous nature notwithstanding, *Tales at the Outspan* is an ideal point of departure for a study of the oral-style story. All of the constitutive elements of this kind of story are contained in the text: a campfire setting, a congenial company of travellers who wish to while away the evening hours by telling tales, and a frame narrator who 'reports' the tales to the reader. However, as has been pointed out, the

---

[16] Another indication of the indeterminate discursive footing of Drayson's work is its use of footnotes supplying factual information. One reads: "The dollar at the Cape is worth about 1s. 6d., and ivory fetches from 4s. to 5s. a pound. A bull elephant's tusks frequently weigh 70 or 80 lbs each" (38).

use of these elements is entirely artless, and it is this that distinguishes the early oral-style tale from its more sophisticated successor.

It is also important to recognize that the oral-style story is used by Drayson to convey an 'authentic' Africa. The voices of the various narrators are not only employed to convey the precise texture of this African adventure but also to *guarantee* its authenticity. Hence the lack of disruption, of authorial interference and subversion.

Drayson's earlier rejection of "tales of adventure," of "light reading," in favour of the anecdotes told "over the bivouac fire" (13) is relevant here. The absence of any discernible irony in his remark is astounding given the reputation of the 'tall tale' told around the campfire. It indicates that the purportedly spoken word, and real, lived experience, is given precedence over the world of the imagination. By implication, a text like *Tales at the Outspan*, which purports to be a series of narratives garnered first-hand, has greater *authority* than "light reading" and other examples fitting, in Drayson's dismissive phrase, "this description of literature" (13).

It is the collocation of oral narrative or anecdote, on the one hand, and *authority*, on the other, that is the important point here. The textual presence of the voices of the various narrators, in other words, is a guarantee of the authenticity of their stories. There is also no evidence in the text to suggest that Drayson regards his role as mediator in this regard as a complicating factor – that in 'reporting' the tales he is unavoidably changing them. This lack of selfconsciousness is another conspicuous characterizing feature of the early oral-style story.

The authority of *Tales at the Outspan* is also closely tied to notions of 'realism' or 'verisimilitude,' which Ernest Pereira identifies as one of "the hallmarks of the orally transmitted tale or personal anecdote" (1986b: 105). As will be seen in subsequent chapters, one of the constants in the early colonial short story is the claim that the 'plain truth' is being told. The fact that a large part of the appeal of these early stories for their metropolitan readership is precisely this 'realism' or 'authenticity' may account for the curious amalgam of fact and fancy that one encounters in early collections of South African short stories. Many of the stories Drayson recounts (and this is also the case with other later writers) are palpably improbable or, at the very least, highly exaggerated. Nonetheless, the claims for authenticity are rarely absent in the prefaces of these collections.

Significantly, also, the 'authority' of Drayson's tales is predicated upon their being told by white men. The "Totties" and "Kaffirs" are merely objects of curiosity or derision, and the implication is that they do not have tales worth telling – that their narratives of Africa either do not exist or are unworthy of being heard.

— Ω —

Before the more established writers of the late nineteenth century are discussed, a brief look at two intervening collections. Stories by Frederick Boyle and Joseph Forsyth Ingram have been selected because, along with Drayson's work, they illustrate other facets of the nineteenth-century oral-style tale. Taken together, the stories of these three writers demonstrate in different ways the 'hybridity' of the stories of this period. None stakes its claims to noteworthiness on purely fictional grounds: Drayson mixes in travelogue, Boyle oral history, and Ingram folklore research.

Now, while the stories of Drayson, Boyle, and Ingram share the characteristic of generic indeterminacy typical of writing of this period, there are differences to be observed in the way they engage with Africa. Drayson's complacent racism leads him to exclude African voices from his tales. As will be seen in the discussions that follow, Boyle and Ingram both attempt to incorporate African voices in their stories, and this suggests an ideological development in the South African oral-style story in the period 1860–1890.

Frederick Boyle

The dedication of Frederick Boyle's *The Savage Life* (1876) is an ingratiating acknowledgement extended to one Joseph Mayer, not a few of whose many "benefactions," we read, have "been allotted to the exploring of barbarous lands." Boyle goes on to remark:

> Were these stories fiction, I should not have ventured to put them under your *numen*. Some have changed in characters, locality, or other detail; for one cannot always tell a fact in its plain reality. But I may conscien-

tiously declare that no tale in the collection is without its solid foundation of truth. [unnumbered prefatory page]

Again we encounter the stock claim of virtually all the tales of this
period that they purport to tell 'the plain truth.'

Another conspicuous feature of these early tales of Africa is their
presentation of race relations as entirely unproblematic. In Drayson's
Tales at the Outspan, the natives of Africa are presented as compliant
servants or hunting guides, and their voices are entirely absent from
the discourse around the campfire. Where the African appears in
Boyle's *The Savage Life*, it is merely as a decorative feature of a text filled
with details about high adventure. However, it is important to note that
an African's story has at least been deemed of sufficient interest to
warrant reporting, and this marks an important distinction between
Drayson and Boyle.

As is to be expected from the date of his collection, most of the tales
Boyle tells about South Africa deal with aspects of the Northern Cape
diamond fields. The text opens with a note on the ignorance of "some
English people" concerning this aspect of South African life: "as returning diggers are few in number, and those who test the market by
experiment are not apt to tell their doleful story, the public is still very
ignorant as to what we have done and found out yonder" (1876: 1). The
inclusive pronoun immediately signals Boyle's orientation and intent:
he is writing for an abysmally ignorant English public and clearly
intends to bring them up to date about life in South Africa. Accordingly, the tales are full of informative data regarding the circumstances of
diggers at the diamond fields, the size of their claims, the price of
diamonds, and so forth.

The most interesting of Boyle's attempts to "tell a fact in its plain
reality" is his tale entitled "My Kaffir Chawles." (The corruption of the
chief character's name suggests an incomplete cultural metamorphosis:
"Chawles" merely mimics "Charles" and has to be content with being
an imperfect copy.) The eponymous character, who is the narrator's
servant on the diamond fields, is also chief of a Zulu tribe in Nomansland (present-day East Griqualand):

For a chief he was the most ragged rascal to be found in camp, the
blackest and the biggest-mouthed. It was awful to see Chawles grin. He

> threw his head well back as a preparation, showing an ivory set of
> dominoes, clean-ranged in a pink-silk case. (205–206)

This description is followed by Boyle's analysis of the "Kaffir" language, which he describes as "the strangest speech in the world" (206):

> Its peculiarity lies in the "clicks". Before beginning to talk you must press
> your tongue to the palate; then twist your mouth awry, and let the air in
> sharply, as old people do when they urge a horse [....] "Click, clack, tza"
> has a very tremendous significance in South Africa, if you intersperse a
> few syllables of "baby talk." (206–207)

Adding that it was this difficulty with language which "routed our missionaries" (207), Boyle then proceeds with Chawles's tale. One day Chawles comes to him with the news that his second wife is dead, and requests leave to return home. Six months later he returns with "an enormous scar" and a tale to tell. The author prefaces Chawles's tale with the remark: "I shall not try to render the story in his own language, for the good fellow's English would be almost as difficult to set down as the clicks of his native Kaffir" (208).[17] The story, then, is told in "plain words," and "[c]onfirmation [of it] will be found in government reports" (208). Again, the dimension of fictionality is absent, and the tale is relayed instead as a piece of oral testimony.

The tale concerns the skirmishes between Adam Kok's Griquas and the Nguni tribes of the region. At the point at which Chawles returns to Nomansland, the balance has swung in favour of the newly militarized Griquas:

> Chawles felt very sad – "much sick," as he expressed it; but such a
> sudden desolation did not strike him, a savage, as it would have struck
> us. Grieved he was, and surprised, but not dumfoundered, as would
> have been an Englishman, finding a smoky desert where his home had
> lain. If a tribe live by plunder, by plunder it may expect to die; and this
> rudimentary principle is understood, if not honoured, amongst the
> Kaffirs. (209–10)

---

[17] Significantly, the difficulty of 'setting down' the tale is merely touched on here. It is precisely this question of translation from an alien tongue into the English language – a process which is simultaneously a matter of translating an alien culture into terms that would be comprehensible to the English reading public – which should have vexed these early storytellers but which, in the complacent manner typified here by Boyle, was typically merely passed over by them.

The explicit comparisons between savage and Englishman, barbarism and civilization, so conspicuous in Drayson's *Tales at the Outspan*, are also prominent here. The savage is not to be equated with the colonizer; his sensibilities are not as refined, his emotions not worthy of unqualified empathy.

Chawles now finds himself surrounded by enemies and only just manages to evade the marauding bands of victorious Griqua. At this point the author–narrator interpolates a "moral":

> Nowhere are the joys of savage life more apparent than among Zulus; nowhere are the savage virtues more prominent; but give the Zulu man a taste of civilisation, of law and settled order, he is foremost to uphold a system he can scarcely comprehend, and to abandon the delights of independent action. (211)[18]

After this remark, it is no surprise to read that Chawles reached the point where, hungry and tired, he "thought wistfully of the elysian [diamond] fields, and the police thereon" (211). He escapes the killing fields of Nomansland and returns to the diamond fields with two of his sisters, who had miraculously escaped harm. Chawles's story, the narrator remarks, was considered to be so improbable that he "obtained credence from no one until we had it on official authority that the government found itself obliged to interfere in Nomansland" (216). The tale ends with the following note: "This story will explain to a puzzled public why the death of Adam Kok was telegraphed, in large type, some weeks since for the information of Europe. He had made himself not only famous, but an actual 'question'" (216).

Chawles's tale is thus reported as a piece of oral testimony which is later corroborated by "official authority." Again, as with Drayson's tales, the dimension of fictionality – with the attendant elements of artifice and irony – is suppressed. The author professes merely to be relaying a true story, and the footnote to the tale confirms the notion that "information" is being imparted to the metropolitan reading public.

It is, of course, significant that an African's story is being retold here – in his complacency, Drayson felt no need to incorporate African

---

[18] The paradoxical tensions in colonial attitudes to the Zulu – markedly present in this passage – are, as Dan Wylie (1995) comprehensively documents, present in most of the writing about Shaka in this period.

voices. However, it is also significant that Chawles's tale is entirely re-cast in the author's re-telling of it. Boyle displays a glib confidence in domesticating his servant's tale: there is no sense that Chawles is an autonomous agent who tells a story which has inherent merit and therefore warrants circumspection in its re-telling. The attitude of the frame narrator to his informant is condescending, and narrative author-ity is firmly vested in the act of re-telling the story – a re-telling that is, significantly, bolstered by "official authority." Chawles's harrowing experience thus become the occasion for the relaying to Boyle's metro-politan audience of an illustrative tale of savagery.

J. Forsyth Ingram

If Drayson's writing illustrates the point that the South African oral-style story is partly rooted in tales about travel in Africa, and Boyle's that oral anecdote or testimony is another important generative source, Ingram's collection illustrates the point that there is close contiguity between the oral-style story and folklore.

Despite the fact that Ingram's collection appeared some thirty years after Drayson's, it is from the point of view of this study generically anterior to the work of Drayson and Boyle. Whereas the discursive footing of Drayson's and Boyle's tales is ambiguous enough to allow the suspicion that the narrative frame is partly *conventional* – that these writers, in other words, are not entirely serious in their claims to authenticity and literal transcription – there is no sense in *The Story of a Gold Concession, and Other African Tales and Legends* (1893) that merely the convention of the oral-style tale is being deployed. Indeed, in his Preface (quoted in full below) the author claims to have produced a collection of carefully documented African folklore:

> The following collection of stories and wild legends are [sic] the result of much careful inquiry amongst certain of the native tribes in South-East Africa.
>
> For the most part they were told round the camp-fire by natives during the journeys undertaken by the writer. As far as possible the idiom and spirit of the original narratives have been retained. Here and there slight departures have necessarily been made therefrom, in order to render the translations intelligible to general readers. Those who are familiar with Africa and African legendary lore will recognize the faith-

fulness of the reproductions. Many of the stories were related to the writer by those travellers and adventurers of the desert who are so rapidly becoming extinct. Though some of the incidents related by them border upon the fictitious, they are for the most part based on fact.

The illustrations are from photographs from nature, and as such are calculated to portray, more forcibly than mere engravings, the savage people and wild places touched upon in the stories. (1893: v–vi)

What credence does one grant to Ingram's claims? He claims to have "retained" as far as possible "the idiom and spirit of the original narratives." This implies that he had actual informants who related the tales which he then "reproduced" as accurately as translation would allow. This "reproduction" is enhanced by a number of illustrations from photographs, interspersed at appropriate points in the text. The frontispiece, for example, is captioned "Where the Gold Was Found," a reference to the title-story. Other illustrations from photographs (of historical figures, chiefs, important personages, traditional African settings and the like) are located at the relevant juncture of the text.

There can be little doubt that Ingram believed himself to have produced an authentic work documenting the lore of a part of the African continent. The other possibility – that the text is an elaborate device masking a deeply ironic hidden purpose – is not only exceedingly unlikely on the internal evidence of the text itself, but would also be entirely out of character with the period. As this study will show, it is only towards the turn of the century with Glanville and, most notably, a little later with Perceval Gibbon that the South African short story of the oral-style variety manifests this kind of irony.

However, the substance of the tales themselves undercuts the claim that they are "for the most part based on fact." While there may have been an attempt to reproduce them "faithfully," the tales themselves are, by their very nature, highly improbable. They are a miscellany of personal anecdotes, folklore, myths and legends.

The title-story, for example, purports to be the true record of how a particular sea captain acquired his fortune in gold. Exasperated by ceaseless speculations about his ill-gotten gains, the "gruff old Captain K—, the African millionaire" (4), the narrator remarks, "set down his history in crabbed characters on large sheets of foolscap, and, calling a select few of his friends together, he delivered himself of the true and authentic history of his life" (6). His life story is then the focus of the tale told by the frame narrator, who, at the end of the captain's narrative, reports: "At this point the old mariner gathered his papers together and handed them to me for publication" (48).

Of interest here is the bid for authenticity made by the frame narrator. His contextualizing remarks about how he came across the story (the reader is led to assume that he was one of the select company at the original telling of the tale), the references to the "crabbed" handwriting, and the concluding remark about being given the papers for publication serve this purpose.

The written tale, then, claims to be a transcription from 'authentic' oral sources. All of the tales in *The Story of a Gold Concession* take this form: they all employ narrators who tell stories about their personal experiences. The book as a whole thus positions itself at the interface of oral and written discourse, the literary convention of an intradiegetic narrator presumably being adopted in an attempt to convey the mode in which the tale was originally encountered by the author.

While the title-story concerns the adventures of Europeans in the African hinterland, most of the other tales employ African narrators who tell tales of African mythology. The narrative voice that frames the tales can be identified as that of the author, and his purpose in writing the tales can be inferred from his relationship with his informants. There is no discernible irony in this relationship: whether it is the voice of a grizzled gold-hunter or that of an African tribesman that is heard, the relationship between narrator and frame narrator is stable and inviolable. The latter clearly understands his role as being that of purveyor of the lore of a little-known continent to a metropolitan audience.

There are several textual signals that "faithfulness of reproduction" rather than irony and subversion is sought after. In the title-story, the captain's embedded narrative is prefaced by the remark: "Taking up the thread of the worthy old mariner's narrative, I will allow him to tell his story in his own way and almost in his own words" (7). The handing over of the sheaf of papers already alluded to is a further indication of the relationship of trust and fidelity that exists between informant and author–narrator.

Another example prefaces "The Story of Zaweete," a tale about a wise king who dies and becomes a forest deity. Munyosi, the narrator of the tale, remarks: "'White men, as a rule, laugh at the legends of the black tribes, but nevertheless these same legends are of great value to us, who cannot see the thoughts of books or listen to the whispers of the black marks on the papers which are always in the hands of the white men'" (79–80). Clearly, the author is an exception to the rule, and the tale is accordingly told without fear of ridicule. "The Story of Zaweete" prompts a recollection by another man seated at the fireside. Munyosi urges this man on with the words: "'Tell the master the story; for, lo, he understandeth the truth of these the histories of our country'" (87–88).

However, the author's role in this act of cultural exchange is not confined to that of being an attentive and sympathetic ear. Munyosi's evocation of the orality–literacy distinction suggests another aspect of this relationship. Munyosi will tell his tale, and will in turn benefit from its preservation in the form of "the black marks on the papers." *The Story of a Gold Concession and Other African Tales and Legends* thus takes itself to be performing the role of transcribing oral sources which would otherwise be threatened with extinction. Not only does the authorial persona understand (and take seriously) the 'truth' of the oral histories recounted to him, he also translates them from one language, culture and ontological mode into another.

What is lacking from Ingram's tales – and what would make them more likely progenitors of the oral-style tale proper – is any indication of ironic interplay between the various levels of narrative. It is easy to see how the kind of earnest ingenuousness that permeates Ingram's work could become subverted or parodied in later, more sophisticated varieties of the oral-style story. The stories themselves are ripe for the kind of subversion one finds in Gibbon and particularly Bosman, but no advantage is taken of this. Even the superficial humour one occasionally encounters between the "Africans" and travelling hunters in *Tales at the Outspan* (which never goes beyond banter of the most trivial sort) is entirely absent from *The Story of a Gold Concession*.

— Ω —

No sense of technical advancement in the early oral-style story can thus be discerned in the thirty years from Drayson's work through Boyle's to Ingram's. What the work of the three writers illustrates, rather, is that the 'raw materials' of the later oral-style story are to be found in the various indeterminate discursive modes current in the mid- to late nineteenth century – among them travel-writing (Drayson), oral testimony (Boyle), and folklore (Ingram).

What *can* be discerned in this thirty-year period is some progression in consciousness: as has been pointed out, Drayson entirely excludes African voices from his narratives; in Boyle's story, the African servant Chawles's story is told, but in the voice and manner of his white master; Ingram, for his part, appears genuinely concerned with allowing his narrators a voice, and most of his informants are African. Thus, between 1862 and 1893 there appears to have been a growing awareness of the importance of allowing indigenous voices to be heard.

Drayson's collection falls squarely into what Manfred Nathan calls the "Age of the Great Hunters," which he periodizes as 1854–1871 (1925: 20). The pre-industrial, paradisal landscape of Drayson's South African hinterland would give way progressively to the more complex social relations engendered by European encroachment after the mineral discoveries of the late nineteenth century. Accordingly, the simple tales of high adventure typical of the nineteenth-century South African short story would gradually become displaced by more complex story forms.

However, this is not yet reflected in Boyle's story, which falls into Nathan's "Romantic Age," 1867–1880 (1925: 20). There is no sense in Boyle's story that race relations have become in any way problematic and therefore the subject of more complex fictional strategies. (Indeed, as has already been noted, Chawles escapes the killing fields of Nomansland and returns gratefully to the "elysian fields" of Kimberley.) Chawles's story of savagery does not ask questions about the growing European usurpation of mineral-rich territories, but merely forms a useful footnote to recorded history, and, of course, a diverting and informative tale for Boyle's metropolitan readership.

The seriousness with which Ingram takes his project signals a departure from the light-hearted romanticism that permeates the stories of both Drayson and Boyle. However, as was pointed out, his earnest desire faithfully to reproduce oral testimonies positions his stories at an even earlier phase of development than in the case of Drayson and Boyle. In terms of their awareness of the importance of capturing indigenous voices, though, they represent some sort of ideological advance upon the two earlier writers and anticipate Scully's more throughgoing attempts in this regard.

This 'advance,' however, should not obscure the commonalities in these early examples of South African frame narratives. Unlike Gibbon and Bosman, who employ a more complex variety of the oral-style story, none of the authors discussed above attempts to subvert or ironize either the content of the framed narratives or the tellers of these narratives themselves. They all treat very ingenuously the stories told by their various informants, even when these stories are palpably fantastical.

This ingenuousness is also reflected in the positioning of authorial voice. Not only do the various frame narrators of the respective stories fail to exploit the power with which they are technically endowed to subvert their internal narrators, but there is often also a collapsing of the distinction between author and frame narrator. The potential for a multi-layered narrative structure, with each level resonating ironically against all the others, is thereby forgone in favour of an attempt at an unmediated presentation of an African experience.

The notion of *authority* is intimately bound up in this 'artless' narrative structure: the author speaks in his own voice, and he 'reports' the tales he garners with the view to presenting an 'authentic' Africa invested with the authority of first-hand experience – hence, of course, the various attempts to persuade the reader that the 'plain truth' is being told. This authorial stance is predicated upon a view of Africa as uncontested terrain. Once resistance to European colonization, the divisive effects of the Second Anglo-Boer War, and the social upheaval consequent upon urbanization begin to impress themselves on the narrativizers of the African continent, a very different form of oral-style story emerges.

———————— ❧ ❧ ————————

3 The 'Artless' Oral-Style Story
W.C. Scully and Percy FitzPatrick

 ∾ ───────────────────────────────────

T HE LATE NINETEENTH CENTURY witnessed a proliferation of collections of South African short stories. The appearance of Scully's *Kafir Stories* in 1895 was followed rapidly by H.A. Bryden's *Tales of South Africa* and Ernest Glanville's *Kloof Yarns* (both 1896). The year 1897 saw the appearance of Percy FitzPatrick's *The Outspan: Tales of South Africa*, Glanville's *Tales from the Veld*, and Scully's second collection, *The White Hecatomb and Other Stories*. Bryden's second collection, *From Veldt Camp Fires: Stories of Southern Africa*, appeared in 1900.

A notable aspect of all of these collections is the presence of elements of oral discourse in the written form. This is most conspicuous in stories by Scully and FitzPatrick, and they have therefore been selected for detailed discussion here. However, the work of Bryden and Glanville also evinces this tendency. Many of Bryden's stories are anecdotes related in the first person, and the campfire setting and the device of the frame narrative are also used. Some of the titles (from *Tales of South Africa*) themselves – "The Secret of Verloren Vlei," "A Desert Mystery," "A Legend of Prince Maurice," "Vrouw Van Vuuren's Frenchman" – reflect a desire to unlock some of the raw mystery of an obscure reach of Empire, itself an impulse typical of the age.

Glanville's tales are more noteworthy, largely because they make sustained use of a larger-than-life fictional narrator, Uncle Abe Pike. This character, remarks Ernest Pereira, "is in the tradition of Baron Munchausen and other tellers of tall tales, but his immediate predecessors must be sought in the American Mid-West, where incredible yarns are spun to bedazzle and dupe innocent greenhorns." Pereira adds that, the Eastern Cape setting of Glanville's Abe Pike stories notwithstanding, "neither the style nor the humour could be described as indigenous" (1986b: 110). Pereira's first remark is accurate, but the inference he draws is debatable. There is no question that Glanville has drawn extensively on the yarn tradition of the American mid-West, but there are also aspects of his stories which point to a strongly indigenous grounding, as will become clear in the course of the next chapter. I have devoted a separate chapter to Glanville's tales because, in addition to making sustained use of a fictional narrator, they also represent a formal advance upon the stories of Scully and FitzPatrick.

Scully's place in a nascent short story tradition in South Africa is an important one, and he has produced three collections of stories worthy of note. FitzPatrick, for his part, has vividly evoked the campfire-yarn sessions of the transport riders in the late nineteenth century, and his "The Outspan" is therefore examined in some detail below.

In this chapter it will be argued that the stories of Scully and Fitz-Patrick can be characterized as 'artless' oral-style tales. Neither writer exploits fully the potential for irony latent in the genre; indeed, in many ways their stories maintain some sort of continuity with those of the writers examined in the previous chapter: the narrators of the stories discussed here still claim 'authenticity' for the tales they report, they do not attempt to subvert them in any way, and the same desire to convey faithfully the true 'spirit of Africa' is apparent. Moreover, their use of the oral-style story genre is sporadic: Scully's three volumes of tales use a frame narrator only intermittently, and the only good example of such a tale by FitzPatrick is his title-story.

However, the stories of Scully and FitzPatrick do differ from those of their predecessors in one important respect: there is a greater degree of selfconscious 'artistry' to be observed. Thus, while Scully and Fitz-Patrick do not exploit the ironic potential of the oral-style tale to the full, there is a new 'aesthetic' dimension to be observed in the late nineteenth-century oral-style tale.

W.C. Scully

Scully's contribution to the development of an indigenous literature was noted by Herman Charles Bosman, whose effusive "Scully is better than nine-tenths of the *contemporary* English authors whose works are prescribed for the

Witwatersrand University courses in English" (Bosman 1986a [1948]: 94) is notable more for its patriotism than for its accuracy. And in the opening lines of his own "Old Transvaal Story" which, interestingly, first appeared at the same time as the original article containing the remark above, Bosman makes an entirely different gesture of acknowledgement, and one which amounts to nothing less than a back-handed compliment: "As Scully, I think, knew – have you ever chanced upon his 'Ukushwama'? – the Transvaal seems to have had only one ghost story" (Bosman 1963 [1948]: 107). *Pace* Stephen Gray's remark that Bosman then "took over a W.C. Scully tale [...] and reworked it more successfully without humiliating the old man" (Gray 1986: 29), the conceptual distance between Scully's ingenuous 'ghost story' and Bosman's metafictional version shows why Bosman is remembered and Scully is all but forgotten. (The implications of the differences involved will be taken up in greater detail in the chapter on Bosman.)

Scully has also been the subject of intensive research by Jean Marquard which has issued principally in two forms: her doctoral thesis, "A Neglected Pioneer in South African Literature: W.C. Scully" (1984a), and her useful collection of selected stories by Scully entitled *Transkei Stories* (1984b).

Marquard devotes a chapter of her thesis to Scully's short stories, where she begins by noting his method: "Scully combined the functions of fiction and anthropology in a very natural way. Of the two major sources for the history of South African tribes, which are the records of European explorers and oral rendition, Scully, situated far away from libraries or archives, adopted the 'oral' method" (1984a: 190).

Scully had himself detailed his *modus operandi* for collecting stories:

> Occasionally I heard of some old Native who had been an actor in the tremendous drama of the Tshaka wars. Such men I always made a point of visiting. I have sat for hours next to such a patriarch, feeding him, as he lay on his mat, with teaspoonfuls of brandy and soup, endeavouring thus to stimulate his flagging memory. I was thus enabled to collect some valuable historical information which would otherwise have been irretrievably lost. (Scully 1913: 274)

The historical value of data naively collected in this way is doubtful, but this need not detain us here. What both Marquard and Scully himself reveal is the latter's close acquaintance with Nguni oral culture and

his attempt to work this into short stories, and it is this that is of consequence for this study.

Many of the stories in Scully's three volumes – *Kafir Stories* (1895),
The White Hecatomb (1897), and *By Veldt and Kopje* (1907) – contain
elements of (mainly Nguni) oral lore: "The Quest of the Copper," from
Kafir Stories, is a fictional reconstruction of the adventures of an expedition commissioned by Shaka to find copper; "Ukushwama" (also from
Kafir Stories) takes the form of an anecdote related in the first person in
which is embedded a tale of local legend about tragic lovers; "Gquma;
or, The White Waif," from *The White Hecatomb*, concerns the mythical
origin of an exclamation uttered by the narrator's African companion;
while the title-story of this volume is the narrative of "the daughter of a
'common man of the Amangwane tribe' caught up in the commotion of
the Shaka era" (Marquard 1984b: xxi); "The Imishologu" (also from this
volume) is an old man's account of a family tragedy and, like "Ukushwama," takes the form of an embedded narrative; "The Writing on the
Rock," "By the Waters of Marah," and "The Hunter of the Didima,"
from *By Veldt and Kopje*, all employ internal narrators – an old Boer
farmer, an Englishman living in the wilderness, and an old African
hunter respectively – and Scully has therefore captured in this volume
an interesting range of nineteenth-century South African voices.

However, none of Scully's three volumes has anything like the
structure of a story cycle, and in none of them is the internal narrator
used with any consistency or towards any discernible greater design.
Citing the evidence of letters to his wife, Marquard (1984a: 188) argues
that all of the stories that Scully was to publish in book form were
written before 1897, the date of publication of his second volume of
tales. On the internal evidence of the stories themselves, and from the
data Marquard assembles from his letters, it would therefore appear
that all three volumes are miscellanies rather than consciously designed
thematic entities. There is also no discernible development in the three
volumes – in them Scully mixes personal reminiscence, internal narration, and first- and third-person narration in roughly equal measure –
and I have therefore selected only certain stories for mention, and one
for detailed discussion, in order to illustrate Scully's particular use of
the oral-style story.

Marquard distinguishes two kinds of story used by Scully: one is what she calls "pure fiction, using atmospheric or 'defamiliarising' devices common to Romance writing of the period"; the other "claims to deal in factual events and uses the device of internal narration":

> The second group is connected to oral and folkloric traditions and usually involves a 'listening' narrator, who reports back to the reader, verbatim, a tale told him usually of bygone times by an old resident with a long memory. In his use of the internal narrator, Scully shows that he is fully aware of the oral tradition in Africa and of the uses to which it can be put in fiction of a European order. (1984a: 199)

Marquard's notion of "verbatim" reportage by a "'listening' narrator" in Scully's stories fails to include the necessary observation that this is literally impossible and that it is therefore merely a convention that Scully has adopted in some of his stories.

Examples of stories which fit into Marquard's second group have been listed above. I wish to focus primarily on one of these, "Ukush-wama," in which Scully employs the device of a storyteller figure. (And, as I have already noted, the story also has the distinction of being singled out and embellished by Bosman, a fascinating piece of inter-textuality to which I shall return in the chapter on Bosman.)

As is the case with many of the stories of this period, "Ukushwama" is a frame narrative related in the first person. In the course of his business as the colonial administrator of a region of the Transkei, the narrator encounters a local myth about a pair of star-crossed lovers whose tragic demise haunts the region. The headman of the area, Numjala, warns the narrator that the forest he must pass in order to reach home is impassable on horseback on the night of the new moon. The narrator initially discounts the story as an example of local super-stition. Predictably, his dismissiveness is rewarded by a close encounter with the local shades: his horse indeed refuses to pass by the forest in which the lovers are buried and he is forced to return to the headman's kraal. This then provides the occasion for the embedded narrative (Numjala's tale), in which some regional wisdom is imparted to the once-sceptical administrator.

Numjala's tale concerns an ill-fated love affair between his eldest daughter, Nomalie, and a young man, Xolilizwe, who is attractive and worthy in character, but of poor social standing. Nomalie has caught the eye of the chief of the tribe, Lukwazi, who persuades Numjala to allow her to become the latest addition to his household of twelve other wives. However, soon after the marriage Nomalie returns to her father's kraal complaining of ill-treatment at the hands of Lukwazi and vowing to die rather than return to him. Lukwazi is unable to reclaim her and Xolilizwe returns with enough cattle as a "down-payment" for Nomalie's hand in marriage. Numjala consents and the two are married and go to live in Xolilizwe's uncle's kraal. Three months later the feast of the first fruits ("Ukushwama") is celebrated and this ritual requires, among other things, that the chief eat fruits (a pumpkin or a mealie-cob) stolen from another chief's territory and mixed by the witchdoctor in the skull of a man killed for the purpose. After the ceremony it transpires that the skull used by Lukwazi is in fact Xoli-lizwe's, and his headless corpse is found near the Ghoda forest. In a fit of grief, Nomalie drowns herself and is buried alongside Xolilizwe. Four months later, on the evening of the fourth new moon after the feast of the first fruits, the drunken Lukwazi is thrown by his horse near the grave-site and breaks his neck. "'Since then'," Numjala con-cludes, "'no horse will ever pass the Ghoda bush between sunset and sunrise when the Moon is new'" (1895: 182).

The story ends with the resumption of the narrative frame: the administrator leaves Numjala's kraal the next morning and rides past the Ghoda, alongside which he observes two piles of stones lying close together.

How, then, does Scully's tale compare with the earlier, 'artless' stories of Drayson, Boyle, and Ingram?

Scully, like Ingram, shows a genuine interest in African culture, and this illustrates the point that there is a progression away from the complacency of Drayson's view of Africa to be discerned in the South African short story. Almost all of Scully's stories engage in some way with Xhosa society, and many of them attempt to convey this engage-ment on a formal level – the manner in which the stories are told, in other words, often accords with their content. (The stories by Scully listed above, for example, mostly employ internal narrators in an attempt to convey something of the atmosphere of the oral tale.)

On the level of narrative structure, there is a small but significant shift away from the early oral-style narratives of Drayson, Boyle, and

Ingram. I argued that the stories of the latter writers conform to the Bakhtinian notion of "simple" *skaz* narratives: there is no ironic interplay between the various levels of narrative, and although two (or more) voices are heard, and these voices may speak in stylistically distinct discourses, the tales are all unidirectional in tendency. There is, in other words, no internal 'dialogic' structure in these stories whereby ideologically opposed voices are placed in competitive 'dialogue' with each other.

The beginnings of such a competitive dialogue can be observed in Scully's "Ukushwama" (in the form of mild authorial self-irony, as I shall go on to demonstrate below) and this marks a small development in the internal complexity of the oral-style tale. The narrative structure of the tale thus warrants closer examination.

"Ukushwama" has two clearly demarcated narratives (labelled parts I and II of the story) with clearly distinguishable narrators. The frame narrative uses the voice of a first-person narrator (the colonial administrator) to set the scene for the presentation of the framed story told by Numjala. In a concluding paragraph, the voice of the frame narrator takes up the story once more. The embedded narrative is obviously relayed via the first-person narrator, and employs standard, grammatical English, but the author attempts to preserve some of the characteristics of the oral narrative: some Xhosa words are used ("*metja*," "*lobola*," "*ikazi*," "*imfe*" – with the English equivalents in parentheses) and direct translations from the Xhosa are also present ("great son," "the feast of the first fruits," the "great place").

Numjala's narrative also bears several of the hallmarks of the oral tale. Numjala himself possesses many of the distinctive characteristics of an oral storyteller: he is old enough ("well over sixty years of age"; 166) to be rich in experience, is engagingly eccentric ("a man of parts"; 166), and has wit and intelligence (his verbal sparring with the narrator over the contentious parallels between Christianity and African witchcraft reveals this tellingly). Finally, he is hospitable, and this quality provides the occasion for the story in the first place – an occasion, it should be remarked, that is celebrated in a setting standard for the telling of a tale: the smoking of pipes after supper and the story unfolding beside the open fire.

In accordance with the style of oral tales, the characterization in Numjala's tale is also schematic: Nomalie is the misprized princess, Xolilizwe her ill-fated lover, his social status incommensurate with his attractiveness, and Lukwazi (who forces Nomalie to become his thirteenth wife) is the arrogant, drunken king, who misuses his power and spreads misery around him. He brings about the tragedy of the two lovers, but gets his just deserts soon afterwards.

The last point here is a further indication that Numjala's tale conforms to the characteristics of the oral tale. A common feature of oral tales is their didactic intention. The use of human character-types rather than unique individuals is integral to this intention: the outcome of the story will often be evident to listeners merely on the presentation of characters at the outset. Numjala's narrative has a clear message: interference with the natural course of love, arrogance (Lukwazi), and greed (Numjala himself, in 'selling' his daughter) bring unpleasant consequences.

The presence of all of these features in Numjala's tale suggests that Scully has attempted to convey a Xhosa oral legend as 'authentically' as possible, and herein lies the bulk of the story's appeal. Whereas in the stories of Gibbon and Bosman the reader's attention is principally drawn to the rivalry between the various narrators and the irony that lies in the discrepancy between the internal narrator's attitude and that which we are meant to infer from the frame narrator's tacit signals, in Scully the embedded tale is left largely undisturbed by the reporting narrator and is the main focus of the reader's attention.

However, what is noticeable in Scully's tale – and absent from the stories examined earlier – is a greater degree of sophistication, which manifests itself, first, in a more selfconscious aestheticism and, secondly, in what may be taken to be the beginnings of ironic interplay between internal narrator and frame narrator.

The first of these elements is demonstrated in Scully's deployment of the conventions of the ghost story: the coincidence of the new moon on the night that the administrator visits the area, the building of suspense, and the unsettling sense of the supernatural afoot – all testify to the presence of consciously deployed literary techniques.

The ending to the story also points to a conscious aestheticism:

Next morning I dismounted at the Ghoda, and walked into the forest. I
found the large umgwenya tree without difficulty, and underneath it
were the two piles of stones close together. They were much overgrown
with ferns and creepers. A large bush-buck leaped up and crashed
through the undergrowth. His doe followed immediately afterwards,
passing so close that I could see the dew-drops glistening on her red,
dappled flank. (182–83)

The way in which the seemingly coincidental encounter with the buck
is made to refer elliptically to the two slain lovers is a deft touch, and is
one example of the greater degree of artistic skill Scully demonstrates in
comparison with his literary predecessors. With Scully, in other words,
the oral-style tale is in the process of becoming an 'art form.'

The second of the elements that indicate a development in the oral-
style story with Scully is the presence of irony. Numjala's seemingly
accidental use of the aphorism about hubris at the beginning of the
story – "'He who always says of the thing he does not understand,
"This cannot be," is in danger of being put to shame'" (168) – prepares
for the ironic disruption of precisely this quality in the frame narrator
himself. The frame narrator's rationalist scepticism is destabilized by
Xhosa 'superstition,' and he has to revise his assumptions accordingly.

Scully also prefaces his story with a short poem (by the author himself, under a nom-de-plume):

> "No ghosts, they say, What is a ghost? –
> Nay, what are thoughts and stars and winds?
> They cannot tell – they show at most
> Those formal swathes the pedant binds
> Across clear eyes, the while he plugs
> The apertures of liberal lugs." (165)

Inscribed "SHAGBAG *on Dogmatism*," this epigraph is clearly intended,
like the aphorism about hubris, to reflect ironically on the attitude of
the frame narrator of the story – and, by extension, on Scully himself.

Marquard also touches on a degree of 'artfulness' in Scully when
she remarks that in his stories he "effaces his personal involvement,"
and introduces the "first person magistrate [...] as a fictional character"
(1984a: 191). It would appear, then, that unlike Drayson, Boyle and
Ingram, who make no attempt to fictionalize their frame narrators,
Scully tries to create some distance between his own speaking position

as author and that of his first-person narrator (who often appears as a magistrate or administrator).

However, the only notable example supporting Marquard's assertion is "Kellson's Nemesis" (from *Kafir Stories*), where the magistrate (perhaps because of his morally reprehensible act of siring a son and then deserting mother and child) is cast as a fictionalized character who is not to be identified with Scully himself. Elsewhere, the magistrate appears as a thinly disguised authorial persona and is easily recognizable as a kind of literary stand-in for Scully himself. Thus the distance maintained by Scully between himself as author and his magistrate persona as narrator is seldom exploited fully.

The purpose of pursuing this line of argument is to show that, despite the presence of some elements of greater sophistication, Scully's oral-style stories have not yet reached the stage of 'artfulness,' where the various levels of narrative are used to allow the author to remove himself almost entirely from the story itself. The irony that does exist in Scully is confined to the kind of self-deprecation exemplified above, and it does not become the dominant *mode* in which his stories operate. Where internal narrators are used, the tales they tell are relayed without authorial interference, and as such they do not significantly depart from the intention ascribed to the earlier authors to 'speak Africa' in an 'authentic' and unmediated way.

While Scully does not invest his oral-style stories with the pervasive irony found in Bosman (and, to a lesser degree, in Glanville and Gibbon), it would be wrong to conclude this discussion of him without acknowledging what he does contribute to the development of the oral-style story. Most importantly, Scully (unlike Drayson in particular) recognizes the integrity and importance of African culture in its own right, and many of his stories centre on aspects of this culture. This involves providing the colonial subject with a 'voice,' and, as we saw, such a subject can 'speak back.' The upstaging of the administrator in "Ukushwama" does not amount to unseating him, but it can readily be seen that we have already come a long way from Drayson, with his silent "dark visages" around the campfire, and are beginning to anticipate the more thoroughgoing irony found in Gibbon's tales.

As a way of explaining Scully's greater self-awareness and respect for African culture it can be observed that his attitude to Empire and

British superiority was by no means a simple one. In her Introduction to *Transkei Stories*, Marquard provides ample evidence to indicate that Scully had profoundly ambivalent feelings about British imperial rule, and showed considerable sympathy for the subjugated indigenous tribes and (later) also for the Boer cause:

> Although he was "a man of his time" and a civil servant of unusual talent, Scully's faith in the colonial order often faltered [...] From his writing-desk in isolated magisterial residencies, he lamented the industrialisation of the landscape and the deterioration of humane values in an urban, technocratic culture. Moreover, he thought that by undermining the principles of justice and democracy, whites in South Africa betrayed the highest ideals of Western civilisation. Like his famous contemporary, Olive Schreiner, Scully became increasingly disenchanted with the kind of Imperialism represented by Rhodes [...] he was ultimately pessimistic about the eventual triumph of Western civilisation in Africa. (Marquard 1984b: xvii)

Marquard's last comment here captures the central ambiguity in Scully's attitudes. Is Western civilization bound to fail because of its own problems, or because of the intractability of the subject African tribes? Marquard concludes her Introduction thus: "The character of his fiction is marked by exotic, artificial and crudely simplified rhetorical patterns. The habit of locating 'laws' of nature in problems of an empirical nature exposes many of the underlying prejudices and limitations which are an integral part of the colonial imagination" (xxiii).

It would appear that the combination of two factors account for Scully's status as a "neglected pioneer": the first is his racism and condescension; the second the inherent weakness of his work itself. The latter aspect would not in itself consign the author to literary oblivion, as his work would still have socio-historical interest alongside its minor artistic merits, but it is the combination of this with the racism typical of the age that has no doubt contributed to Scully's relative obscurity.[1]

---

[1] In response to Jean Marquard's attempts to rescue Scully's racist "Umtagati" in the name of "good art" (Marquard 1978: 20–21), David Maughan Brown (1984) has argued convincingly that Scully's racism is indisputable and that any assessment of his contribution to South African literature must take this into account rather than attempt to explain it away.

Percy FitzPatrick   Sir Percy FitzPatrick's collection of stories,
The Outspan: Tales of South Africa, first appeared in 1897, two years after the appearance of Scully's *Kafir Stories*. The title-story of the collection is of particular interest here, as it employs a fictional narrator and evokes the fireside ethos of the oral tale.

A major figure looming large behind writers who, like FitzPatrick, were writing in the last decade of the nineteenth century and in a colonial setting is, of course, Rudyard Kipling. Stories which would have been known to writers like FitzPatrick are those contained in Kipling's *Plain Tales from the Hills* (1928 [1888]), the "The Indian Railway Library" series (also published during the course of 1888) and, most particularly, the first volume in this series, *Soldier's Three*, which features Privates Mulvaney, Learoy, and Ortheris. (This volume later appeared in an edition entitled *Soldiers Three, The Story of the Gadsbys, In Black and White* [1895].) In his early critical essay on Kipling's stories, Andrew Lang remarked that among Kipling's "discoveries of new kinds of characters, probably the most popular is his invention of the British soldier in India" (1971 [1891]: 73). Indeed, as subsequent criticism shows, these characters were to become immensely popular with the British reading public and Kipling was to use them repeatedly in later collections. Using such characters as narrators enabled Kipling to locate his tales at the level of the common man's experience, and he rendered this textually by imitating the regional accents of his narrators (Terence Mulvaney's broad Irish accent, in particular, came in for repeated and highly effective use by Kipling). Other narrators used repeatedly by Kipling include the German Hans Breitmann (borrowed from Charles Godfrey Leland's *Hans Breitmann's Ballads* of 1857) and Petty Officer Pyecroft, the naval equivalent of Mulvaney in the army stories.

While none of these tales closely resembles those told by FitzPatrick and later South African users of the oral-style tale,[2] there can be little doubt that Kipling's deployment of narrators as character 'types,' his comic imitation of their verbal styles, and, in general, his predilection

---

2 Kipling's "Mrs. Bathurst" (see footnote 4, below) is closest in structure and style to FitzPatrick's "The Outspan." However, the story appeared for the first time only in 1904, several years after FitzPatrick had written his tale, so there can be no question of direct influence in this case.

for oral-style narratives,[3] influenced the colonial short story of the 1890s and early-twentieth century.

FitzPatrick's "The Outspan" is in fact an outstanding example of the kind of colonial fiction with which Kipling is so closely associated. Writing of this kind was occasioned in South Africa by the presence of the motley band of expatriate adventurers who flocked to the diamond- and gold-fields in the last two decades of the nineteenth century. The region's communications and transport infrastructure was at this stage rudimentary, and supplying the mining towns of Kimberley and the eastern Transvaal, and later those on the Witwatersrand, involved the use of transport riders, who travelled great distances from the ports to the hinterland. The social ethos that evolved under these circumstances was conducive to the swapping of yarns and anecdotes, which usually took place at the evening outspan. FitzPatrick's "The Outspan" is a fine example of just such a tale and the milieu on which it draws.

The story is headed by an epigraph worth noting. It reads "There is no art in the Telling that can equal the consummate art of the Happening!" (1897: 1) and is prompted by the recollections of a man "in the fields" who recounts to the narrator an extraordinary tale of coincidence. The narrator in turn remarks (to the reader): "And I only recall the remark because it must be my apology for telling plain truth just as it happened" (2–3). What follows this prefatory passage – the substance of the story – is a series of loosely connected anecdotes which focus mainly on an enigmatic character called "Sebougwaan." Predic- tably, just such a coincidence as was related by the narrator's informant at the outset occurs in the story that unfolds. However, the main point here is that, like the writers discussed earlier, FitzPatrick again invokes the "plain truth" of his tale as a guarantee of its value.

Part of the ethos of the period under discussion is the priority accorded the world of action over that of (literary) reflection. This pre- disposition is symptomatic of the unease the class of person attracted to the fields would have had with the life of the imagination. The men that populate FitzPatrick's stories are essentially men of action, 'do-ers'

---

[3] Indeed, Kingsley Amis remarks that Kipling's tendency to over-use the oral style of narration actually weakened his stories: "What happens in a Kipling story is hard to remember afterwards – the telling is what counts: an exact comment on his weak narrative power" (Amis 1975: 110).

in a socio-economic context that rewards such an attitude. Paradoxically, however, the same social context also encouraged the development of narrative (the very stuff of fiction) in the form of the personal anecdote, the fireside yarn, the relaying of news and gossip to the information-starved men in this far reach of the Empire. These contradictory impulses – suspicion about loquacity, on the one hand, and the desire, on the other, to fill the idle evening hours – would readily lead to a literary form whose claims to legitimacy hinge on its faithfulness to actual events. Its proclaimed closeness to lived experience bestows upon it an authenticity that recommends it to the attentions of the metropolitan reader thirsty for glimpses into the exotic outposts of the colonies.

"The Outspan," as the title suggests, draws its subject-matter from a fireside yarn-swapping session. The first-person narrator is unnamed, but is a clear presence from the opening passages of the story. He provides the frame for the main story: several travellers are encamped one night under the stars and, as is customary in this kind of setting, the telling of stories soon commences. One of the characters at the fireside, "Barberton" (his place of domicile substitutes for his name), supplies the first half of the main narrative, which concerns the unusual life-style of an acquaintance of his who goes by the name of "Seboug-waan." Sebougwaan has two Swazi wives, and has adopted African customs. However, he eventually fetches up among the prospectors in Barberton, and dies a sudden, awful death from fever. Barberton recalls for his rapt audience's benefit the man's last, inexplicable cry: "Oh, my God! my poor wife!" (28).

The enigma – Who was his wife? Why did he leave her? What kind of man was he? – is resolved unintentionally by another member of the party: the "surveyor." (Here a profession substitutes for a name, the inference being that the company that night was composed of men who are interchangeable with others, who are 'types' rather than unique individuals.) The surveyor reports that he had a shipmate who was remarkable for his exemplary character, marred only by one flaw: his inability to forgive. This man suspected his wife of having affairs during his long absences at sea. He therefore settled his whole estate on her and their child and left England, never to return. The surveyor casually mentions his name at the end of his narrative, and a shocked Barberton recognizes his own "Sebougwaan."[4]

In the framed story, then, there are two clearly identifiable narrators who unwittingly provide two parts of the same story. Their two-part narrative is interrupted frequently by interlocutors: one anecdote merges with the next, the story as a whole displaying a singular lack of economy. Indeed, FitzPatrick is overwhelmed by his material: "The Outspan" teems with narratives, some of which interrupt others, while yet others are merely alluded to, serving as digressions from the main story.

The relationship between the frame narrator and the participants in the fireside yarn-swapping session is nonetheless a very simple one: he is a bystander who simply 'reports' the tales that unfold. There are six participating narrators in "The Outspan," and the story as a whole is a loosely structured collection of anecdotes. However, again, as with Scully, the voices heard do not compete in any ideological sense. The interest in the story is the overall lack of authorial management: there is no evidence, in fact, that any attempt at economy was made. The 'competition' between the voices, then, is more a consequence of bad stage-management than ideological conflict.[5]

---

[4] Kipling's famous tale, "Mrs. Bathurst" (1904), has a similar structure. Two narrators each provide a part of the tale about the New Zealand widow and hotel-keeper Mrs Bathurst and her (never fully disclosed) relationship with a man by the name of Vickery who jumps ship in Cape Town and is later found dead, having been struck by lightning. Pyecroft (a naval petty officer used as a narrator in several Kipling stories) provides the first part of the narrative, while the frame narrator's acquaintance, the railwayman Mr Hooper, provides the (much shorter) part about the discovery of Vickery's corpse. As in FitzPatrick's tale, it is a chance encounter between the narrators (brought together in Kipling's story through the agency of the frame narrator) that enables the full tale to be told.

[5] It is interesting in this regard to note the tone of Peter Randall's Foreword to the 1987 Lowry edition of *The Outspan*. Randall begins by observing: "Very few, even amongst his staunchest admirers, would be so bold as to claim that Sir Percy FitzPatrick is a major literary figure, or even that he possessed significant literary talent." He goes on to note that FitzPatrick was "inevitably subject to the racist, sexist and chauvinist attitudes of his time" and also possessed "an uncritical acceptance of the rightness of the imperial cause." The chief value of FitzPatrick's stories, Randall avers, is that they "provide, if nothing else, an excellent example of colonialist literature, with all the faults that this implies" (Randall 1987: unnumbered

Indeed, FitzPatrick's story is a model of ideological complacency. There are two main thrusts to "The Outspan," neither of which suggests any critical awareness on FitzPatrick's part. The first of these is the frame narrator's desire to evoke something of the life-style of the transport-riders, prospectors and others present in the interior at the time. He devotes much of his energy to glorifying this mode of life: "When a man has spent some years of his life [...] in the veld, in the waggon, or tent, or bush, it is an almost invariable rule that something which you can't define germinates in him and never entirely dies until he does" (3).

Clumsily inserted into this evocation of veld life is the second thrust of the story, the frame narrator's attempt to address the familiar colonial bogey of civilization's descent into barbarism upon its encounter with Africa. Sebougwaan 'goes native' and pays for it – "[c]ivilisation," as Barberton puts it, "scorned and flouted, being the instrument of its own revenge!" (12). There is no discernible irony here – no evidence that the frame narrator would dispute Barberton's ideologically loaded claim. The various narrators may speak with different inflections, but they are all companions around the campfire and as such enjoy a kind of comradely equality. This also applies to the frame narrator, whose task it is simply to relay the ethos of fireside yarn-swapping in nineteenth-century Africa. In the context of the period, the story's appeal would rest on its evocation of 'real-life adventure in Africa.' The close relation to 'lived experience' which the story claims gives it a quality of 'authenticity' that was no doubt intended to appeal to the metropolitan reader fascinated by the more exotic outer reaches of the colonies.[6]

In his incisive reading of "The Outspan," Gareth Cornwell demonstrates how the hierarchy which FitzPatrick sets up at the outset between "Telling" and "Happening" – between the recounting of an

---

prefatory pages). My own purpose in discussing FitzPatrick's work here is precisely to show, in technical terms, these "faults."

[6] "Induna Nairn," also included in the collection, has a similar peripatetic quality to "The Outspan": it is a long, semi-coherent narrative cloaked by a chauvinistic (in both senses) Victorian morality and all of the accompanying prejudices. Another story, "The Pool," as David Maughan Brown (1984) has argued, mixes the racism of colonial ideology with the melodrama favoured by the age, with similar results.

event and the original event itself – is subverted and undermined by the paradoxes and tensions within the story as a whole:

> What has happened is that despite the overt attempt to give substance to a cultural myth by invoking the authority of Happening, FitzPatrick's narrator has been obliged, in deference to the integrity of his narrative project and the discourse which frames it, to provide a psychological explanation for the dark night of Sebougwaan's soul. In so doing he implicitly rejects Barberton's pseudo-scientific ideology of racial determinism. (Cornwell 1983: 22)

As its subtitle "Deconstructing the Fiction of Race" indicates, Cornwell's article shows how FitzPatrick's story deconstructs itself: it believes itself to be doing one thing while in fact it can be seen to be doing something entirely contradictory: "paradoxically, the signifying system of FitzPatrick's narrative relies upon the agency of another, contradictory logic simultaneously at work in the text, undermining and inverting the hierarchy" (19). Presuming to illustrate the deterministic thesis expounded by Barberton – namely, that civilized Europeans "can't throw back to barbarism at will," that "settling down among savages" will always, as is demonstrated by the fate of Sebougwaan, end in "tragedy, trouble, ruin, call it what you like" (FitzPatrick 1897: 10) – which attests to a belief in what Cornwell calls "a structured, deterministic universe constantly communicating its nature to men through the medium of the experience which they undergo" (19), the story is forced by the conventions of narrative realism to provide a psychological explanation for Sebougwaan's undoing.

Cornwell makes this point succinctly at the end of his discussion of "Induna Nairn," another of the stories in *The Outspan*, in which the unfavourable comparison between a black woman and a white woman who is taken to epitomize the 'good woman' in fact reverses itself: "Thus once again the sheer irrationality of racial mythology comes into conflict with the moral–psychological logic of the realist narrative, hopelessly compromising its integrity" (25).

Cornwell's concern is to demonstrate the discursive dissonance in examples of nineteenth-century colonial fiction. He includes a brief commentary on Scully's "Kellson's Nemesis" and refers also to Sarah Gertrude Millin's *God's Stepchildren* in order to argue that the attempt to embody the ideology of racial determinism in realist fiction produces textual anomalies:

> In each case, the attempt by the author to seal off the narrative in the envelope of this determinism results in a falsifying contradiction, for the epistemological premises of classic realism must inevitably come into conflict with a priori theories of human nature. (27)

FitzPatrick's "Telling," finally, has ironically come to dominate and configure the formerly ascendant "Happening."

This argument is a sophisticated demonstration of the ideological discontinuities and contradictions of racist colonial texts like "The Outspan." In showing up such discontinuities and contradictions, Cornwell illustrates Pierre Macherey's point in *A Theory of Literary Production* that there is no book "which is completely self-conscious, aware of the means of its own realisation, aware of what it is doing" (1978: 27).

My concern with the story has been to point out the absence from the text of what Bakhtin would call a dialogic structure, hence a degree of authorial 'artfulness.' The voices of various narrators are heard, among whom "Barberton" and "the surveyor" are the most dominant, but no irony in the use of the spoken discourse of others is discernible, and the story is therefore monologic in structure. To take up Cornwell's point: if there is another voice to be heard (in ideological terms), then it is that of the text's 'unconscious.'

There is no evidence that FitzPatrick was conscious of the irony in the fact that his story, which is meant to illustrate a thesis about racial determinism, is in fact forced by the conventions of narrative realism to provide a psychological explanation for Sebougwaan's undoing. It is precisely the question of *control* over this kind of irony that distinguishes the ingenuous oral-style story from its later, more artful and sophisticated successor. Had FitzPatrick 'set up' his narrators in a manner which implied that there was a clear discrepancy to be detected between their views about racial determinism on the one hand, and those of the reporting frame narrator on the other, his use of the oral-style story would more closely approximate that of Glanville, Gibbon and, particularly, Bosman.

— Ω —

"Ukushwama" and "The Outspan" were chosen as the principal focus of this chapter because they are both outstanding examples of a certain kind of oral-style story –the 'artless' style. Such tales lack the sophistication that we shall observe in the "Vrouw Grobelaar" stories of Perceval Gibbon, but they can be seen to be attempting a greater degree of artistic 'crafting' than was evident in the tales by Drayson, Boyle, and Ingram. Scully's attempts in this regard were discussed above. Fitz-Patrick shows less control over his narrative, but it is significant that he actually attempts devices like narrative parallelism (the prefatory tale about remarkable coincidences and the ensuing main story illustrating just such a coincidence) and the concealed ending – however clumsily these are executed.

Scully and FitzPatrick can thus be seen as 'transitional' figures in the development of the oral-style story. In the tales by Drayson, Boyle and Ingram, the constitutive 'raw materials' of the genre were seen to be present, although these were not exploited in a humorous and ironic way, and they were not used to reflect obliquely on any serious themes. Instead, these writers laid the stress on verisimilitude, underplaying any fictional dimension that may have been latent in their material. Such a procedure is also present in the tales of Scully and FitzPatrick, although there are small but significant shifts of emphasis to be observed in these later stories. Whereas the work of the earlier writers revealed a large degree of generic indeterminacy – suggesting, I argued, that these writers had not achieved an entirely coherent mode in which to give expression to the 'African experience' – Scully and FitzPatrick are more consciously 'telling tales.' They may still claim some degree of authenticity for their stories, but it is less clear that they are being entirely ingenuous in these claims.

The 'fictionalizing' of the frame narrators of their stories is one indication of this. Whereas in the collections by Drayson, Boyle, and Ingram a collapsing of the distinction between author and frame narrator frequently occurs, Scully and FitzPatrick maintain this distinction. Despite the fact that Scully's frame narrator frequently appears as a thinly disguised authorial persona (as I have argued), and that Scully does not take advantage of the potential for ironic interplay between the various levels of narrative of his tales, he does at least attempt to sustain the illusion that his frame narrator is not to be identified in any simple way with himself as author. The same is true for FitzPatrick: nowhere in *The Outspan* can there be an automatic identification of FitzPatrick as author with the "I" of the first-person narratives (which make up four of the six tales in the volume).

In the tales of Scully and FitzPatrick discussed above, the oral-style story thus moves closer to its more advanced, ironic mode. The discursive footing of the stories by these writers is firmer than that of the earlier oral-style tale, they are more consciously 'fictionalizing,' and there is more evidence of an 'aesthetic' dimension in their work. However, they have not taken the oral-style story to the stage where the various constitutive elements of the genre become entirely *conventional* – where, in other words, any 'authenticity' that is claimed is patently part of an elaborate illusion which is simultaneously asserted and undermined. As we shall see, it took Perceval Gibbon to introduce this decisive shift into the oral-style story. But it is Ernest Glanville, with his "Uncle Abe Pike" creation, who brings the oral-style story to the cusp of 'artfulness,' and I wish to consider him before moving on to Gibbon.

———————   ᧞ ᧞   ———————

4 On the Cusp of 'Artfulness'

Ernest Glanville's "Uncle Abe Pike"

∾ ───

I REMARKED AT THE BEGINNING of the previous chapter that Glanville's collection, *Tales from the Veld* (1897),[1] was the first example in South African literature of a sequence of oral-style stories consistently using the same internal narrator, but that his style of story, according to Ernest Pereira, had more in common with yarns told in the American mid-West than with tales told in the South African veld. The discussion that follows will show that Glanville's tales are in many ways very firmly rooted in the soil of the Eastern Cape province, and do in fact make an important contribution to the development of the South African oral-style story.

Glanville introduces his narrator in the following way:

> Abe Pike – Old Abe Pike, or Uncle Abe as he was variously called – lived in a one-horse shanty in the division of Albany, Cape Colony. I won't locate his farm, for various reasons, beyond saying that there is a solitary blue-gum on the south side of the house and the rudiments of a cowshed on the north. Uncle Abe was not ambitious; he was slow, but he was sure. So he said. One blue-gum satisfied him, and as for the cowshed he meant to complete it during the century. I don't introduce him as a tree planter, but as a narrator of most extraordinary yarns. He called them facts – but of the truth of this the reader may judge. (1897: 1)

Several things are immediately obvious in this introductory passage. There is, to begin with, a clear indication that the first-person frame narrator treats his subject, Abe Pike, with a degree of amused scepti-

---

[1] The first fifteen stories in *Tales from the Veld* are reprints of the tales from Glanville's earlier collection, *Kloof Yarns* (1896), and I have therefore chosen to use the later, better-known text.

cism. The "various reasons" for not being more precise about the location of Uncle Abe's farm are not specified, but the implication is that the farm is not entirely salubrious. That Uncle Abe "was slow, but he was sure" is followed immediately by the cautionary "[s]o he said," and this suggests that the narrator does not accept his subject's word at face value. The humour in Abe Pike's intention to complete his cow-shed "during the century" reinforces the reader's growing sense that Abe Pike is a lazy layabout with a penchant for stretching the truth, and the narrator's description of Pike's tales as "most extraordinary yarns," which he regards as "facts" but which the reader must treat with a great deal of scepticism, merely confirms this impression.

We are immediately aware, in other words, that we are dealing with an entirely different sort of tale from those of Glanville's predecessors. With remarkable economy, the opening passage of the collection establishes the setting and style of tale which the reader will be likely to encounter – the 'tall tale.' Accordingly, the teller of these tales – the raconteur Abe Pike – must not be taken seriously: his tales are told to amuse and divert rather than to instruct and enlighten. Thus a new form of oral-style story appears in South African literature – one which exploits the conventions of the oral narrative in order to place an ironic distance between teller and reporter of tale and thereby to infuse this style of story with humour.

Glanville's best-known story, "Uncle Abe's Big Shoot," is a good example of this. The frame narrator, a man young enough for Abe Pike to try his yarns out on but not gullible enough to believe them, arrives at the old man's homestead to "crow over" his achievement of shooting a brace of red-wing partridges (1897: 8). Far from being impressed, the old man proceeds to tell his young companion a yarn about shooting two birds with an "ole muzzle-loader" (9). His fantastical yarn grows in the telling, however, and he ends up claiming to have bagged a buck, a nine-pound barbel, a brace of pheasants, a hare, and a porcupine – all with a single shot! To the young man's incredulous response, the old man retorts:

> "I was there – you weren't. Tis easy accounted for. When I pulled the
> trigger the fish leapt from the water in the line, and the bullet passed
> through him inter the buck. I tole you the gun kicked. Well, it flew out
> o' my hands, an' hit the hare square on the nose. To recover myself, I

threw up my hands, an' caught hold o' the two pheasants jest startled
outer the bush."

"And the porcupine?"

"I sot down on the porkipine, an' if you'd like to 'xamine my pants
you'll find where his quills went in. I was mighty sore, an' I could ha'
spared him well from the bag. But 'twas a wonderful good shot. You're
not going?"

"Yes, I am. I'm afraid to stay with you." (13–14)

This humorous exchange exemplifies the tone of Glanville's collection
as a whole, and in it can be seen the various elements already discussed: the sceptical distance of the frame narrator, the mock-seriousness
of the yarnster, and the setting and style typical of yarns of this sort.

Malvern van Wyk Smith remarks that Abe Pike, Glanville's "most
memorable invention [...] told the most marvellously tall stories in a
homely vernacular that borrows much from Mark Twain and anticipates Bosman" (1990: 24). Twain's influence (indeed, that of the entire
mid-West frontier-yarn tradition) is indubitable; where Glanville anticipates Bosman, however, warrants a little more attention. Van Wyk
Smith is correct in identifying this latter connection, but there are differences as well as similarities to be discerned between the two writers.

As should be clear from the foregoing discussion, Glanville's
achievement is to have infused the oral-style tale with humour and a
degree of irony, and in this way he departs significantly from the
ingenuousness with which his predecessors tell their tales. He also de-
lights in giving his narrator a "homely vernacular" (Van Wyk Smith),
and this adds much to the oral 'stylization' of his tales. Following
Bakhtin, Glanville does not so much display "an orientation toward the
oral form of narration" (Eichenbaum's formulation), as "an orientation
toward *another person's discourse*" (Bakhtin 1984: 192; emphasis added).
In other words, it is precisely the idiosyncratic nature of Abe Pike's
verbal style that Glanville is intent on capturing.

Bakhtin characterizes the first type of oral narrative as "simple *skaz*,"
the second as "parodistic *skaz*." Parodistic *skaz* deploys a storyteller
figure precisely because of the idiosyncratic nature of this figure's
verbal style. This, argues Bakhtin, is distinct from the author's own
style, and a dialogic structure is thereby established in which author (or
frame narrator) and internal narrator speak in stylistically and ideo-

logically distinct discourses. The purpose of establishing this dialogic structure is to parody the storyteller and indirectly suggest that the author has a different attitude to that expressed by his narrator.

Where in this schema does one place Glanville's tales? I have already suggested that they are demonstrably more sophisticated than those of his contemporaries Scully and FitzPatrick (and certainly more so than those by Drayson, Boyle, and Ingram). But are they invested with the same degree of sustained irony later used by Gibbon and Bosman? Addressing this issue hinges on how one interprets the character Abe Pike and the nature of his relationship with the young frame narrator – and, at a further remove, the implied author.

Uncle Abe Pike is a more complex creation than would appear at first sight. As the sequence unfolds, it becomes clear that he is used in a variety of ways by the author. In his guise as entertaining raconteur telling patently fantastic yarns, he is the butt of the frame narrator's scepticism and is merely an object of amusement for the reader. However, as with Oom Schalk Lourens, the reader is never entirely sure whether Abe Pike is always in earnest.

For instance, in the story "The End of the Tiger," Abe finally succeeds in killing an old "tiger" (a black leopard) that has been raiding the young frame narrator's herd. For once, his tale – in which he recounts the killing of the tiger – actually plays down his achievements. He claims that the beast was in fact killed by an old baboon, and that his bullet had gone wide of the mark. However, the frame narrator later comes to interpret events differently:

> I have reason to believe that Uncle Abe maligned himself for the sake of the yarn. On examining the tiger's skin subsequently, I found no traces of the baboon's teeth, but exactly between the eyes was a bullet-hole. The old man had held his gun straight in the dark kloof. (117)

This tale is used, I believe, to show that Abe Pike is concerned more with telling a good tale than with faithfully recounting the pedestrian facts of the matter at hand – even when such a 'tale' actually underplays his achievements.

Indeed, upon closer scrutiny of his yarns it appears that he is gesturing towards an interpretation that goes beyond literal adherence to the facts. For example, he earlier recounts a fantastic yarn ("Abe Pike and the Whip") about losing the thong of his whip-stick at a particularly awkward time: it is dark and he is unable to recover the thong, which he requires in order to drive his oxen home and out of danger of the marauding black tiger. A further problem is that the oxen are tired and simply refuse to budge. At this point, he remarks, he learnt something which gave him "'a better understandin' o' the spread o' kindness overlaying things'" (27). He goes on to say that a whip-snake thoughtfully attached itself to the end of his bamboo stick and, of course, the oxen respond to the first strike of the new 'whip' with amazing energy, thus getting the old man out of his predicament. The frame narrator responds, "'Uncle Abe Pike! Do you expect me to believe that?'"; to which the old man replies, "'I have my hopes, my lad. But when yer gets older you'll get more faith [...] I tell you there's a heap o' goodness among animiles an' reptiles, tho' this is the fust time I 'xperienced the thoughtfulness o' a snake'" (29–30).

It is possible to interpret Abe Pike's yarns as being something more than the manic ramblings of a deluded old man. At times they seem to take on some of the attributes of the fable – or even the parable. Beneath the surface level of the fantastic yarn, in other words, there appears to be a deeper level of signification which fulfils the purpose of conveying some useful lesson or moral. The point of the tales, the old man seems at times to be implying, is not their literal veracity or otherwise, but whether they offer some understanding of life's circumference. The yarn itself may be patently untrue, but the broader human vision it illustrates may in the end be more significant.

Interestingly, not all of Abe Pike's tales are light-hearted yarns. Although humour is never absent, tales like "Abe Pike and the Kaffir War," in which Abe recounts his experience of the violence of the Frontier Wars, or "A Bugle Call," a moving story about the brutal death of the boy bugler of the 94th Regiment, or, again, "The Young Burgher," in which a Boer woman loses both husband and son at the hands of the marauding Zulu hordes, clearly belong to another genre in Abe Pike's extensive repertoire. In these tales (and others dealing with the Frontier Wars) Pike becomes the seasoned frontiersman, battle-hardened and resourceful in adversity. Although one does not, of course, accept these tales at face value, there is a distinct sense that the young frame narrator (who is clearly intended to guide the reader's responses) is less cynical in his attitude, and more eager to learn from the experience of his older companion.

The appearance of the Xhosa witchdoctor and friend of Abe Pike's, Bolo, adds a further area of interest to the tales. Like Abe Pike, Bolo is a skilled storyteller, and beneath the surface banter and mock-rivalry which characterizes their interactions there is a clear sense of their mutual respect. The best example of this occurs in the story "Abe Pike and the Honey-Bird," in which the frame narrator follows the spoor of a cow and her calf stolen from his herd – suspiciously, it must be added, around the time of the hasty departure from his farm of Abe Pike and Bolo.

The story is ambiguous. The frame narrator tracks the spoor to Abe Pike's farm, and there it is obliterated by the hoofmarks of Abe Pike's own herd. Pike seems to know a little too much about what the younger man is after, but covers up with a typical piece of eloquent obfuscation. We learn from Pike, however, that Bolo has also just left his farm: "'He quitted last night. No, he ain't gone off with your cow. He was skeered'" (52). What Bolo was "skeered" of is then the substance of what appears suspiciously to be an elaborate diversionary yarn about a honey-bird leading Bolo to the black tiger's lair. The young man then proposes to go off on the tiger's spoor, an idea which is headed off by yet another Abe Pike yarn. This last concerns Pike's encounter with a spiteful honey-bird which leads him to a "bee-tree" belonging to another bird. Abe Pike chops the tree up for the honey, but is interrupted by a "bird court-case" in which a jury, consisting of an oriole, a spreuw and a mouse-bird, and a judge (a crow), pronounce the honey-bird guilty of usurping another bird's property. The unlucky bird is then decapitated by a fiscal shrike and its body is devoured by the crow. Abe Pike concludes: "'I went home then, thinking as how they might try me for aiding and abetting a crime'" (59).

Pike is, of course, alluding to the "crime" of being party to a raid on another bird's "bee-tree," but the story as a whole is ambiguous enough to suggest that the actual "crime" Pike is alluding to might well be that of helping Bolo steal the young man's cattle.

Abe Pike is, in fact, a deeply ambivalent representative of frontier society. His closeness to Bolo, his respect for Xhosa culture (in "Abe's Diamond Mine" Pike defends the Xhosa custom of *lobola*), and his idle and shiftless ways all suggest that at least part of Glanville's intention in creating such a character was to satirize notions of settler industry, loyalty to the colonial authorities and, indeed, 'civilization.'

These purported attributes of settler society are conspicuously called into question in the tale "End of the Scouting," which begins with the frame narrator praising Abe Pike for his "industry" in stamping mealies with a wooden pestle and mortar. Pike responds thus:

> "Industry be blowed – it's my teeth! They're worn down, and not equal to chewing hard mealies. You take pattern by me, sonny, and keep your teeth. Lor' love yer, when I sees young boys and gals with half their teeth missin', I'm jest thinkin' that there's no ignorance like that of the civilised man. Take me, or take an ord'nary Kaffir turned sixty, and look at his mouth. Teeth as white and soun' as a animile's – 'cos why? – 'cos he ain't loadin' his inside with all sorts o' hots and colds, an' sweets, and thingammies painted yeller an' red – an' 'cos he polishes up his grinders with a bit o' wood and heaps o' water." (198)

Under pressure from his young friend, Pike is forced to concede that "Kaffirs" take to the white man's "civilised" ways all too readily when given the chance, but concludes pointedly that "'When you start to civilise a Kaffir you give him toothache, and fill him as full o' wickedness an' sickness as a white man'" (199).

This can, of course, be read as a homely version of the post-Enlightenment idea of the Noble Savage, perfect in his 'natural' state, but prone to corruption by Western influence. And, indeed, Pike's respect is for the "kaffir" in his 'natural' state, untainted by foreign interference (notice the telling comparison above between "Kaffir" and "animile"). In this 'natural' state he is respected as a worthy adversary – proud, war-like, and athletic. He is also credited with a great deal of cunning, and is able, Pike has ample occasion to remark, to run rings around the colonial government. The latter, Pike remarks in "Abe Pike and the Kaffir War," is "a ass – alus was a ass, and alus will be a ass [...] so blamed ignorant that any Kaffir chief could best it every time" (131–32).

From the above it can readily be seen that Abe Pike is a complex creation, at once an unbelievable yarnster and a respected frontiersman, a man professing loyalty to the Queen (this is illustrated in the story

"The 'Red' Kaffirs") and derisive of the colonial administration – anti-nomian and law-abiding, racist and humane.

The complexities inherent in the presentation of Abe Pike carry over into his relationship with the 'reporter' of his tales, the young frame narrator. As has been suggested above, this relationship is not an entirely stable one. For the most part, the young man merely fulfils the role of being an incredulous but absorbed listener to the fantastic yarns. At times, however, the old man plays the role of avuncular counsellor to his younger companion, and the stories in which this occurs are, accordingly, both more credible and more serious.

This, in turn, suggests an ambivalent authorial attitude on Glan-ville's part. Is his purpose merely to parody his creation as an incredible Munchausian figure[2] planted in the Eastern Cape landscape, or is there some sympathy between author and character? From my argument so far, it should be clear that although an element of the former runs through *Tales from the Veld*, there is a stronger pull towards some sort of identification between author and character.

This latter tendency is most clearly revealed in the story "A Kaffir's Play," which begins with a long discursive passage about the nature of the "kaffir":

> The red Kaffir is a man with a good deal of character, which he does his best to destroy. The pure kraal Kaffir, who lounges negligently in his red blanket or squats on his loins by the fire at night, telling interminable stories about nothing in particular, has many points which mark him from the "town boy" – the spoiled child of civilisation, who treads tenderly in his hard "Blucher" boots, and covers his corduroy trousers with bright patches of other material; who has to support his weary frame against every pillar and post and corner he comes across, and who is generally shiftless, saucy, and squalid. (232)

The narrator goes on to identify a range of other defining characteristics ("stern pride of race," "sullen reserve," "national impulse to fight"; 233), reiterates the myth about the descent of the Bantu people from "the valley of the Nile, the hot nursery of fierce races," and quotes Pringle's poem "The Caffer" for its "vivid picture of the Kaffir" (233–

---

[2] See note 1, in Chapter 6 (Slater), on the connections between Glanville's cre-ation and Baron Munchausen.

34).[3] Concluding that the "Kaffir thrived" under the "fierce ordeal of war," and that he is "the victim of civilisation" (234), the passage ends with a plea for him to be allowed "a plot of land sufficient for his wants" in order that he "retain some of those characteristics which made conquerors of his warrior ancestors" (234).

This long prefatory passage is narrated not by Abe Pike (as should be clear from the uninflected register), nor even by the frame narrator, but by an intrusive authorial voice. Significantly, it is followed by a tale by Abe Pike, who, as if in agreement with the foregoing, begins: "'Yes [...] the Kaffir can use two things better'n a white man, easy – his tongue and his stick. I seed a Kaffir onct get the better of a fencing master'" (234–35).

I have quoted the opening passages of this story at length because I believe they clearly reveal the degree of consonance between author and character. Scattered over a dozen stories, although expressed in a more demotic register, can be found an echo of these views in the voice of Abe Pike. This suggests that, while Pike may well serve as a figure of amusement in the stories, there is also an underlying strain of ideological sympathy with him on the part of the author.

On a formal level, the intrusion of an authorial voice constitutes a lapse of authorial control over the sequence of stories. The structural distance between author, frame narrator and storyteller is momentarily disrupted and any illusion that the last is an element in a sustained ideological parody or critique is dispelled. This recalls the ideological collusion between Scully and his magistrate persona, where one can be seen to be the fictional representation of the 'real' other. The effect is the same: the notion of authorial distance from, and manipulation of, a character for the purposes of satire and parody evaporates.

What must immediately be added, however, is that, while the multiplicity of voices heard in *Tales from the Veld* (principally those of the internal narrator, frame narrator, and implied author) resolves itself, in the final analysis, into a single-voiced discourse, this discourse is in

---

[3] Glanville gives a free version of Pringle's poem, rather than an accurate quotation. "The Caffer" originally appeared in *Thompson's Travels* in 1827, but it is likely that Glanville used the better-known *Ephemerides* (which appeared in 1828) as his source. In a still later version of the poem, which appeared in *African Sketches* in 1834, the original Dutch "kloof" was replaced by its Scottish equivalent "cleugh" (Pereira & Chapman 1989: 111). Glanville uses the Dutch form in his quotation.

itself ideologically ambivalent. A genuine dialogic structure – in which the internal narrator is 'set up' by the frame narrator and/or author to speak in a stylistically and ideologically distinct discourse – is thus not a feature of the Abe Pike stories, but the overall ideological thrust of the tales is by no means unambiguously supportive of the colonial effort in South Africa.

To return, then, to the question posed earlier: where does one place Glanville's tales in the sequence of oral-style stories which are the focus of this study? That we have come a long way from the colonial complacency of a Drayson or a Boyle should be abundantly clear from the discussion above: not only does the native now have a voice, he actually also elicits a marked degree of sympathy from (even, perhaps, colludes with) the main narrator in the tales, and this figure is himself supported by the authorial voice which intrudes conspicuously at one point.

However, we have not yet reached the point where an internal narrator is used for the clear purpose of setting up an ironic, dialogic narrative structure – a structure in which a parody of the internal narrator's verbal style and ideological bent is clearly the main purpose of deploying an oral style of story. As we shall see, it is in this respect that both Gibbon and Bosman are different.

That Glanville is thus on the 'cusp' of the 'artful' oral-style story is demonstrated by going back to examine the Preface he writes to his tales, a Preface which, with some qualification, is very similar to those adorning collections by his predecessors:

> The tales here set forth are, subject to a generous allowance for Uncle Abe's gift of imagination, true to the animal life and the scenery of a district in the Cape occupied by the British Settlers of 1820 – a tract rich in incidents of border warfare, hallowed by the struggles of that early band of colonists, saturated with the superstitions and folk lore of the Kaffirs, and thoroughly familiar to the author – who passed his boyhood there. [unnumbered prefatory page]

Again, as in the prefaces of earlier collections of tales, it is asserted that the stories are 'true' to the character of their human and natural setting – a setting characterized by "incidents of border warfare," and "hallowed by the struggles" of the early colonists. That the author "passed his boyhood there" is a further bid for 'authenticity.'

The significant thing about Glanville's preface, however, is the allowance made for the unreliable 'filter' through which the stories are percolated. The oral-style story's inherent potential for irony and subversion is indirectly alluded to here, and this is a tacit signal from the author that a story's mediation through oral narration, far from guaranteeing 'authenticity,' is more likely to prove a complicating factor requiring greater interpretative rigour from the reader. The 'tall tales' that then ensue in such fantastical profusion retrospectively invest this early signal with added significance.

Glanville's tales thus represent a further step in the development of the oral-style story: the stylization of the internal narrator, the humour that the distance between this figure and the frame narrator allows, and a greater sense of the unreliability of this sort of tale are all indications that the genre is becoming more complex. In the next chapter, it will be seen how the potential for ironic interplay between the various narrative levels of the oral-style story is more fully and consistently exploited in the "Vrouw Grobelaar" tales of Perceval Gibbon.

———————— ✒ ✒ ———————

5 The 'Artful' Oral-Style Story

Perceval Gibbon's "Vrouw Grobelaar" Sequence

☙ ————————————————————————————

T HE FOREGOING DISCUSSION OF WRITERS of the closing years of the nineteenth century has brought us to the brink of the new self-awareness that now begins to manifest itself in the South African oral-style story. It will be seen here that Perceval Gibbon's achievement was to take all of the elements present in the stories examined so far and to infuse them with a new selfconsciousness and artistic purpose.

Gibbon's *The Vrouw Grobelaar's Leading Cases* (1905)[1] is thus an important (and unjustly neglected) contribution to the development of the South African short story. It has unfortunately long been out of print, and this perhaps testifies to its marginalized status in South African literature. The collection is of great interest by virtue of its many intrinsic merits, some of which should emerge in the discussion that follows, but it is especially undeserving of neglect in that it represents an important stage in the development of the South African oral-style story. Gibbon's "Vrouw Grobelaar" is a key literary antecedent to South Africa's most celebrated fictional narrator: Bosman's Oom Schalk Lourens.

---

[1] There is another collection of tales of this period which, in outward appearance at least, bears a striking resemblance to Gibbon's *The Vrouw Grobelaar's Leading Cases*. This is Herbert Noyes's *Jan of the Thirstland: Being for the Most Part Reflections of the Vrouw van Renan of Renanshoek* (1910). The Vrouw van Renan is not, however, the principal narratological feature around which the tales are organized. She features in only a few of the tales, and the collection as a whole therefore more closely resembles C.R. Prance's *Tante Rebella's Saga: A Backvelder's Scrap-book* (1937), which is briefly discussed in the chapter on Blignaut.

The Vrouw Grobelaar's Leading Cases has received some critical attention. An appreciative contemporary reviewer, noting that the Vrouw
Grobelaar "cannot fail to attract the admiration of all readers" with her
"shrewd common-sense, sharp tongue and clever philosophy" (anon.
1907: 517), clearly failed to see any irony in Gibbon's use of his narrator.
Indeed, the reviewer also applauds the "keen insight" Gibbon gave in
his racist earlier work *Souls in Bondage* "into the half-caste world which
exists near the centres of civilisation in South Africa" (517).

By contrast, Geraldine Constance uses *The Vrouw Grobelaar's Leading
Cases* as the transitional text in her dissertation examining the development from "Manichean allegory" to the "beginnings of enlightenment"
in Gibbon's three South African works. Between the nakedly racist pot-
boiler *Souls in Bondage* (1904) and the altogether more sophisticated
Margaret Harding (1911), argues Constance, comes the ideologically
ambivalent *Vrouw Grobelaar*, in which "Gibbon structures the stories so
as to avoid authorial responsibility for this ideology by the inclusion of
specific narrators" (1992: 26). She notes that some of the seventeen
stories in *Vrouw Grobelaar* appeared before the publication of the
volume in 1905, and "without the frame narration which affects reception of the collection" (27).[2] "It is therefore unsurprising," she argues,

---

[2] Constance's references (1992: 27) are vague and/or inaccurate. She notes that
"A Good End" appeared in the *Natal Witness* in 1901 as "Van der Linde's Dying"
and that "Unto the Third Generation," "The Dreamface," and "The Avenger of
Blood" were published in the *Edinburgh Magazine* in 1904. The latter reference is
surely incorrect, as the *Edinburgh Magazine* ceased publication long before this.
(The *Edinburgh Review* – which was still functioning in 1904 – contains nothing by
Gibbon for this year, and is in any event very unlikely to have published such
material.) Two other Gibbon stories which Constance cites as having appeared
earlier are "The Post Cart" and "Dissipation in Dopfontein." These, says Constance, appeared in the *Rand Daily Mail* in 1902 (she provides only years of publication in all cases, and her bibliography contains no details about these stories).
However, neither of these stories re-appears in *Vrouw Grobelaar*.
These inaccuracies (outright errors?) aside, the interesting thing about these
stories is that none contains, as a key ingredient, the kind of racist sentiments from
which Gibbon might have wanted to distance himself. They are all concerned with
matters pertaining to internal relations in the Boer community itself (the poignancy
of a son having to kill his father; the bitter rivalry between father and son; the
infatuation of a man for an imaginary woman), and any irony that would be introduced by the use of a frame narrator would not bear upon racial sentiments. This,
of course, may itself be significant: if Gibbon did publish these stories in an earlier

"that contradictory and racist notions persist in the stories" (27). None-theless, she adds, there is a development to be observed away from the authorial position in *Souls in Bondage*, for Gibbon "has shed responsi-bility for the racist attitudes which are visibly those of the storyteller, Vrouw Grobelaar, an elderly woman and a member of a particular community to which he does not belong" (27). Constance concludes her chapter on *The Vrouw Grobelaar's Leading Cases* by remarking that the final story in the collection ("Her Own Story") and its position in the sequence "suggest that Gibbon has become unsure of his racial beliefs and that he is trying to point to the difference between the Vrouw Grobelaar and himself" (40).

Constance is possibly correct in identifying a central ambivalence in authorial attitude in *Vrouw Grobelaar*. The journalist in Gibbon probably shrewdly judged that his more prejudiced readers would see in his tales accurate renderings of South African life, complete with an un-questioned racial hierarchy, while for the more enlightened there would be no easy identification of author with racist narrator.

Ernest Pereira is a more sympathetic analyst of *The Vrouw Grobe-laar's Leading Cases*. Citing the masterful opening story "Unto the Third Generation" as an example, Pereira remarks: "Unlike the largely comic, plot-orientated tales of his contemporaries, Gibbon's are studies in psychology and human relationships which in many ways anticipate the stories of Pauline Smith" (1986b: 111). And Gibbon ends this story, Pereira adds, in a way that Bosman, with his "acute sense of the close contiguity of the comic and tragic in our lives, would have appreciated" (112): "The Vrouw Grobelaar, to point a weighty moral, turned her face upon Katje. But that young lady was sleeping soundly with her mouth

---

form, then he may have selected those which at their core did not express views with which he felt uneasy.

The one possible exception (and thus the only story worth examining in this connection) is "The Avenger of Blood," as it deals with the peculiar death of Fanie van der Merwe, a young white man who accidentally kills a young black boy and is avenged by the boy's elderly black companion. Even here, however, the story is, if anything, critical of the young man's racism, and so the introduction of a frame narrator would not significantly alter it in this respect. (In any event, the story has proved untraceable in its putative earlier form, and it appears that Constance her-self never saw it.)

open" (1905: 11). Pereira thus ascribes a greater degree of self-awareness and ironic critique to Gibbon than Constance would allow.

My own reading of *The Vrouw Grobelaar's Leading Cases* is that while
Gibbon was undoubtedly prone to some of the stock racial notions of
the time, his stories demonstrate a far greater selfconsciousness than
was evident in those of his contemporaries Scully and FitzPatrick, and
this is reflected in his skilful use of literary artifice. In the discussion
that follows, I shall point out the inconsistencies that exist regarding
authorial attitude to the Vrouw Grobelaar's racism, but I shall argue
that, taken as a whole, *The Vrouw Grobelaar's Leading Cases* tends to
question rather than endorse the prejudices of the times. It is no
accident, in other words, that a great deal of 'artfulness' now enters the
South African oral-style story.

— Ω —

The Vrouw Grobelaar's Leading Cases is a collection of seventeen stories
which all feature an internal narrator, the Vrouw herself. An early indication of Gibbon's artfulness is his care in setting the scene. In the
opening passages of the first story, "Unto the Third Generation," he
describes his narrator as "a lady of excellent standing, as much by
reason of family connections [...] as of her wealth" (1905: 1):

> Her face is a portentous mask of solemnity, and her figure is spacious
> beyond the average of Dutch ladies, so that certain chairs are tacitly con-
> ceded her as a monopoly. The good Vrouw does not read or write, and
> having never found a need in herself of these arts, is the least thing impa-
> tient of those who practise them. The Psalms, however, she appears to
> know by heart; also other portions of the Bible; and is capable of spitting
> Scripture at you on the smallest provocation. (2)

Her extended household – "some half-dozen of nieces, a nephew or
two, and a litter of grandchildren" (3) – does her the service of providing her with an audience: "It was in no sense an unwilling service, for
her imagination ran to the gruesome, and she never planted a precept
but she drove it home with a case in point" (6). Katje, one of her nieces,
is the Vrouw's chief interlocutor, and provokes the tales mainly by
expressing a contrary view.

The fact that the Vrouw Grobelaar cannot read or write makes her
gift the richer. Like storytellers in a primary oral culture, she is accomp-

lished in the art of verbal exchange – be it mere banter or a fully-fledged tale. She relies on a conversational turn of phrase and a store of memorable phraseology derived mainly from the Old Testament, itself a rich source of oral lore.[3]

The Vrouw's context is very much a rural one: the community of Dopfontein is dependent on land and cattle for survival and is bound to the seasons. These God-fearing people are relentlessly engaged in a stark confrontation with the elements and a baneful fate which presides over the entire landscape. The Boers, Gibbon's frame narrator remarks, "are a lonely folk and God's finger writes large in their lives." This, he says, is the reason for the Vrouw's "stores of tales" being "often horrible enough" (6).

The Vrouw Grobelaar's stories thus portray a typical Boer farming community of the late nineteenth century. They have wholly sub-jugated the local population, have an Old-Testament fear of God, and have placed the local predikant at the centre of their religious cosmo-logy. Theirs is a deeply prejudiced society in the grip of a conceptual narrowness which breeds superstition and gossip, and whose members take a thinly concealed pleasure in the misfortune of others. The flat continuity of their lives is broken only by human contact, or, more spectacularly, by the tragedies that surface periodically, which, if memorable enough, enter local oral history.

As is typical in this kind of society, conversation on the stoep during the evening leisure hours modulates into the telling of tales. The ab-sence of any alternative entertainment and the curiosity stimulated by their dull routine provide a fertile matrix for the oral tale. Casual and desultory conversation usually prompts the Vrouw to invoke a moral to encapsulate the topic of discussion, which, in turn, is usually illus-trated by a story.

Having introduced his storyteller and her milieu in the opening passages of the first story, the frame narrator introduces himself, albeit in outline only. He is Katje's lover, whom she meets "with the readiest lips and the friendliest hand in the world" (4). We learn later that he is an Englishman and a schoolmaster (attributes which, of course, provide conventional distancing and ironizing elements), but

---

[3] In their study of the short story, Stone, Packer & Hoopes (1976: 26–29) cite Genesis as an early influence on the development of the genre.

he is not given a name nor is he described in any further detail. However, we do learn at the end that he and Katje are to be married, and this elicits the last tale in the collection, "Her Own Story," in which the Vrouw relates her own experiences of married life. This detail suggests that Gibbon is concerned to present a cohesive sequence of stories with a teleological dimension. The frame narrator's repeated visits to the homestead in his pursuit of Katje provide the occasion for the stories, but they work towards a conclusion. The implication is that the convivial storytelling evenings will come to an end when he and Katje get married and move away.

The frame narrator goes on to present the contextualizing detail which frames the stories themselves:

> I almost think I can see it now – the low Dutch kitchen with its plank ceiling, the old lady in her chair, with an illustrative forefinger uplifted to punctuate the periods of her tale, the embers, white and red, glowing on the hearth, and the intent, shadow-pitted faces of the hearers, agape for horrors. (6–7)

Thus the constitutive elements of the oral tale – an intimate physical setting, a riveting storyteller, long evening hours to while away, and a receptive audience – are all deftly introduced here, before the onset of the first story proper.

The Vrouw's first story is provoked by Katje's indignant remark to her aunt that her grandfather's character has nothing to do with hers, and this remark provides the catalyst for the tale itself in the pattern noted above. Gibbon's stories are thus constructed in a manner which gives them a structural resemblance to the oral tale proper: the pre-amble and stimulus to the story itself are rendered in the 'mini-frame' preceding each story. This pattern is followed consistently throughout the sequence.

Before the Vrouw takes up the story, the narrator remarks: "The tale was in plaintive Dutch, the language that makes or breaks a story-teller, for you must hang your point on the gutturals or you miss it altogether" (7). It should be noted at this point that, this remark not-withstanding, Gibbon does not attempt to reflect the cadences of the Dutch language as Pauline Smith and Bosman would do later. Whereas both later writers attempt to create the illusion – mainly via syntactical constructions – that Dutch-Afrikaans is being spoken by their characters, Gibbon, having informed the reader about the language medium, is content to revert chiefly to standard English, with the occasional idiomatic expression or Dutch word thrown in for effect.

"Unto the Third Generation" is a story about the Vrouw's husband's uncle, who "'drank so much and carried on so wickedly that his wife died and his girls married poor men and never went to stay with their father'" (7). The man's son Barend reaches the point where he can bear this no longer, and, one evening, when his drunken father attempts to cajole him into drinking, the situation erupts into the first fist-fight that the two men have ever had. Having bested his father, Barend disowns him and tells him to get out of the house. He drags the old man out of the house and across the yard to the gate leading onto the open veld. His father at last responds:

> "Leave me here," he said, speaking slowly and painfully. "Leave me here, my son. Thus far I dragged my father." (11)

The frame narrator's concluding remark, quoted appreciatively by Pereira, is worth repeating: "The Vrouw Grobelaar, to point a weighty moral, turned her face upon Katje. But that young lady was sleeping soundly with her mouth open" (11).

The Vrouw clearly intended the story to be a cautionary tale about the power of heredity in human affairs: Katje, in other words, should not be too complacent about the negative character-traits of her forebears lest she unconsciously fall into patterns of behaviour which lead to her undoing. The irony in this particular story is light but comic: the "weighty moral" which should serve as the *pièce de résistance* of the storytelling event falls on (literally) deaf ears.

It can be seen from this opening story that the narrative structure of Gibbon's stories is a great deal more sophisticated than that of his predecessors. His centrepiece is the engaging Vrouw Grobelaar herself, and this commanding old woman finds an ideal foil in her young niece Katje, whose provocative responses are better grist to the old lady's storytelling mill than might have been those of a more overtly sympathetic interlocutor. Katje's youth (and that of her suitor) is itself a provocation to the sage old lady, and the tales are therefore liberally sprinkled with spoonfuls of unsolicited counsel.

Our understanding of the point of the Vrouw's stories is meant to be different from (and superior to) that articulated by the Vrouw herself. The narrative structure of the stories makes it clear that our perspective is supposed to approximate that of the frame narrator, although this device is handled adroitly by the author. Never are we openly invited to ridicule the Vrouw, and she remains the centrepiece of the stories.

Indeed, the frame narrator's reporting of the Vrouw's tales is done from the very margins of the narrative, and this allows the Vrouw and Katje to be foregrounded. The Englishman has a very shadowy presence in the stories, but this does not prevent the Vrouw from directing a few barbed comments in his direction, like her response to Katje's remark (which prompts the second story, "The Dream-Face") that she wished "'a man would come and make me marry him'" (12). The Vrouw retorts: "'Do you think I would let a man – any man, or perhaps an Englishman – carry you off like a strayed ewe?'" (12–13).

The multi-directional nature of these exchanges indicates that several layers of irony are activated in the narrative structure of *The Vrouw Grobelaar's Leading Cases*: the mock-adversarial nature of the relationship between the Vrouw and Katje provokes the tales in the first place. Then the nature of the relationship between the two young people is such that it invites the Vrouw to respond with a mixture of scorn and pity, and the frame narrator's Englishness merely intensifies this response. Stage-managing all of this is the author himself, who has removed himself by way of this elaborate 'masking' device and is free to manipulate characters at will.

The Vrouw Grobelaar does not have it all her own way with her young niece. In "The Dream-Face," she attempts to persuade Katje that young Fanie van Tromp is a suitable marriage partner for her. Having bluntly remarked that Fanie will inherit his father's "'very large property',"* she goes on to note his handsomeness:

> "His beard is as black as – "
> "A carrion-crow," added Katje promptly.
> "Quite," agreed the Vrouw Grobelaar, with a perfect unconsciousness of the unsavouriness of the suggestion. (14)

Gibbon is not averse to letting other characters (and, of course, the reader) having a laugh at the old lady's expense, and the relationships between the characters are thus lively and variable.

There is a great deal in *The Vrouw Grobelaar's Leading Cases* that reminds one of Bosman. The use of a stable fictional narrator is one obvious element of similarity, but there are many other points of comparison. The ironic humour that pervades *The Vrouw Grobelaar's Leading Cases*, for example, is something that immediately brings Bosman's stories to mind. This irony is located chiefly in the distance between the Vrouw's perception of events (or, very frequently, the moral she draws from a story) and that which we as readers are encouraged to adopt.

The Vrouw is apparently unaware of the comic contradictions in the views she articulates. "Counting the Colours," for example, describes the unhappy marriage of a forbidding old patriarch and a fun-loving young slip of a girl. The girl eventually poisons the old man and runs off with a young Irishman. With unconscious irony, the Vrouw describes this young man's musical ability thus: "'With him, in a black box like a little coffin, he had a machine he called a banjo, upon which he would play lewd and idolatrous music which was most pleasing to the ear'" (77). Gibbon's acute consciousness (and the Vrouw's unconsciousness) of the collision between the society's moral sensibility and its sublimated desires is communicated in this way.

Throughout the book there is a disconcerting mixture of the comic and the tragic, a feature of the stories which (as Pereira suggested) anticipates Bosman. For instance, in "The Peruvian" – which, the narrator informs us, is a blanket term for anyone for whose nationality the Vrouw has no name – the Vrouw warns against the dangers of dabbling in witchcraft. A young girl of the neighbourhood mysteriously disappears, and her family, having exhausted every other method, resolves to use the reputed divining powers of an itinerant Greek "smouser." The girl's two burly brothers chance upon him after returning from another fruitless search. The 'capture' is described thus:

> "The smouser, of course, whined and squirmed, but Piet was the man
> who broke the bullock's neck at Botha's kraal, and he made no difficulty
> of tying the little man's wrists to his off stirrup. All his trinkets and fallals
> they left behind, and riding at a walk, talking calmly between themselves

of the buck with wide horns that the Predikant's cousin missed, they
dragged the little smouser to the homestead." (162)

This casual brutality has a burlesque quality which makes it all the
more shocking. The local witchdoctors, who are also coerced into
aiding in the search for the girl, "'would have been glad enough to find
her, for they were flogged from morning to night, and Barend van der
Byl beat the life out of one who did not seem to be doing his best'"
(160). The gross injustices inflicted upon the subject native populace are
reflected in this deliberately casual fashion. This conveys a muted sense
of outrage that they should be there merely to suffer somewhat
arbitrarily the ire of any Boer in the vicinity.

The Bosmanesque quality in the throwaway comment about "'the
buck with wide horns that the Predikant's cousin missed'" is unmistakable. A similar Bosmanesque turn of phrase is used in "The Dream-
Face," when Katje remarks of a hapless suitor: "'He is as graceful as a
trek-ox, and his conversational talents are those of a donkey in long
grass'" (15). As can be seen from these examples, the tales in *The Vrouw
Grobelaar's Leading Cases* are in many ways mere pretexts for a show of
authorial verbal skill. This, too, distinguishes Gibbon from his lack-
lustre forebears, and allows us to see how he anticipates later writers
like Bosman.

Although, as has been remarked, the frame narrator is never fleshed
out in any detail, we learn a great deal about him through the remarks
he silently interpolates into the Vrouw's narratives. In "The Dream-
Face," which organizes itself around the Vrouw's warning "[s]ome-
times the thing we want is at our elbows, and we cannot grasp it
because we reach too far" (16) and is provoked by Katje's derisive
remarks about her young suitor just quoted, he has occasion to remark:
"The Vrouw Grobelaar had never heard of Beatrice and her Benedick,
but she had a notion of the principle" (15). Remarks like these (in this
case a reference to Shakespeare's *Much Ado About Nothing*) establish a
cultural and cognitive distance between frame narrator and storyteller.
They also, of course, tell us something about the frame narrator himself
– and, by extension, about the speaking position of the author, who is
clearly educated, culturally distant, and sceptical.

The story in question ("The Dream-Face") also illustrates something
of Gibbon's artistic range. It is a poignant tale about Stoffel Struben,

who, says the Vrouw (with her storyteller's skill at whetting an audience's appetite with a paradox), "'nearly went mad for love of his wife'" (16). Stoffel chooses for his wife a woman who has qualities of gentleness and patience, and for a long time thereafter he hankers for a more exciting partner. The situation is exacerbated when he strikes his head on a rock after falling off his horse. In his delirious state he sees a "dream-face" and upon recovering is haunted by it: "'If ever God gave a thing to a mortal man','" he muses, "'he should have given me that woman'" (19–20). Some time afterwards, his wife dies of fever, but with her dying breath she provides him with the knowledge that will tantalize and taunt him forever: "'That face – you – saw ... was ... mine!'" (28).

The slightly melodramatic nature of this story (exaggerated in my synopsis) is offset by the delicacy of its telling, and the sadness and misunderstanding engendered by human frailty are convincingly and movingly conveyed.

Melodrama is also a feature of "The Avenger of Blood," a story prompted by Katje's derisive remarks about witchcraft, and which concerns a young man with whom the womenfolk (including the young Vrouw herself) had fallen in love. However, Fanie van der Merwe had one nasty habit: he was unable to pass a black man without striking him. Says the Vrouw:

> "What I didn't like about him was his way with the Kafirs. A Kafir is more useful than a dog after all, and one shouldn't be always beating and kicking even a dog. And Fanie could never pass a Kafir without kicking him or flicking his whip at him." (32)

One day, with an irony too pointed to be incidental, Fanie, who is bearing the news of the Predikant's father's death, recklessly vaults a wall near the homestead on his horse and accidentally kills a young black child. A mysterious old black man, who was the child's companion and is visibly enraged by the tragedy, removes some of the child's blood from the horse's hooves and marks Fanie's shoes with it. Fanie is aghast at this, but soon responds with his customary ire, lashing the old man with his whip. A few days later, on his way home after another visit, Fanie encounters a ghost at the kloof nearby and comes galloping back ashen and perspiring. Oom Jan (the Vrouw's uncle) supplies the explanation: "'You have done murder!'" (37). Some time later Fanie is discovered dead in a nearby spruit, and when his shoes are removed a little drop of blood – still wet – is discovered on his toe.

Again, it is interesting to note that although there is a distinct element of melodrama in Gibbon's tale, it nonetheless contains moments of real poignancy. The old black man's grief at his young companion's death is registered by the Vrouw Grobelaar's family, and they adjust their attitude to young Fanie van der Merwe accordingly. Indeed, there are several indications earlier on in the story that the Vrouw (who is a young girl at the time of the event) herself felt ambivalent about Fanie, and her comment about his racism quoted above is remarkably akin in tone to that later adopted by Oom Schalk Lourens: beneath the surface humour of the derogatory comparison between blacks and animals ("'A Kafir is more useful than a dog after all'") there lies the implication – tacitly mooted by the Vrouw herself – that such racist attitudes are morally indefensible.

However, one has to juxtapose this with the attitudes enunciated by the Vrouw in the story that follows, "The Hands of the Pitiful Woman." "'Kafirs',," she says, "'are not men, whatever the German missionaries may say. I do not deny we have a duty to them, as to the beasts of the field; but as for being men, well, a baboon is as much a man as a Kafir is'" (41). Stung by Katje's mirth at such unreconstructed racism, she retorts: "'Did you hear how the Vrouw Coetzee came to die? Well, I will tell you, and you will see that we must hold the Kafirs with a hand of iron or they will destroy us'" (42).

The Vrouw Coetzee is left alone on her farm with her little baby while her lawyer husband is away in Pretoria. Soon afterwards the farm labourers refuse to work or to obey her instructions. They then surround the house, into which the woman has barricaded herself, and demand liquor. Things rapidly get uglier when the men have drunk the brandy she hands them through the window. She kills one of the labourers, who enters the house through the chimney, but then hears the others removing a part of the roof to gain access. Believing that her time has come, she strangles her baby to prevent him from falling into the hands of the vengeful labourers. Unbeknown to her, a group of farmers from neighbouring farms have come to her rescue, but they arrive minutes too late, and the physically unharmed but permanently insane mother dies a year later. The Vrouw Grobelaar concludes: "'So you see that, after all, a Kafir is – Katje, what are you crying about?'" (51).

Geraldine Constance uses this story to clinch her argument about the Vrouw Grobelaar's racism and the frame narrator's unwillingness to demur: "Neither the Vrouw Grobelaar nor the frame narrator asks whether the belligerent workers on Vrouw Coetzee's farm were prompted by any more serious motive than lack of supervision and a desire for brandy" (Constance 1992: 34). And, indeed, such questions do arise. The Vrouw Grobelaar seems to contain within herself contradictory attitudes to black people (now sympathetic and indulgent, now implacably hostile) and, of course, this can be accepted as an authentic fictional creation on Gibbon's part, given the Vrouw's time and context.

But the question remains why the frame narrator is content to let the story unfold without any kind of intervention. Had Gibbon wanted to register authorial distance from the sentiments expressed by the Vrouw, he could have used this persona to interpolate a remark, as he does elsewhere. However, the Vrouw's last remark – "'Katje, what are you crying about?'" – may suggest something else about the story. The story is indeed powerful and moving, despite its questionable use by the Vrouw as an exemplum, and it is arguable that Gibbon judged the story to have enough intrinsic power to carry the reader over the Vrouw's obvious racism. On this reading, the story is tragic and moving in its portrayal of the mother's desperate act of being forced to kill her own child. *Why* she is forced to kill the child is of secondary importance. The reader would then primarily be overwhelmed by the tragic nature of the act itself and not the circumstances culminating in this act.

This, of course, does not exonerate Gibbon of racism by implication, but it does shift the focus of the debate from a political plane to an aesthetic one. Were he to have carried this story off successfully, Gibbon would have had to present the genuine pathos of the story, without diluting its raw impact; but also – and this is where he fails so conspicuously – he would have had to distance himself from the Vrouw's crass sentiments. A last silent observation by the frame narrator on the power of the story despite the questionableness of the use to which it is put may have achieved this purpose. As the story stands, however, the only other conclusion is the one Constance arrives at: Gibbon implicitly endorses the Vrouw's racism by his frame narrator's silence.

The story "Like unto Like" is another demonstration of the Vrouw's racism. This time, however, there is a clear indication of a divergent authorial viewpoint. One of the Vrouw's nephews, Frikkie Viljoen, has become enamoured of a girl of a lower social class. "'Her grandfather was a *bijwohner*[4]',," she warns, "'Pas op! or she will one day go back to her own people and shame you'" (63). Frikkie's laughter at this remark then provokes the Vrouw to tell the story of a man who marries a woman who is socially beneath him and feels compelled to kill her out of shame when, some time later, he finds her dancing naked with "Kafirs" in a nearby location. There was "'something in the colour of her skin and the shaping of her lips and nostrils'," the Vrouw remarks, that caused her to say to herself, "'Ah, somewhere and somewhen your people have been meddling with the Kafirs'" (65).

The central concern of the Vrouw's tale is, according to Jean Marquard, "the idea of a reversion to savagery by Europeans in touch with the primitive darkness of Africa" (1978: 20). Marquard notes that this theme is "tentatively treated" here by Gibbon, and that he "anticipat[es] the more profound and conscious examination of this idea in European writers disenchanted with ideals of Empire – Conrad's *Heart of Darkness* is the most obvious example" (20). Marquard goes no further than this (her brief mention occurs in her Introduction to *A Century of South African Short Stories*), but her phrase "tentatively treated" does suggest that Gibbon is not entirely sure of his artistic purpose; which accords with the spirit of Geraldine Constance's reading of *The Vrouw Grobelaar's Leading Cases*.

My own reading is that Gibbon is more skilful than he is given credit for. The Vrouw is seemingly unconscious of the fact that she uses a cautionary tale about racial determinism to warn her nephew about the problems he will encounter as a result of class determinism. Two things are being satirized here: the Vrouw's race and class prejudice (she implicitly endorses the atavistic racism of the protagonist of the story), and her logical confusion. She thus becomes an object of ridicule as the author stands back and allows her to undo herself. Gibbon thus

---

[4] A *bijwohner* (also as *bywoner*) is a tenant farmer.

artfully exploits the distance he establishes between his first-person narrator and his storyteller. He understands the Vrouw's prejudices intimately, positioning her in such a way that her closed-mindedness becomes apparent and a source of amusement to the reader.

Like Oom Schalk, the Vrouw Grobelaar is part-comic and part-sage. Deeply stamped by prejudice, she nevertheless has an ability to knit compelling narratives around a moral or an anecdote, and possesses a broader humanity which safeguards against the reader's alienation from her. Her very innocence of the irony in what she says is manipulated by the author for ironic effect. An example of this is provided in the story "Tagalash," about the water spirit who hypnotizes young girls and abducts them to be his underwater brides. When Katje laughs derisively at this piece of superstition, the Vrouw retorts "'you laugh in the face of wisdom and counsel as they laughed in Sodom and Gomorrah'" (171), thereby comically bestowing upon a heathen myth the sanctity (in her eyes) of Christianity. Interestingly, her uncritical mingling of Christian and pagan beliefs is a product both of illiteracy and her immersion in a religious society where orthodoxy is strategically coupled with local superstition.

The interplay between the different levels of narrative (the embedded tale, the frame narrator's reporting of it, and the authorial attitude to be inferred from this) is evident in almost all of the stories. In the opening passages of "Morder Drift," for example, the frame narrator – unusually – alludes to himself directly:

> The business was something before my time but I can remember several versions of it, which were commonly current when I first came into the Dopfontein district. It was not much of a tale as a general thing, except that, if you happened to have a strain of hot blood in you, it discovered a quality of very picturesque pathos. However, as you shall see, only the tail-end of the story is generally known, and it was the Vrouw Grobelaar, the transmitter of chronicles, who divulged it to Katje and myself one evening in its proper proportions. (108)

The frame narrator then goes on to render a version of the tale as he first heard it. The putative audience is constituted by Katje and the Vrouw – the latter "dozing like a dog, with one ear awake" (111) – although direct speech is not used, and, as the vocative "you" in the passage above indicates, the reader rather than this audience is thus addressed. The Englishman's tale about a young Boer woman who is found cradling the head of her murdered husband at Morder Drift while smiling contemptuously across the river draws a response from the dozing Vrouw Grobelaar. The Englishman remarks: "When my tale was finished [...] the contempt of the artist for the mere artisan moved her to complete the record" (111).

The Vrouw begins by remarking "'You are wrong when you say the truth never came to light'" (111), then sets the record straight:

> "It is not a tale to carry abroad," observed the old lady. "It concerns some of my family. The woman was Christina van der Poel, a half-sister of my second husband, and what I am now telling you is the confession of Koos van der Poel, her brother, on the day he died. I remember he was troubled with an idea that he would be buried near her, and that she would cry out on him from her grave to his." (112)

She then proceeds to put flesh on the bones of the Englishman's tale, in the process showing that she is indeed "artist" to his "artisan."

Her reference to an extended family (so extended in this case that the reader could be forgiven for inferring that all local stories touch on the Vrouw's family in some way) indicates something about the nature of oral lore and its transmission: the Vrouw is the repository of local gossip and legend and, in choosing her as his narratological centre-piece, Gibbon has located his collection of stories at the very nexus of Boer oral lore. He is therefore able to draw on the power of an oral tradition distilled by generations of retellings and give voice to this tradition through an 'authentic' spokesperson.

Unlike his predecessors, however, Gibbon introduces the possibility of ironic intervention in this oral tradition through the device of a sceptical frame narrator. The ideological tension between narrator and storyteller is not always exploited (as we saw in "The Hands of the Pitiful Woman"), but Gibbon constantly indicates that he is alert to the possibility of ironic interplay between them. Describing the girl who is at the centre of the family drama in "Morder Drift," the Vrouw remarks, "'Christina was a wild fanciful girl'" (112), adding, significantly: "'she might have had her pick of all the unmarried men within a day's ride, and there used to be some very good men about here'" (113).

The Englishman gets his own back in "A Good End," a story about an ailing father – an upright and respected man in the community and a Christian to boot – who persuades his reluctant son to shoot him when all attempts to ease his painful illness fail. The subject of the conversation which precedes the story is death, a matter with which, says the narrator, the Vrouw Grobelaar was awe-inspiringly familiar:

> She was as opinionative in this regard as in all others; she had her likes and dislikes, and it is my firm belief to this day that she never rose to such heights of conversational greatness as when attending a deathbed. It is on record that more than one invalid was relieved of all desire to live after being prepared for dissolution by the Vrouw Grobelaar. (128)

"Never," he concludes, "were her reminiscences so ghoulish and terrifying, and never did she hurl her weighty moralities over so wide a scope" (129).

The Vrouw, for her part, uses the tale to instruct Katje on how to die effectively: "'It will be a lesson to you, Katje, and I hope you will think about it and take it to heart'" (130). At the conclusion, however, when she describes the pathos of the good man's end at the hands of his son, she cannot resist the droll remark "'the shot was a true one, and the work was well and workmanlike done'" (141), and Gibbon allows her niece the last word: "'It must have spoiled the sheets,' observed Katje" (141).

The exchanges between the three characters are skilfully managed by Gibbon, and a significant part of the appeal of the stories is precisely his artfulness in shifting the ground beneath his three interlocutors. Attention is thus often diverted away from the content of the stories and towards the nature of their telling. This is an illustration of the 'selfconsciousness' which, as I remarked earlier, now begins to manifest itself in the South African oral-style story.

Gibbon's use of his storyteller figure is thus controlled and effective, and there are indications in the text of how deliberately he proceeds. The title of the book itself suggests that the stories included in the volume are only a selection of those heard by the frame narrator. The implication is that the Vrouw Grobelaar had a vast store of tales, of which the present ones are simply the most memorable. He also supplies the Vrouw with a mien appropriate to a storyteller. We hear, for example, that she "adjust[s] her voice to a narrative pitch" (88) before picking up the thread of a tale.

He has therefore skilfully 'showcased' his storyteller and uses this device to various ends. The distance he creates between frame narrator and storyteller, as has been argued above, allows for oblique but trenchant commentary on the society's prejudice. However, by anchoring his stories in a figure like the Vrouw Grobelaar – a local sage privy to all regional gossip and legend – he also allows the reader 'authentic' glimpses into the Dopfontein community.

A good example of this is provided in the story "The Coward," which concerns the marriage between a Boer renowned for his marksmanship and a robust and courageous farm girl, Anna, who discovers soon after their marriage that her husband is a coward. He refuses to cross a river which is in full spate, and she is left to drive the team of oxen across. Some years later he is called up for service with the local commando when a local tribe rises in rebellion. After some days have elapsed, Anna visits the commando on the pretext of bringing her husband provisions. Night falls, and she finds herself trapped between the Boer lines and the advancing horde. Her husband finds her, and they resolve to shoot each other rather than be taken alive. To the last, he remains a coward, and it falls to her to take their lives.

On a narratological level, "The Coward" is of interest because it demonstrates Gibbon's adroit use of multiple narrators. At one point in the story, Anna hears news of how the battle is proceeding from the mouth of a wounded burgher who returns from the front. Her informant supplies a vivid description of the events, to which she could not possibly have been a witness. At this point the story is filtered through three levels of narrative: the burgher; Anna; and the Vrouw Grobelaar herself. Relating all of this to the reader is, of course, the shadowy first-person narrator himself. The various levels of the narrative are exploited so skilfully that the mechanics of the process are scarcely perceptible. Here and elsewhere, the Vrouw Grobelaar's oral cadences fade as the author takes up the narrative, providing descriptions and insights that could not realistically be placed in the mouth of the more pedestrian Vrouw herself.

For example, in "The Sacrifice," which describes a predikant's desperate recourse to the occult in his ill-fated attempt to save his ailing wife, we get the following description of the doctor, which could not conceivably be ascribed to the Vrouw Grobelaar: "The doctor sat beside the bed and watched the sick woman, and heard her weak murmur of children born in the dreams of fever. It was a still night, cool, and hung with the glory of stars, and the point at which life and death should meet and choose drew quickly near" (225).

Gibbon has thus skilfully harnessed the power of the oral tale without forgoing the benefits that the written story can bring. The illusion that oral tales are being heard by the reader is carefully sustained. Oral tales have a predilection for strong and compelling story-lines: stories told before an audience must possess economy and irresistibility to keep the listeners engaged. The short story can afford to be more impressionistic, lyrical, even poetic; but the tale must be drawn in bold and memorable lines.

Paradoxically, however, it may digress (or appear to digress) in the matter of adducing detail. The audience's desire to be entertained requires that the tale must cover a certain distance. Where the framework of the plot allows, the listeners can be entertained by the storyteller with a host of seemingly irrelevant details. These constitute the storyteller's paces as he or she unfolds the narrative. A story told is an *event*: it occupies a spatial and temporal dimension and must be of a certain duration. Often details can lure the listener into a state of suspended animation, and this makes the climax that much more effective.

In *The Vrouw Grobelaar's Leading Cases*, a critical balance is struck between spareness of narrative and a proliferation of decorative detail. The Vrouw herself is for the most part firmly in control of her narrative (although not of its 'meaning'), and this attests to Gibbon's skill in his use of a fictional narrator. Where she is expansive, she alludes to the curious and unexplained aspects of people's characters. Why is it that Barend Voss (in "Unto the Third Generation") never had "'a word of good or bad to throw away on any one'," but nevertheless had "'the face of a violent man'" (8) and is capable of killing his drunken father? And how is it that Jan Uys (in "Counting the Colours") can beat his young wife mercilessly and treat her like a slave, and then, after she has poisoned him, allow her to escape with her lover? Or, again, how is it that Stoffel Struben (in "The Dream-Face") can be described as being "'shallow'," as having "'the mere capacity for love'" (17), and yet be entirely devoted to the "dream-face" he sees when he is near death after striking his head on a rock?

Much is left unexplained, and it falls to the reader/listener to fill in the gaps. As Walter Benjamin (1973: 91) argued, it is half the art of storytelling to keep the story free from explanation as one produces it. The reader/listener must make the psychological connections between events and interpret things the way he or she understands them. One of the ways in which this process is adumbrated in *The Vrouw Grobelaar's Leading Cases* is by the throwaway references the Vrouw makes to local characters. No explanatory information is supplied, and this evokes the sense of an entire (mostly known) community lying beyond the sweep of the Vrouw Grobelaar's gesticulating hand. The reader becomes, by virtue of this technique, a privileged outsider allowed a glimpse of the life of the community via the agency of the storyteller.

Gibbon has thus skilfully allowed his reader insights into the community he describes via his Boer storyteller, but he holds open the possibility of ironic intervention by his frame narrator. The Vrouw articulates the dominant ideology of her society at the time, while the first-person narrator maintains a critical distance. This narrative structure enables Gibbon to deliver an oblique but powerful indictment of the prejudices of the age.

——————— ৵ ৩ ———————

6 The Taller the Tale
Francis Carey Slater's "Oom Meihaas"

ᔥ ───

PERCEVAL GIBBON provided South African literature with its first fully-fledged Afrikaner fictional narrator and, as we saw, invested a great deal of irony and humour in the narrative structure of the tales she tells. A closer prototype of Bosman's Oom Schalk Lourens, however, emerged just three years later in the form of Francis Carey Slater's "Oom Meihaas." Not only is this figure male, he is also lazy, dissembling and cunning:

> Oom Meihaas was a tall, bony man, somewhat loosely built, but tough and wiry. He had curling chestnut hair, a wavy golden beard, twinkling blue eyes, and a ruddy complexion. His dress was simple; it consisted of a pair of rough, mouse-coloured cord trousers (creaky, and rather pungent in odour), a coarse grey flannel shirt, veldschoens which had once been brown, now of a nondescript colour, and a battered, soft felt hat decorated with a much frayed band of crape. Luxurious articles of attire, such as socks, collars, ties, etc., were out of Oom Meihaas' line: he saw no use for them; they were only worn by the extravagant, who had more coins in their bags than sense in their pates.
>
> Oom Meihaas was rather a famous man in his way: he had the reputation of being the biggest liar and the laziest man in the whole district. This was no mean honour; especially if we come to consider the numerous competitors from whose deserving brows these laurels were snatched. (Slater 1908: 139–40)

It is at once evident that Slater has drawn a 'type' here – a typical backveld, "takhaar Boer" – which would find its most famous embodiment in Bosman's Oom Schalk Lourens some twenty years later. Not only do the two characters resemble each other in physical appearance, they both also possess a penchant for telling tall tales:

> Ever-smiling, easy-going, good-natured and loquacious, Oom Meihaas
> was excellent company. This latter fact was also largely due to his flex-
> ible imagination, and the airy manner in which he passed off the
> spurious coinage of his brain as guineas minted from the furnaces of his
> life. The thought of any one ever doubting his veracity never occurred to
> Oom Meihaas; indeed, such an idea would have filled him with indig-
> nant surprise. He had so long dwelt in the realms of imagination that he
> found the country of truth strange and unreal; so naturally, he preferred
> to stay where he felt most at home. (141)

We encounter this Oom Schalk prototype in Francis Carey Slater's
collection of tales *The Sunburnt South* (1908), where he appears in the
story "Monologue of Oom Meihaas." The narrator comes across Oom
Meihaas "sitting in the shade of a peach tree, smoking" (139). His wife
and sons are hoeing in the hot sun, and when the narrator chances
upon him Oom Meihaas rather sheepishly claims that he was sitting
there trying to recover from a bad headache.

This brings up the topic of ill-health, and Oom Meihaas at once em-
barks on an anecdote about how he once worked through influenza,
despite his wife's tearful entreaties:

> "My vrouw came to me crying and begged me to stop. She said that I
> was going to die; that the way I was working was unnatural and un-
> canny; that she had never seen me working like that in all the twenty
> years of our wedded life. But I did not heed her; I went on working and
> would not stop for a moment. She came to me two or three times a day
> and gave me little *soopjes* of *dop*: I swallowed the *dop* as I worked and
> kept steadily on. And will you believe, in three days I *skoffeled* a 'land' of
> potatoes which had taken my wife and three of my sons a week to do the
> previous year. And I cured my influenza too! Ja! that is the way to
> work," he added with a laugh which sounded like a distant rumble of
> thunder, as he noticed the astonishment and admiration depicted upon
> my innocent countenance. (142)

The tell-tale textual signals – "'she had never seen me working like that
in all the twenty years of our wedded life'"; "'will you believe'"; "the
astonishment and admiration depicted upon my innocent countenance" – immediately register both the narrator's dissimulation and
his listener's scepticism. Neither – and the listener in particular – fully
believes the tale, but both are prepared to suspend disbelief momentarily in order for the tale to proceed.

Inevitably, it leads to another:

> "You see my *vrouw* there," he went on, "she works like a young girl, and
> yet she is the mother of twelve children. I trained her to work, and now
> she could not live without it. She leaves the girls at home to do the
> house-work, and she comes to the 'lands' to work with us. She never had
> a sickle or a hoe in her hand before she married me, and now she will
> use them as well as any living man except" (he added modestly)
> "myself." (143)

In his "modest" way, Oom Meihaas then proceeds to tell the tale about
how he wooed his well-to-do wife, in the process cunningly throwing
off a more eligible suitor. Koos Prinsloo is the rival, "'a miserable looking little skunk with a dirty, scrubby beard and yellow, squinting
eyes'," (143) but, unfortunately, young and wealthy. Fierce competition
for the young Sannie Marais's hand then ensues, Prinsloo's wealth
being traded off by the parents against Oom Meihaas's better nature.

The latter's native cunning enables him to deceive and flatter
Sannie's father, Oom Willem Marais. Says Meihaas: "'He and I often
went out shooting together; and, though I was admitted to be the best
shot in the district (and I'll tell you some of my shooting experiences
some other time) I was always careful to allow the old man to bag more
than I did'" (146–46). (A tall tale about shooting would follow later in
Slater's work, and I shall return to this in due course.)

Things come to a head when Oom Willem Marais suddenly falls ill
and it is feared that he will die. Sannie brings the news to Meihaas and
also tells him that Koos Prinsloo has been dispatched to fetch old Mrs
Smith, a herbalist. The race is then on to win the family's favour. Meihaas overtakes Prinsloo and tells him that Oom Willem has died and
that his wife has requested that Prinsloo break the news to the
neighbouring families and tell them that the funeral will be the next
afternoon. Having thus duped his rival, Meihaas then presses on to Mrs
Smith's, returning with the old lady, who promptly cures the sick man.
Meihaas thus shows himself to be an "*oprecht*, hardworking, young
kêrel" (154–55) and Prinsloo incurs the family's wrath for his "lies."
Needless to say, Meihaas also wins the hand of the admiring Sannie.

It should be clear by now that Oom Meihaas tells tales that neither
he nor his audience believes, and he thus takes his place in the tradition
of South African fictional narrators with a gift for stretching the truth.

Curiously, given the potential of this formula, Slater does not include any other "Oom Meihaas monologues" in his first collection of tales and the old yarnster only reappears in his novel *The Shining River* (1925). Here Oom Meihaas (now re-christened "Oom Mias") tells a set of yarns (including the one discussed above) which are taken up again in Slater's later collection of tales *The Secret Veld* (1931). (This volume contains versions of all of the stories in Slater's earlier collection.)

The first tale, retitled "The Saddle," appears here along with two others: "Good Hunting" and "Great Snakes." The first of these is apparently the one Oom Mias threatened to tell earlier, and again concerns the rivalry of Mias (who is now supplied with a surname – Van Biljon) and Koos Prinsloo in their courtship of Sannie Marais. Oom Willem, Sannie's father, suggests that they have a shooting contest to settle their wranglings over who is the best shot in the district. He supplies the young men with two of his guns and two rounds each – one bullet, one shot – and the contest is set for the next day.

The two men settle down to sleep the night at Oom Willem's house; Mias notes with disgust Koos Prinsloo's "'snoring [...] like an overfed pig'" while he himself "'smoked quietly [...] and made [his] plans'" (1931: 256). Unlike Prinsloo, he doesn't undress fully before getting into bed – presumably so as to be first off the mark the next morning. "'To tell you the truth'," he remarks in parenthesis, however, "'I seldom take off my trousers and shirt when I go to bed – it's such a needless labour'" (256). In an oblique manner, Mias's slothfulness is thus once again revealed.

Predictably, Mias has a good shoot. His first shot fells no fewer than twenty-nine guinea-fowl, which, he says, "'rained down like dead leaves from a tree'" (257). Fearing incredulity on his listener's part, he quickly adds: "'I know you won't believe me, but I counted them over carefully, three times, there and then'" (257). He then sets off for the river to shoot the buck he knows he will find there. Sure enough, not one but two buck appear, and Mias takes aim:

> "There was a terrific explosion; the gun kicked like a horse (Oom Willem had overdone the powder this time) and fell from my hands.
> "I clutched wildly in the air, to save myself from falling, and fell upon my back. When I reached the ground I found something wriggle under me. Will you believe it, two pheasants had flown up from the

rushes, frightened by the gun-shot and I had clutched them as I fell; under me was a hare that had jumped from its form (also evidently frightened by the gun-shot)." (259)

Fearing that this was "all" he had bagged with his second shot, he looks around for the two buck he had aimed at:

> "Well, you can believe me or not as you like, but, as sure as I am sitting here, *four* bucks lay dead at the river side; there was the ram, the ewe and two fine kids. (I have never known bush-bucks to have twin kids before – but it was so in this case.) Will you believe me, those kids had come abreast of their parents and I had failed to see them in each case; the bullet (thanks to Oom Willem's extra allowance of powder) had gone clean as a whistle through three of the animals, and we subsequently found it lodged in the fourth!" (260)

Not content, he robs a bees' nest of honey cakes on his way back to his camp and only then makes for the homestead. With an inspired bit of cunning, he returns empty-handed, convincing the family that he has been unsuccessful and duping the triumphant Koos Prinsloo (who has shot a mere duiker-ram and four guinea-fowls) into parting with another of his horses (one was part of the wager) before revealing all. He then concludes: "'Not a bad morning's work, was it? And if you can tell me of any man who has shot as much game with two cartridges, I'll know what to call you'" (263).

Of course, Glanville's Abe Pike trumps Oom Mias on two counts: not only had he achieved better with one cartridge; he had, moreover, told the tale several years before Oom Mias![1] This bit of intertextual banter indicates that South Africa's yarnsters were already beginning to gesture in each other's direction, thus anticipating the more sustained instances of intertextual cross-references that occur between Blignaut's Hottentot Ruiter and Bosman's Oom Schalk. The latter's remark in "The Selons-Rose" that he does not "know any new stories" (1963: 133) is tacit recognition of the extent to which storytellers (and, of course,

---

[1] Of course, the tale is not original to Glanville, either. An early version of this tall hunting-tale occurs in Chapter Three of *The Surprising Travels and Adventures of Baron Munchausen* (Raspe 1901 [1785]), in which the Baron claims to have killed "fifty brace of ducks, twenty widgeons, and three couple of teals" (1901: 16) with one shot. See John Doyle's commentary in this regard, quoted in note 2, below.

their authors) shamelessly plunder the stores of oral lore garnered by their forebears.[2]

Oom Mias's last tale, "Great Snakes," is another fantastical yarn about his encounters with snakes. One such encounter finds him leaning against the trunk of a fallen tree having a smoke after shooting a duiker-ram. He is horrified when, a little later, the trunk begins to move. He then discovers that it is a large snake which is beginning to swallow the buck he has just shot. He shoots the snake, cuts open its mouth and retrieves his kill, then coolly rubs it on the grass and carries it home.

The second encounter is with a cobra which wraps itself around his leg one night when he is playing his concertina for Sannie on the stoep of her father's house. Being "'*almost frightened*'," he remarks, he nonetheless continues to play "'as sweetly as ever'" (279). However, he discovers that as soon as he stops playing his "'slow, sweet tunes'" the snake begins to hiss angrily. Having a "'happy thought'," he suddenly switches to a "'rollicking dance tune to set the snake in motion'" (279), Sure enough, after a few bars of "Vat jou goed en trek Ferreira!" the snake slips off his leg and starts dancing about on the stoep, allowing him to alert Sannie and get her father to shoot it.

"'It's all very well'," continues Oom Mias, "'you can laugh as much as you like, but what I have told you is the *living truth*'" (280). Having thus assured his listener, he proceeds to tell another tale, about a ringhals cobra which pursues him one day when he is returning from

---

[2] When Oom Mias tells this story in Slater's novel *The Shining River*, another storyteller character, "Uncle Eb," responds with the words: "'Well, Mias [...] I am disappointed in y'u; I thought you were too good a liar to steal another man's yarn. That story 'bout the buck, the pheasants, the hare and the honey is one my old friend, Bill Silver, used to tell, on'y y'u've altered it to suit your own ends'" (1925: 246). This is a clear indication of Slater's desire to acknowledge (albeit indirectly and humorously) earlier users of the tale.

John Doyle's (very brief) remarks about Oom Meihaas and the tradition in which he is to be located are worth quoting in this connection: "In Oom Meihaas the author presents a South African Baron Munchausen. With little doubt, he was collecting these stories rather than creating them. Here a reader sees Slater's most extensive use of folk materials, yet nothing is peculiar to South Africa. This kind of character and this type of story is found in every community in the world" (Doyle 1971: 32). Doyle's remarks draw attention to the universality of such tales, and also to Slater's awareness that he was re-using elements of an old folk culture.

Alice with a bottle of brandy for "Old Ackermann" (who wished to rub the brandy on his back to cure his "lumbago"). "'Though naturally of a courageous disposition'," Oom Mias remarks, "'I got a bit of a fright'" (281). Trying to turn the tables on the snake, Oom Mias then relates how he loosened the cork from the brandy bottle and prepared to throw the contents in the snake's eyes. The snake received the first splash of brandy in its mouth instead and, finding it to its liking, wrested the bottle from Oom Mias's grasp and tipped the entire contents down its throat. The snake, of course, became "'hopelessly drunk and looked so jolly and happy'" that Oom Mias did not have the heart to kill it, and instead left it "'lying coiled round the bottle and beginning to snore quite loud'" (282–83). Old Ackermann, Mias concludes indignantly, would not believe his story: "'Will you believe me when I say that he was rude enough to suggest that I had drunk his precious brandy myself?'" (283).

That Oom Mias is in the Abe Pike tradition of telling Munchausen-like tales with manic levels of exaggeration should be clear from the above synopses. Like Abe Pike, he does not believe his own stories, but cannot resist telling them on each occasion that arises. And, like Abe Pike's young companion, Oom Mias's listener is merely amused. Indeed, the tales have no more serious purpose that this – to be mere 'entertainments' for the diversion of the reader.

However, two developments can be observed. Slater has created an Afrikaans narrator, a 'type' from whom such yarns are entirely to be expected. A gross caricature rather than a carefully delineated individual, this figure is nonetheless clearly cast in the same mould that Bosman was later to use.

Secondly, Slater is more economical in 'framing' his yarns. As we saw, the first Oom Meihaas tale introduced a narrator who is never identified but whose scepticism is unambiguously registered. This persona does not reappear in the later tales, both of which clearly assume the reader's familiarity with the formula and merely begin with the narrator's opening words: "'Yes,' said Oom Mias thoughtfully [...]"; "'Snakes,' said Oom Mias, 'are not things to be played with [...]'" This more economical formulaic opening anticipates Blignaut and Bosman very strikingly.

Another area of interest is the patently spurious use of "the living truth." If anything, Slater takes Glanville's scepticism about such a quality being found in a tall tale on a few paces. Not only is he implicitly ridiculing this stock claim, he also shifts the focus from an earlier interest in 'authentically' revealing the mystery of the dark continent (Drayson, Boyle, Ingram – and Scully and FitzPatrick to an extent) to a concern with the intrinsic humour of the yarn – the taller the tale, the better (Glanville and Slater).

With Glanville and Slater, in other words, humour becomes the main objective of the oral-style story.[3] This humour is partly a function of the new scepticism with which both writers now use the genre: the yarn is no longer invested with the awe that accompanies the exploration and narrativizing of a largely unknown continent; it is, rather, exploited in order to satirize the genre's tendency to relay fantasy posing as the 'plain truth.'

However, Slater's advances upon Scully and FitzPatrick should not be exaggerated. He wrote only three "Oom Mias" tales, and his collections otherwise contain very much the same kind of story as those written by the two earlier authors. "Lena of Lion Kloof," for example, is a frame narrative about a beautiful but psychologically disturbed woman whom the frame narrator encounters when he overnights at a farm. This woman's father reluctantly tells the tale of her life when prompted by the curious traveller. "Dirk's Dirge" follows a similar pattern: the traveller is told a tale by his host about a young man who loses his young lover tragically and who then becomes an eccentric recluse. Both are strongly reminiscent in theme and structure of Scully's "Ukushwama." Other stories are folkloric in nature ("The Forest Urn"; "The Tinktinkie"), or frame narratives of the loose, digressive sort written by FitzPatrick ("The Mermaid"; "'Wonderful Women'"; "The Minstrel"). There are also, in the author's own words, "studies of Bantu life and character" (1931: 13) which are akin to tales told by both Scully and, later, Frank Brownlee. "'Soete Aapie'" is noteworthy in that it uses the myth about a human being brought up by baboons treated by

---

3 The element of humour is also, of course, present in Gibbon's tales. My point here is that it is the foremost element in Glanville and Slater, whereas Gibbon's collection as a whole deals with more serious themes.

Gibbon ("The King of the Baboons"), Fred Cornell[4] ("The Proof") and
Bosman ("Birth Certificate").

In none of these stories is there the ironic subversion, the
foregrounding of the artifice of the tale, and the skilful activation of the
different narrative levels that we saw in Gibbon. Indeed, Slater's
Preface to his first collection contains a statement which is strongly
reminiscent of earlier avowals of telling the "plain truth": "[the writer]
has endeavoured throughout to give authentic pictures of the veld and
its people; and, while rambling through the forest of fiction, has ever
kept in view the gleaming wings of the white bird – truth" (1908: viii).

Furthermore, that Slater wrote only three "Oom Mias" tales and
then 'recycled' them suggests that, like Pauline Smith (as we shall
shortly see), he also did not possess Bosman's capacity for invention
within a formula. That these tales are very light, derivative, and memorable only for their manic exaggeration also suggests that Slater had not
found a style of story that he could use repeatedly and to good effect
(unlike Glanville and Gibbon and, of course, Bosman later) and
resorted instead to compiling (and recycling) loose miscellanies of, in
his own words, "simple tales and sketches of life" (1908: vii).

Slater's contribution to the oral-style story genre is thus slight but
noteworthy. In "Oom Mias" Oom Schalk Lourens finds his closest fore-
bear: both figures are Afrikaans and male, and possess a native cunning

---

[4] Fred C. Cornell, another writer of this period, tells a number of stories in his *A
Rip van Winkle of the Kalahari and Other Tales of South-West Africa* (1915), which use
the device of the frame narrative. One of a party of prospectors, simply called
"Jason," tells his companions tales about the Kalahari and German South-West
Africa. "The Follower" is a ghost story, while "The Proof," as remarked above,
deals with the old myth about a human being brought up by baboons. In "'The
Drink of the Dead'" "Jason" again features, although this time as a character, the
narrator of the embedded ghost tale being, appropriately enough, the ghost of a
Portuguese adventurer who had perished in an ill-fated treasure-seeking expedition. The last story of the collection, "The Waters of Erongo" again uses an embedded narrative, this time narrated by one Jim Blake, the expedition's cook. Here
Cornell imitates his narrator's cockney accent in the telling of the tale. In none of
the tales is there any of the irony used to such good effect by Gibbon, and the collection as a whole appears to have the straightforward intention of imparting
something of the mystery and beauty of a little-known part of Africa. That (like
Slater) Cornell repeatedly uses a narrator, however, suggests a great deal about the
presence of such characters in South African society of the early-twentieth century,
and also about the narrative possibilities they suggested to writers of the period.

and an ability to dissemble. However, the fact that Oom Schalk is capable not only of stretching the truth but of doing this more often and more skilfully, and that he is, moreover, capable of doing it in a manner which touches more profoundly on the human condition, explains why he is remembered and Oom Mias is all but forgotten.[5]

---

5 Doyle makes a comparison between the two types of "tellers of tall tales" used by Slater in *The Shining River*. Here Slater juxtaposes Oom Mias with another raconteur, Uncle Eb (Ebeneezer Ripple), and the latter is shown to be superior. Doyle offers an astute analysis of the differences between the two narrators:

> Uncle Eb's stories always proceed on two levels. There is the surface narrative, with its exaggerations, its fantastic action; but there is also the reader's awareness that the raconteur knows what he is doing and expects the listener to get the humor on the level of "not being taken in." At times the fun can be created by the reader's seeing the listener fail to grasp the situation. A number of effects are possible. Much less range is achieved from the direct lying and the personal achievement stories of Oom Mias. The audience always laughs at Oom Mias but with Uncle Eb. (1971: 73)

Doyle's argument is supported by the different responses of the internal audience in the novel (the listeners at the storytelling events) to the two raconteurs. Oom Mias is called "a queer customer," "a lazy old liar," and "an old waster" (1925: 148) behind his back, and is openly challenged with humorous rejoinders after his tales, whereas Uncle Eb's tales are more respectfully received.

Doyle's distinction between "being laughed at" and "being laughed with" also applies when narrators like Oom Mias and Oom Schalk are compared. Oom Mias's fantastical yarns will always be received (by internal audience and reader alike) with amused incredulity, while with Oom Schalk one is never sure whether the sly old raconteur is in earnest or in jest (this latter quality is also, as we saw, a feature of some of the Abe Pike stories). And, of course, Oom Schalk (unlike even "Uncle Eb") tells stories in which tragedy and burlesque are disconcertingly mixed. All of this points to the greater complexity of Bosman's creation.

7 Half a Step Forward?
Pauline Smith's "Koenraad Tales"

〜 ───────────────────────────────

PAULINE SMITH IS BEST KNOWN for her collection of short stories, *The Little Karoo* (1925), and her novel, *The Beadle* (1926), neither of which bears in any significant way upon the themes of this study. Outstanding in many other ways, both works also testify to Smith's remarkable ability to capture the contours and cadences of the rustic Dutch spoken by her Little Karoo characters, and this demonstrates her acute awareness of the texture of this oral culture. (A similar penchant for capturing the contours of the spoken word is evident in her collection of children's stories, *Platkops Children* [1935].) However, with one exception, none of her best-known work attempts an 'oral style' as a principle of narrative composition.

Attention will thus be devoted here chiefly to Smith's two "Koenraad tales," which, bearing as they do a marked resemblance to Bosman's Schalk Lourens stories, are very different from the work for which she is better known. It will be argued that these stories mark Smith's place in the oral-style story tradition in South Africa but that, despite structural affinities with Bosman's stories, they are in important ways less complex than Gibbon's Vrouw Grobelaar sequence.

Smith's engagement with the oral tradition of the Little Karoo also points to the prevalence of oral-style stories in the corpus of the pre-Second World War South African short story. This study has already discussed such stories by writers like Drayson, Boyle, Ingram, Scully, FitzPatrick, Glanville, Gibbon, and Slater. The use of this kind of story by one of South Africa's foremost writers indicates that it still had purchase on South African life in the early decades of this century.

— Ω —

"The Pastor's Daughter," from *The Little Karoo*, is the closest we come to an oral style of presentation in Smith's acknowledged work. In this story, the main character, Niccoline Johanna, tells the (unidentified) first-person narrator the story of her life. The story begins:

> I was teaching school for Miss Cherry in Platkops dorp when Niccoline Johanna told me her love-story. Niccoline lived then in the old Bergh house opposite Miss Cherry's garden, and Christoffeline, her little adopted niece, lived with her [...] As we sat sewing together one afternoon, re-making a little white dress for her niece, she said to me suddenly:
>
> "Tell me now! Whose child do they say Christoffeline is?"
>
> "Why, Niccoline," I cried, "she is your uncle Hans's child, and her mother died when she was born!"
>
> And Niccoline, putting down her work and looking out across the garden, answered: "She is not my uncle Hans's child. My uncle Hans had no child. She is Paul Marais's child. Wait! I will now tell you!"
>
> And here is what she told me. (1925: 121–22)

The frame narrator, who is unnamed but (the reader assumes) is close enough to the internal narrator to trade confidences, begins by relating the circumstances under which she came to hear the story that she goes on to relay. Just enough information is conveyed in the narrative frame to allow the reader to place the characters in a setting, understand something of their relationship and how the embedded story was elicited in the first place, and to provide some background to the subject-matter of the story itself. The stage is now set for the embedded story to begin.

Niccoline's story concerns her ill-fated love affair with Paul Marais. She promises to marry Paul and is then forced to retract this promise when her mother reveals that she has cancer and will therefore not be able to look after Niccoline's father for much longer. The aggrieved Paul then marries an Englishwoman, who later leaves him. This woman's brother comes to Paul some time later with the news that his sister is dead, and Paul returns to Niccoline and tells her that they are now free to be married. (Niccoline's father has also died in the mean-time.) This time it is Paul who is forced to retract his promise when he discovers that his wife is still alive and in desperate circumstances. The couple are reunited and leave for the Transvaal. Some time later

Niccoline hears that Paul has consumption and that his wife is expecting a child. Paul's wife dies in childbirth and Niccoline leaves to nurse Paul and look after the baby. When Paul himself dies, Niccoline returns to Platkops with the little girl, whom she gives people to believe is her uncle's child. The story ends thus:

> For a little while after Niccoline Johanna ceased to speak we sat together in silence, and when at last I looked at her on her strong sallow face there was neither bitterness nor sorrow, only a quiet resignation.
> "You see this dress that I am making for Christoffeline?" she said. "It is the same that I was making that night for my wedding." (140)

The story has all of Smith's characteristic stark power and tragic vision, and there is much that can be commented upon in this regard. However, what is of more immediate concern here is its use of the frame-narrative convention. The passages quoted above are the opening and closing parts of the narrative frame, and the story is thus a prime example of this convention in operation. Significantly, the story's power derives partly from its mode of narration, because it is the intimacy and immediacy of personal experience that are conveyed via the frame narrative. This convention creates the illusion that it is a person's life-story that is being conveyed, in her own words, and that the reader has been brought as close as possible to the source of this experience.

It is instructive to compare this 'bid for authenticity' with attempts by the writers examined earlier. In all cases, the frame narrative has been invoked in order to bring the reader as close as possible to the narrative source, as it were. The writer's purported role in this kind of story, then, is merely to be the narrative interface between informant and reader.

A crucial difference between Smith's use of the frame narrative and that by Drayson, Boyle, and Ingram, however, is that she makes no attempt to signal, overtly or tacitly, that this is a 'real' voice that has been captured in print. Indeed, the power of the story derives in good measure from the reader's sense that the story is profoundly fictional. Niccoline's story is thus not unique, narrowly personal, confined to an empirically observable moment in history. Her story is one variation on an abiding human archetype, a story that will be told again and again, and experienced in different ways by different human subjects. This is the source of its power: it is curiously familiar, as if it has surfaced from the wells of a shared human unconscious.

Thus, while Smith may (like her less skilled literary forebears) be exploiting the potential of the frame narrative to convey the impression of immediacy, the ontological footing of her work is utterly different: there is no artless 'authenticity' being ingenuously sought after here; her work is indisputably 'fictional' and her object is the deeper 'truth of life' rather than the narrower 'truth' of a personal anecdote or oral testimony 'faithfully reproduced.'

Before passing on to a discussion of stories by Smith which are less well known – but which pertain more to the themes of this study – it is worth noting that five of the ten stories in the second edition (1930) of *The Little Karoo* employ first-person narrators, and that, of these, "The Pastor's Daughter" is not the only story to use a narrative frame. "Ludovitje," which comes immediately after "The Pastor's Daughter" in the sequence, is also a frame narrative of a sort. However, here the frame narrator has no textual presence and is merely to be inferred from the story's narrative structure. The story begins: "Out on the stoep in the moonlight Alida spoke of her son Ludovitje" (1925: 141). There-after, Alida takes up the narrative and there are no further textual indications of a reporting narrative presence.

The repeated use of first-person narration, and twice within a narra-tive frame, suggests something about Smith's awareness of the oral nature of the culture she so accurately depicts. That such narrative styles are merely conventions (and not forms of narration emanating in a primary, direct way from the milieu of the Little Karoo) should not obscure the point that Smith's artistic task was to convey the ambience of her chosen milieu in a way that was consonant with its character. Her use of these narrative strategies enables her to achieve this goal.

— Ω —

A more striking engagement with the oral tradition of the *Little Karoo* occurs in two little-known tales by Smith. These are "The Cart" and "Horse Thieves," which first appeared in the *Cape Argus* in December 1925 and January 1927 respectively.[1] Both stories employ a narrator, by

---

[1] Although I first encountered the "Koenraad tales" in their *English in Africa* reprinting alongside Scheub's article (1981; see Works Cited), I have used Ernest

name Koenraad, and deal with the pranks farmers in the district get up
to ("boere-verneukery" is the apt term used by Pereira [1986b: 112] to
describe the subject-matter of this sort of story).

In "Horse Thieves" (which, despite the publication date, was written before "The Cart") Koenraad describes the practical joke he and his
brother Hans played on the district sheep-inspector, a little man "who
was forever boasting of the great things he had done and the fine
horses he had owned" (Smith 1993: 24).

> "The sheep-inspector, I must tell you, for all his boasting, knew so little
> about horses that my brother Hans would often say he was sure if we
> put him on his own horse in the dark he'd ride it through the night and
> never know it to be his own. And the last time that that little man came
> out to us we made a plan together to prove it." (24)

Together the brothers contrive a plot to convince the sheep-inspector
that his horse is stolen by Mitchell and Kavanagh (two notorious horse-
thieves in the district) while he is up on the last night of his stay talking
to them in the farmhouse. Disguising the inspector's brown horse as
one of their own by painting it grey, the brothers persuade the coloured
farmhand, Abram, to gallop past the house on another horse while the
brothers are talking to the inspector. Convinced that he has been the
latest victim of the pair of horse-thieves, the inspector sets off in
pursuit, accompanied by the brothers, who have got him to mount
what he believes to be their father's horse, but which is in fact his own.
Koenraad then relates the following:

> "'Man,' I said to the sheep-inspector when I made up to him, 'she
> goes well, eh, my father's grey mare?'
> "'She's an elephant,' groans the sheep-inspector, 'I'll never get any-
> where near my Lady on this!'
> "'Keep up your heart,' I shouted to him. 'You don't know the horse
> you're riding yet! Go on with Hans to the cross-roads and then divide.
> I'll take the kloof here and meet you as you come down, and if he's in
> the kloof we'll get him. That is if Mitchell isn't with him,' I said." (26)

Having thus devised a way of separating from the inspector, the
brothers reappear in disguise as the horse-thieves, Mitchell and Kava-

---

Pereira's collection, *The Unknown Pauline Smith* (1993), as a more convenient (and
generally available) source.

nagh. They then get the terrified inspector to strip to his shirt sleeves and the pair make off with his horse. Their plan goes awry when their father appears after being roused by the noise. Believing that his sons are indeed the horse-thieves, he opens fire on them, striking Koenraad in the leg. Koenraad concludes:

> "Yes, for a long time after that my father would say that if he was not mad then surely his sons were. But afterwards he also came to smile a little when he thought of the sheep-inspector riding through the night on his own brown mare and not knowing it." (28)

The second "Koenraad tale" also involves the despised figure of the sheep-inspector. This time Koenraad is up-country running a trading store with a friend, Arnoud Ferreira. Ferreira shares Koenraad's love of practical jokes and the pair take revenge on the sheep-inspector when he falls ill at a nearby farm and believes that he is dying:

> "I saw quickly that it was colic that was wrong with him and gave him some of my grandmother's droppels. And presently Arnoud said to me:
> "'How looks he to you, Koenraad?'
> "'No, man,' I said, 'he looks to me very bad. He looks to me dying.'
> "'Man,' said Arnoud, 'that's how he looks now to me also ... a dying man ... and the ground so hard that we can never get it dug ... '
> "And we stood there looking at the sheep inspector, whose eyes were starting out of his head." (33)

Having designs on the inspector's cart, the pair persuade the groaning inspector to part with it in exchange for the magical "grandmother's droppels" as part payment. This is duly effected before the inspector recovers from his colic and reassumes his customary peremptory manner.

Koenraad and his accomplice want the cart for their timid friend, James the Englishman, who believes that it will make all the difference in his quest to acquire a wife. Arnoud Ferreira has for some time been cultivating a certain Alida Lategan as a wife for the irresolute James and, after some more pranks concerning the painting of the cart for the occasion, the two go off together to court Alida. The tables are turned on Ferreira, however, when it is revealed that the not-so-timid James has all along been courting Alida's younger sister Lenitje. And Ferreira, who has been developing a half-acknowledged liking for Alida, ends up betrothed to her.

Harold Scheub first drew critical attention to these tales when he published his article "Pauline Smith and the Oral Tradition: The Koenraad Tales" (1981) and reprinted the tales themselves. The raw material for these stories was provided in Smith's 1913–1914 journal, which she kept during one of her visits to the Little Karoo. Among her various notes about her travels, Scheub observes, was "anecdotal material that she greedily gleaned from the Afrikaans oral tradition of the areas she visited":

> Some of the anecdotes were to become the bases for the short stories of *The Little Karoo* and the novel, *The Beadle*. These tales, seemingly little altered, were, in fact, transformed; they were placed into new image environments. Smith thereby reshaped the anecdotes, emphasizing parts of them, adding material, then establishing parallels between anecdote culled from the oral tradition and her own contextual imagery. (1981: 1)

Scheub then undertakes a detailed exploration of Smith's manipulation of this material for her own artistic ends. His chief concern is to show how she manipulated the material culled from anecdotes supplied by her informant, Thys Taute, in line with the 'trickster' formula favoured by various oral traditions:

> Three of his [Taute's] tales were later worked into two short stories by Smith, in which Taute the narrator became Koenraad, a plucky if hapless trickster who, with an ally, deftly builds illusory worlds. The fabrication is a skilfully composed set of images reflecting elements in the real world: through a clever management of fabricated images, the trickster attempts to influence his dupe's perception of real world images. This is the dual arrangement of images typical of trickster narratives in the oral tradition. (Scheub 1981: 1–2)

There is no doubt that Scheub is right about this connection between Smith's tales and the age-old trickster genre, but he makes rather heavy weather of this theme and does not venture any comments about the broader significance of these little-known stories for South African literature in general and for the short story in particular.

Pereira's commentary is more helpful in this regard. Among "several noteworthy features" about the two stories, he argues, are the presence of a fictional narrator and the pervasive use of humour: "That the practical jokes and less innocent pranks the tricksters play on others redound on their own heads adds to the humour and subjects them to the same ironic laughter that Schalk Lourens frequently elicits. But it is the manner or style of the narrative which most markedly calls to mind Bosman's creation" (1986b: 113).

Quoting the opening passages of "The Cart," in which Koenraad idly gazes out at a passing cart from his stoep and is prompted to recall the tale about the cart belonging to the sheep-inspector, who was "such a man that if you had wet your finger and run it down his coat out of the trail there would have come a regulation about sheep" (Smith 1993: 31), Pereira remarks:

> This is pure Bosman: there is the same concern with seemingly irrelevant detail; the same penchant for homely but risible illustration; and the same leisurely use of repetition as Koenraad dwells on the qualities of the sheep inspector he particularly loathes. In her handling of the plot and exploitation of its comic possibilities, Smith proves as adept as – and again uncannily similar to – Bosman. (114)

Arguing that it was unlikely that Bosman ever read Smith's Koenraad tales, Pereira adds that they nonetheless were published before either Bosman or Blignaut had started their respective Schalk Lourens and Hottentot Ruiter series, and that Smith had therefore "stolen the march upon them" (113). He then speculates on the reasons for Smith not pursuing this style of story.

> Having successfully explored a richly comic vein, Smith, one might expect, should surely have written more Koenraad stories. Yet she ap- parently did not, and the reason may be sought partly in personal circumstances, partly in the nature of her creative vision: her interest lies in character and the tragic irony of fate, rather than satire or the human comedy. But I think it is also true that she lacked the imaginative abun- dance that is Bosman's gift. Three of Thys Taute's Little Karoo anecdotes, carefully recorded by Smith in 1913–14, went into the creation of these two comic tales; clearly invention was not her forte, whereas Bosman has the gift of a quick eye and vivid imagination, enabling him to turn the slightest incident or experience to account – repeatedly, but with infinite resourcefulness. (114)

Pereira's qualification of his earlier assertion that Smith was Bosman's equal in "her handling of the plot and exploitation of its comic possibi- lities" is worth noting. The connections between Smith's Koenraad tales and Bosman's Schalk Lourens ones are clear and indisputable, but the differences between Smith and Bosman are just as clear.[2]

Smith indeed anticipates Bosman in a number of ways. Most importantly, she uses an Oom Schalk-like fictional narrator and a Bosmanesque narrative style. Then she uses ironic humour in a way reminiscent of Bosman. And, finally, her rural subject-matter and setting are of a piece with Bosman's Marico tales. The last of these three areas of similarity is both indisputable and also the least significant. The other two, however, repay closer scrutiny.

The question of the narrator and of narrative structure is probably the most important. This is one respect in which Smith anticipates Bosman more closely than Gibbon: she further 'shrinks' the narrative frame of the oral-style story. Whereas Gibbon establishes his in a fairly expansive (albeit skilful) manner, and retains the presence of an audience, one of whom (the Englishman) doubles as the frame narrator, Smith is more economical. As with Bosman, the reporting narrative presence in her tales is never identified: no 'frame' is explicitly set up, and her stories begin *in medias res.* "Horse Thieves," for example, begins: "'I don't know how it is,' said Koenraad as the sheep-inspector rode off from the farm, 'but there is that about a sheep-inspector that puts the devil into a man'" (Smith 1993: 24). Koenraad tells his story to an unidentified interlocutor, and this is signalled by phrases like "I must tell you" or "you must understand."[3]

---

[2] Bosman was, of course, aware of Smith's writing, and his admiration of it is conveyed in his article "Aspects of South African Literature," which first appeared in 1948. The absence in Smith of an "aloof superiority" with regard to matters South African, Bosman notes, "comes almost as a shock." He adds:

> [...] of all the writers of this country Pauline Smith, with her *Little Karoo,* has put forth the strongest claim to the perilous and unhappy garland of genius. A love for South Africa would not appear to be an insuperable obstacle in the way of one's becoming a South African writer. (1986a: 96)

Bosman's wry last remark suggests that it was Smith's ability above all to infuse pathos and seriousness into South African subject-matter that attracted his praise. The inclusion of her profoundly moving story "Desolation" in his anthology *Veld-trails and Pavements* (1952 [1949]), together with his prefatory remark that she has produced "some of the finest short stories in our South African literature" (Bosman & Bredell 1952: 46), reinforces the idea that he appreciated her for her willingness to embrace South Africa as a subject worthy of serious artistic treatment.

[3] "The Cart," it should be noted, contains no such textual signals. It opens with a description of Koenraad watching a cart moving down the road and, before the

Structurally speaking, then, Koenraad and Oom Schalk fulfil the same narrative function: they are both actors in, and recounters of, their stories. The stories in their entirety are narrated by these figures, and the reader is therefore wholly reliant on the versions they offer. Both storytellers occupy the whole 'narrative stage,' as it were, allowing no space for alternative voices.

On the face of it, though, despite its greater economy, this may seem a retrograde step in the development of the oral-style story, in that it precludes the possibility of the irony and parody which are activated only in dialogic narrative structures. As the previous chapter showed, Gibbon exploited the potential for polyphonic discourse inherent in the oral-style story by introducing a dissenting frame narrator. Concentrating the narrating function in one person, upon whom the reader is then entirely reliant, would thus appear to be regressive.

In Smith's case this is indeed so: Koenraad tells his tales without interference from a frame narrator, and the reader is therefore not presented with any divergent interpretations. The 'reporting agency' in the Koenraad tales is passive, and this allows Koenraad an uncontested 'narrative space.'

As we shall see, Blignaut and Bosman adopt a similar narrative structure to Smith, and her Koenraad tales therefore bear a closer resemblance to their "Hottentot Ruiter" and "Oom Schalk" sequences than do the "Vrouw Grobelaar" tales of Gibbon. Neither Blignaut nor Bosman employs an 'active' narrating agency: their narratives are filtered entirely through their respective narrators. A crucial difference, however, is that whereas Koenraad's tales lack any textual signals that his version of events must be contested, it is clear that both Hottentot

---

story he narrates begins, the following statement occurs: "Koenraad watched it lazily as he filled his pipe, then turned to his guest and said [...]" (Smith 1993: 31). It is to this "guest," then, that Koenraad tells his tale and the story as a whole is reported by an invisible third-person narrator.

This slight discrepancy in narrative structure suggests that, unlike Bosman, Smith had not yet arrived at a stable formula for this kind of tale, although it is perhaps unfair to judge a writer on the strength of a mere two stories. Perhaps a better way of expressing this is to say that the "Koenraad tales" were clearly never intended to be part of a larger sequence, but were slight deviations from the artistic route chosen by Smith in her major works.

Ruiter and Schalk Lourens are unreliable narrators, and their renditions are therefore *ipso facto* 'multivoiced.'

That Smith does not avail herself of this narrative strategy means that, in terms of the development of the oral-style story from a simple, monologic narrative structure (Drayson, Scully, FitzPatrick) to a complex, dialogic structure (Gibbon, Blignaut, Bosman), her Koenraad tales are to be located among the earlier, more ingenuous, versions of the oral-style tale. Both Glanville and Gibbon[4] produced 'nascent' fallible narrators that predate Koenraad, and this suggests that Smith does not make significant advances upon Glanville and Gibbon in this respect, despite her more economical narrative style. However, in concentrating the narrative frame of the genre in a single narrator, her Koenraad tales gesture towards the potential that lies in the use of a complex, unreliable narrator so richly realized in the stories of Blignaut and, particularly, Bosman.

To end with, there is the question (the second point listed above) of Smith's use of ironic humour, reminiscent of Bosman. Again, there are indeed similarities in this respect. For example, in "The Cart" the sheep-inspector falls ill, and Koenraad and Arnoud take the opportunity to read to the man from his beloved "little black book" of regulations, saying, "'we can't let a sheep inspector die like a sheep [...] let us read to him'" (Smith 1993: 34). "'When a Caroline man grew ill'," remarks Koenraad in the same story, "'he would send to the store for me, and I would give him some droppels out of a big box of medicines that my grandmother down in Platkops had made up for me. Afterwards, if he didn't feel well, we'd bury him. But it was wonderful how often he got well'" (33). This could be something straight from the mouth of Oom Schalk, and there are various other examples of this in the Koenraad tales.

These similarities should not obscure some crucial differences in the way Smith and Bosman use irony and humour. As can probably be gauged from the synopses above, Smith's Koenraad tales are no more

---

4 Slater's Oom Mias is cast in a similar mould, although it is not clear to what extent his tongue is firmly in his cheek when he recounts his fantastic exploits. His tales involve exaggerations that better even Abe Pike's, but at times he comes across as a simpleton who is the butt of his audience's in-jokes. This is especially the case with his appearance in the novel, and this 'variability' in the way he is presented makes it difficult to judge his complexity as a character.

than light-hearted diversionary stories about the childish pranks of young farmers of the Little Karoo, and as such are markedly different from the stark, tragic stories for which she is better known. They are also different in the same way from Bosman's deceptively simple and humorous Marico tales. Whereas the Koenraad tales are mere 'entertainments,' wholly out of character in both style and substance with Smith's better-known work, Bosman's Oom Schalk stories fuse humour and seriousness in a strikingly effective manner.

——————— ✑ ✑ ———————

8 Casual Sophistication and the Metafictional

Aegidius Jean Blignaut's "Hottentot Ruiter"

෨ ─────────────────────────

THIS STUDY HAS TRACED THE DEVELOPMENT of the oral-style story from its inchoate beginnings (Drayson, Boyle, Ingram), through to the more recognizable shape it achieved in the late nineteenth century (Scully, FitzPatrick, Glanville) and on to its more 'artful,' sophisticated form in the first part of this century (Gibbon and, to a lesser extent, Slater and Smith). After Smith, writing in the late 1920s, there are several other instances of writers working in the genre, although they have been lost in the large shadow cast by their illustrious contemporary, Herman Charles Bosman. Blignaut, the subject of this chapter, has not suffered this fate: his place in the development of the South African short story has been brought into sharp focus precisely because of his association with Bosman.

Other short-story writers of this period have not been as fortunate, despite the fact that they were working in a style broadly similar to that employed by Blignaut and Bosman. These include Francis Sibson (*A Breeze from the Backveld* [1926]), Napier Devitt (*The Blue Lizard, and Other Stories of Native Life in South Africa* [1928]), Philip Townshend (*Tales from Ficksrand and Other Places* [1928]), George Klerck (*At the Foot of the Koppie* [1929]), Anthony Parsons (*Bush Gypsies* [1932]), Alice Werner (*African Stories* [1932]), William Westrup (*Old McBein* [1937]), C.R. Prance (*Tante Rebella's Saga: A Backvelder's Scrap-book* [1937]), and Frank Brownlee (*Corporal Wanzi* [1937]).

Space does not permit a revaluation of the works of all of these largely forgotten writers but, before passing on to a consideration of Blignaut's role in the development of the South African oral-style story, I wish to touch briefly on the last two writers listed here, as their work does have a bearing upon my discussion of the oral-style story.

C.R. Prance and Frank Brownlee have both been referred to by Gray as forerunners to Bosman, and Prance's Tante Rebella is discussed briefly by Ernest Pereira. Both writers used fictional narrators (Tante Rebella and Corporal Wanzi respectively) and therefore have a place in this tradition in South African literature.

Gray's remarks are confined to those already quoted. Oom Schalk, he notes in *Southern African Literature: An Introduction*, "succeeds Gibbon's Vrouw Grobelaar and C.R. Prance's Tante Rebella as the backveld Boer humorist" (1979: 193). And in his Introduction to Bosman's *Selected Stories*, he adds Sanni Metelerkamp's Outa Karel and Frank Brownlee's Corporal Wanzi as other fictional tellers of tales who are forerunners to Oom Schalk (1980: 10).

Pereira does not mention Brownlee, but he does consider Prance at greater length (1986b: 112–13). On the strength of its title alone, C.R. Prance's *Tante Rebella's Saga: A Backvelder's Scrap-book* (1937) would appear to invite comparison with Gibbon's *The Vrouw Grobelaar's Leading Cases*, and its date of publication may suggest that it drew on Gibbon and anticipated Bosman. Pereira notes that many of the stories appeared some time before 1937, and that "Tante Rebella may thus well have been a forerunner of Schalk Lourens: if she was not midwife at his birth, she very probably had some impact on his later development" (1986b: 112). Pereira was probably aware that Bosman and Prance were both contributors to the *Touleier* in 1930, and would in all likelihood have therefore been aware of each other. However, he fails to produce any compelling evidence that Bosman was influenced by Prance's Tante Rebella, apart from noting the Transvaal Bushveld setting of Prance's stories and the occasional example of Oom Schalk's "inconsequential logic" (113); indeed, on the internal evidence of the stories themselves, there is scant reason to pursue this connection.

As Pereira himself concedes, Tante Rebella is not the narrator of Prance's stories, nor does she play any substantial part in them. The title-story opens the collection and introduces Tante Rebella, but she soon fades, even as a nominal point of reference for the tales that follow. The collection is, in fact, little more than an unremarkable miscellany about rural Transvaal life, and Prance makes no attempt to invoke a storyteller figure or the cadences of oral speech. On this evidence, the connections between Bosman and Prance are surely tenuous – if not non-existent – and Prance's position in the oral-style story tradition marginal.

Frank Brownlee is notable for his invention of "Corporal Wanzi," whose tales are contained in a miscellany bearing this name. Somewhat misleadingly, Wanzi fulfils a fairly minor narrative role in this collection. Fewer than a third of the tales have any connection to him, the remainder being a loose collection of anecdotes and tales about rural Transkei related either in the third person or by an authorial persona.

The collection opens with a description of a drill conducted by Corporal Wanzi, who is in charge of "the little native police force" (1937: 11) under the supervision of the magistrate. Wanzi has called the parade because his men "'are all becoming too slack and careless'" (11). He singles out each of his five men for a different offence, ranging from unseemly conduct to dereliction of duty and slothfulness. After a lengthy tirade he dismisses his men with the words: "'Unless I see that you improve in your duties I shall ask the Magistrate to get rid of every one of you'" (13). His men protest at his peremptory treatment of them and demand a hearing. "'Very well'," the corporal responds, "'since you will have it so, as occasion permits I will hear what each of you has to say, and if any is unable to show that he has done something worthy of his place in the police force I will see that he is dismissed'" (14–15).

What then ensues is a collection of five stories, each narrated on a separate occasion by a different member of the police force. The last of these, "Komaniso's Story," concerns a young recruit's discovery of a plot to unleash a native revolt, "'a war against white people'" (50). The sixth story, narrated in the third person, describes the outbreak of rebellion and its successful containment. The last story of the sequence, narrated by Wanzi himself, is prompted by the magistrate, who wishes to know how Wanzi came to injure his arm.

Corporal Wanzi, then, provides the narrative frame for the sequence of stories by provoking a series of 'hearings' at which each of his men tells a tale. His lively exchanges with his men punctuate the stories at key intervals and provide them with continuity. However, the sequence is relayed largely in the third person, with Wanzi being merely one of the group of listeners. Wanzi has a fine turn of phrase, and a character to match, but he is no raconteur and does not occupy a central narrational role in Brownlee's collection as a whole.

Brownlee's stories are, in fact, strongly reminiscent of Scully's, and there is little advance either technically or in ideological orientation. Wanzi and his men are loyal (if occasionally wayward) foot-soldiers of the paternalistic magistrate, and their stories – while revealing something of Brownlee's understanding of Xhosa culture – are little more than diverting items of local colour, already dated at the time of their publication.

— Ω —

Certainly the most direct (and indisputable) influence on Bosman was Aegidius Jean Blignaut, and I wish now to consider this influence at some length.

Valerie Rosenberg's biographical study of Bosman, *Sunflower to the Sun* (1976), uncovered the extent of the mutual influence of these two writers. In a chapter titled "The Bosman–Blignaut Tandem," Rosenberg notes that although the two had met at Johannesburg literary soirées earlier, it was their chance encounter in November 1930, when Bosman was brought to the offices of the *Touleier* by his brother Pierre, that sparked the brief but fruitful relationship between the two writers:

> Jean showed Herman some of the "Ruiter" stories he had written but not yet published.
>
> Bosman was so thrilled with the stories that he and Jean talked far into the night [...] Within a day or so of the reunion between Jean Blignaut and Bosman, Jean received a preface Bosman had written for the "Ruiter" stories in which they were paid enthusiastic tribute. In his covering letter Bosman stated that these stories had inspired one of his own. Typically, when he came to stay in Johannesburg, he left his story behind in Boksburg. He was unconcerned and quite prepared to write another, and had Jean not insisted that they return to retrieve it, "Makapan's Caves" might never have been published. (1976: 71)

Rosenberg goes on to point out several similarities in the "Ruiter" and "Schalk Lourens" stories that were sparked by this association:

> Both used a narrator, and in both instances the narrator [...] was a simple
> man who observed the world with its foibles and foolishness and then
> leavened his observations with his own interpretation. In addition, the
> "Ruiter" tales had that unexpected double thrust at the end which we
> later come to relish in the "Schalk Lourens" stories. Occasionally there is
> even a similarity in incident and anecdote. (73)

Citing, as an example of the last, Bosman's "Dopper and Papist" and
Blignaut's "The Wayside Remedy," in both of which stories a driver of
a cart breathes brandy into the nostrils of his horse to keep it going,
Rosenberg concludes that there existed between the two writers "a
generous hospitality which not only permitted the one to wander in the
regions of the other's ideas, but actually to be welcomed there. In this
way, each enriched the fabric of the other's thinking" (73).

Lionel Abrahams's Introduction to *Dead End Road* (1980) draws on
Rosenberg's research, but also includes its own, more impressive
delineation of the areas in which Bosman is indebted to Blignaut. His
summary is worth quoting in full:

> It is something larger than the specific definable borrowings that Bosman
> is indebted for to the Ruiter stories. It would appear that, having recently
> emerged from prison, he had not yet envisaged the form, the style, the
> approach that could embody and release his pent-up creative energy in
> fiction; his sojourn in Groot Marico as school teacher amid platteland
> folk lay ripe in his memory, a potential source of subjects and inspira-
> tions; the Ruiter stories, providentially encountered at just this moment,
> under the aegis, moreover, of so generous and congenial a spirit as Jean
> Blignaut, gave him precisely the light he needed – demonstrated a parti-
> cular way of employing the narrator, showed how 'Afrikaans experi-
> ence' might be rendered in English, illustrated an appropriate distance
> from realism and a distinctive role for playfulness even in treating tragic
> subjects, exemplified an imaginative blending of romantic and comic ele-
> ments, revealed the potential magic in oblique, off-handed presentations,
> and even provided models of kinds of humorous sallies that would suit
> the spirit of what he had to express. He must have perused Blignaut's
> pages with a rare sense of revelation and artistic liberation. He would
> apply these techniques to a world of fresh material and master every
> borrowed idea so that it was transmuted into something of his very own;
> but he must always have been aware that the key to the art he employed
> so magically to create the Oom Schalk Lourens stories had been handed

to him by Ruiter and Jean Blignaut, a fact he sought to memorialize in his visible borrowings. (Abrahams 1980: 11–12)

Abrahams's summation of Bosman's debt to Blignaut contains the following compelling argument: Bosman needed a suitable form for the expression of his already demonstrated creative drive; his Groot Marico experience provided him with the appropriate material and the "Ruiter" stories suggested the form in which to express this creativity. The "Ruiter" stories, then, principally influenced Bosman in his use of a narrator, his rendering of "Afrikaans experience" in English, his distance from realism as a literary mode, and his use of humour and a casual, 'throwaway' style.

If Rosenberg and Abrahams are right about the extent of Blignaut's influence on Bosman (and their accounts are difficult to dispute), a further question arises: who inspired Blignaut's "Ruiter" character? "Ruiter," as Blignaut reveals in his memoir *My Friend Herman Charles Bosman* (1981), was modelled on a "Hottentot"[1] of the same name who worked on the Blignaut family farm: "Ruiter told me only a few stories," Blignaut remarks, "though he must have known many, because his chuckles to which I put words sounded like wry comments on a string of events. I always saw his wrinkled grinning face carried on ape-like stunted legs through the dust of circumstance with which I surrounded him as proper to his character" (1981: 245).

According to Blignaut, Bosman prompted a visit to the Blignaut family farm, asking whether "we might visit Ruiter's stamping ground" (240). Recalling incidents from his childhood, Blignaut remembers that Ruiter's wife "had been making a nuisance of herself by keeping the household awake at night. She would tap on the windows begging someone to come along and see 'what that damned Hottentot is doing'" (243). In a passage that could have come from one of his Ruiter stories, Blignaut then relates what happened:

---

[1] Blignaut uses this term to denote what must clearly have been a "coloured" man (possibly of Khoi extraction), as the Khoi no longer existed as a race by this time. (The even more derisory "Hotnot" is a much more likely name to have been used.) Blignaut's terminology suggests a degree of racism in his depiction of "Hottentot Ruiter," although there is no doubt that this condescension is mixed with a degree of genuine affection – even admiration for Ruiter's canniness and penchant for survival.

Then one night uncle John went with her to the outhouse where the family lived. He put Ruiter on a scale, telling him his sins were being weighed and the Hottentot woman was pleased to hear that her husband was overweight with the blackest ones. Ruiter chuckled but the nightly racket stopped. In the morning he chuckled again, saying "Black ones: that will be a change from just yellow sins," an allusion to his wife's colour. (243)

Blignaut also recalls Bosman's response to the visit to "Ruiter's stamping ground": "'I can see Ruiter,' Herman said, 'shuffling towards the twin koppies, chuckling'" (244).

That the labourer on the family farm played a role in inspiring Blignaut's creation (and, in turn, Bosman's) illustrates the point that, although it is to literary models that the major share of influence must be ascribed, the oral milieux of late nineteenth- and early twentieth-century rural South Africa cannot be ignored as sources of influence for the oral-style tales that dominated the South African short story in this period.

A similar dual influence is evident in Sanni Metelerkamp's *Outa Karel's Stories: South African Folk-lore Tales* (1914), a collection which invites comparison with Blignaut's, in that it also uses a "Hottentot" narrator.[2] In her Foreword, Metelerkamp professes to

lay no claim to originality for any of the stories in this collection – at best a very small proportion of a vast store from which the story-teller of the future may draw, embodying the superstitions, the crude conceptions, the childish ideas of a primitive and rapidly disappearing people. They are known in some form or other wherever the negro has set foot, and are the common property of every country child in South Africa. (vii–viii)

She also acknowledges a debt to W.H.I. Bleek, whose *Hottentot Fables and Tales* (first published in 1864) looms large behind her own collec-

---

[2] Another writer who uses a "Hottentot" narrator is the Afrikaans writer Toon van den Heever. In his *Gerwe uit die Erfpag van Skoppensboer* (1948), Outa Sem features twice (in "Die Beukelaar van Outa Sem" and "Outa Sem en Vader Krismis") and other stories – "Oom Krisjan oor Kort en Lang Note" is one example – employ an internal narrator. The appearance of a "Hottentot" narrator in Metelerkamp, Blignaut and Van den Heever suggests something about the presence of this figure in the South African physical and cultural landscape of the pre-war era.

tion. So the stories are not 'original' to her, and Bleek's influence is clear and acknowledged. However, this literary influence is balanced by the putative 'real-life' influence of a Khoi man whom she refers to as "the quaint figure of the old Native with his little masters" (viii). That this figure is apparently not the fictional, generalized evocation suggested by her formulation is signalled by a passage which follows immediately afterwards:

> It is nearly three years now since "Old Friend Death" took him gently by the hand and led him away to that far, far country of which he had such vague ideas, so he tells no more stories by the firelight in the gloaming [...] (viii–ix)

So, like Blignaut, Metelerkamp claims to have been partly influenced by a 'real' storyteller figure known to her, while acknowledging the (presumably far greater) influence of the material emanating from Bleek's research and the lore which is "the common property of every country child in South Africa."

It is possible, however, that the first is merely a device employed to bestow greater authenticity upon her tales, and that her influence is wholly 'literary.' Certainly the vague generalities in which she couches her description of her storyteller figure suggest that imagination plays a very large role in this construction. This figure is first described as a representative of "a primitive and rapidly disappearing people" (vii) – clearly the Khoisan people – becomes "the negro" (viii), and ends up "the old Native" (viii). Even if one allows for a degree of unscholarly nomenclature, this semantic slippage suggests that Metelerkamp is constructing a storyteller figure who is a composite of the various indigenous oral traditions of southern Africa, and is thus a largely imagined figure whose outlines are suggested by literary–cultural tradition rather than by an 'actual' encounter.

It is also interesting to observe that her claims to a lack of 'originality' (hence her rootedness in actuality) echo those of earlier writers like Ingram. This signals an important distinction between Metelerkamp and Blignaut: whereas Metelerkamp offers another variation on the familiar claim to 'authenticity,' Blignaut's tales are never presented as being anything but entire fabrications. Indeed, one can only believe that he would have been disdainful of the ingenuous efforts of writers like

Ingram and Metelerkamp, of their pedestrian 'reproductions,' and of their failure to engage in the elaborate flights of fancy in which he and Bosman revelled.

To be fair, Metelerkamp's folktales about how the jackal got his stripe, or why the heron has a crooked neck, or why the hare's nose is slit are intended as tales for children, whereas Blignaut's tales belong in a different category altogether. Metelerkamp's "Outa Karel" is an example of what Pereira calls a "real or reputed author–narrator," who merely provides "a traditionally accepted framework of reference, enabling the reader to identify the 'type' of story he is dealing with and relate it to its appropriate context" (1986b: 103). Such narrators, argues Pereira, "neither intrude upon nor challenge the supremacy of the stories they tell" (103).

"Dead End Road," the opening tale in Blignaut's sequence, immediately signals to the reader that he or she is dealing with a far more sophisticated fictional narrator here – one whose word is not to be taken at face value and whose narratives include metafictional play upon the craft of storytelling itself:

> A storm blew up, but soon spent itself. A short rainbow ladder stood against the air, bending the wrong way with its gaudy rungs.
>
> "Ah! Rain in the sunshine, the time when jackals marry," Hottentot Ruiter said, stretching lazily in the doorway.
>
> "Have you been invited to the wedding?" Kotie, the bywoner's son, asked.
>
> "No; but I'll go all the same when I've rested a bit longer. You see, Kotie, the jackal doesn't wait either to be asked to a lambs' party on the wet grass in the vlei. It just sneaks up along the blue shadows for a bite to eat. Not of grass, though."
>
> Ruiter would have enlarged on the sly habits of the jackal and the bold tactics of the lion, but before he had got set, Kotie had run off with his dog. Ruiter stared at the twin swaths where hurrying feet and paws had brushed the rain-beads from the veld. He shook his head. For he had lost his audience through a faulty start. He should have brought in the lion first thing. It was a pity, because there was a rainbow over the kraal and a fine story in his head in which a dog played a noble part. (Blignaut 1980: 15)

It is in this casual, conversational style that Blignaut begins his story about Jool Meyer's suicide. He approaches his morbid subject oblique-

ly, and constantly juxtaposes humour and seriousness in order not to
allow this subject to weigh too heavily:

> Nobody had taken him [Jool Meyer] seriously. Piet Lategan had even
> spread a story that Jool had drawn up a list of people who would not be
> allowed to attend his funeral. Piet Lategan had added that he was glad to
> hear that Jool had not forgotten the Church, like the good Christian he
> was – he had given the Predikant pride of place on the list. (16)

After one abortive attempt, Jool Meyer succeeds in committing suicide,
and it is left to his faithful servants, Ruiter and Ndobe (who had
exhausted all their ingenuity in attempting to thwart his purpose), to
bury him. The story ends with the burial and with Ruiter being arrested
for 'stealing' the sheep that he and Ndobe had secreted in the hope of
distracting Jool from his macabre intentions:

> Ruiter followed the horseman along the road Ndobe had cleared. Ndobe
> stood at gaze. He was no longer so sure that he had made a good road;
> Ruiter was not being borne along it as smoothly as the coffin had been.
> His feet were so seldom on the ground. (19)

The sudden twist at the end and the casual manner in which it is conveyed are but two of the many Bosmanesque features of the story. The
oblique and deceptive approach to the narrative subject, the economy
and skill with which the story is crafted, its disconcerting blend of the
comic and the tragic, its reflection on the profound ironies of life, and
its implicit commentary on racial injustice are some of the other
features which demonstrate the close correspondences between the
stories of Blignaut and Bosman. Pereira's memorable image of "the
double-yolked egg that Bosman and Blignaut hatched out" (1986b: 108)
encapsulates perfectly the nature of the relationship between the two
writers and its mutually beneficial effect on their stories.

Blignaut remarked in a letter to Abrahams (quoted by the latter in
the introduction to *Dead End Road*) that, in relation to Bosman, he had
"only small talent to set against genius" (Abrahams 1980: 9); however,
his was the spark that ignited the flame of Bosman's talent, and it is
relevant to the concerns of this study to consider precisely what it was
that he introduced to the South African oral-style story that inspired the

foremost exponent of the genre.[3] The discussion that follows will deal
with only nine of the stories contained in *Dead End Road*, as it is these
nine that predated Bosman and can thus be said to have influenced the
development of the 'pre-Schalk Lourens' oral-style story.[4]

No copies of the privately published *The Hottentot's God* have survived, and this means that it is impossible to determine precisely what
Bosman encountered when he first read the original collection.[5] Several
stories have been lost and the sequence of the stories in the original
collection is unknown. Accurate information in this regard would
enable one to consider the original collection as it was conceived in its
totality (and as it was encountered by Bosman). It is also impossible to
determine the number of stories not narrated by Hottentot Ruiter,
which means that one is unable to gauge precisely the narratological
role he plays in the collection as a whole.

This set of related points regarding the original composition of the
Ruiter stories is important: it would be anachronistic to use *Dead End
Road* – a text which appeared only in 1980 – as a point of reference in a
study which discusses stories spanning the years 1862–1947. One also
does not know whether individual stories in *Dead End Road* differ
significantly from their originals in *The Hottentot's God*. In a word, the
impact of Blignaut's creation on the subsequent development of the

---

[3] The sixteen stories that made up the original collection of Blignaut's Ruiter
stories – *The Hottentot's God*, published in 1931 – were all, according to Abrahams,
written during 1930 and published early in 1931. Bosman and Blignaut re-estab-
lished contact only in November 1930, according to Rosenberg (1976: 71); thus Blignaut's Ruiter conception was already far advanced before this momentous occasion. Other indications of this are the fact that Bosman's original preface to *The
Hottentot's God* (reprinted as an appendix to *Dead End Road*) is dated January 1931,
by which point only his earliest story, "Makapan's Caves," had appeared (in December 1930), with "The Rooinek" due to appear in two parts in the January/Feb-
ruary and March editions of the *Touleier*. It would appear, then, that Blignaut had
an important hand in shaping the kind of story that is the focus of this study.

[4] Abrahams, presumably on the basis of information supplied by Blignaut, lists
these stories: "Dead End Road," "Magersfontein," "A Coffin in the Loft," Fire in
the Reeds," "All That Glitters," "Jackal in my Kraal," "The Hottentot's God," and
"Campfires" (Blignaut 1980: 7). (That Bosman himself explicitly refers to seven of
these in his preface corroborates Abrahams's assertion.)

[5] Abrahams remarks that "the whereabouts of any copies of the original collection are unknown today and many of the stories have been lost" (1980: 7). Again,
presumably he is drawing on information provided by Blignaut.

oral-style story is impossible to determine with any precision. The nearest one can come to such an assessment is to confine one's attentions to those stories referred to by Bosman, and to extrapolate from his general remarks about *The Hottentot's God*. (However, using *Dead End Road* as a source for these stories themselves is, of course, unavoidable.)

Bosman's preface begins: "Here is a collection of South African stories; in the main they are related by a Hottentot named Ruiter" (Blignaut 1980: 103). "Dead End Road" is one of these, and it is possible that it headed the original sequence – with its third-person narrative point of view, it provides a view of Ruiter and his setting from the outside, and thus constitutes an ideal opening piece, whereas the other stories of *Dead End Road* are all narrated by Ruiter and therefore do not allow such a perspective.

The main features of the story have already been discussed above, and I wish to confine my attention to those features of this story (and of the other "Ruiter" stories known by Bosman) which add a new dimension to the South African oral-style story.

The opening exchanges between Ruiter and Kotie (the bywoner's son) suggest such a departure from tradition. Ruiter, we read, "would have enlarged on the sly habits of the jackal and the bold tactics of the lion, but before he had got set, Kotie had run off with his dog" (15). What this suggests is that Ruiter's store of tales includes folktales about animals like the jackal and the lion (the kind of story Metelerkamp's Outa Karel tells), and that these stories would be told on occasions when he has an audience, especially one made up of children (as in this case). The tale that then unfolds, however (and this is true of all of the tales in *Dead End Road*), is of an entirely different sort. The implication appears to be that, when left to ruminate freely, as it were, Ruiter's inclination is to tell tales which engage more incisively with issues in contemporary South African life – relations between the races, the effects of the Anglo-Boer War, the injustices meted out to unsuspecting 'Jims' who have 'come to Jo'burg,' and the like.

Perhaps a better way of expressing this is to say that Blignaut assigned his "Hottentot" narrator a more important task than that of merely recounting traditional fables about the jackal and the hare. The difference between "Hottentot Karel" and "Hottentot Ruiter," in other words, is that whereas one is consigned to the museological domain of cultural curiosity, the other is free to engage tellingly (albeit obliquely) with more pressing contemporary issues. Metelerkamp's insulting condescension ("crude conceptions," "childish ideas," "primitive [...] people," "the quaint figure of the old Native with his little masters") is supplanted by a new respect, a new sense that the person on the receiving end of racial oppression may have a very interesting story to tell.

In accordance with this more demanding role, Blignaut's narrator is a far more complex character than his predecessors. Abrahams's apt description of Ruiter as "a humorous, reflective, self-satirical narrator" (1980: 10) pinpoints a crucial difference between Ruiter and earlier South African fictional narrators: the element of reflexiveness, of self-irony. As I argued earlier, Perceval Gibbon's Vrouw Grobelaar has the raconteur's verbal gift, and her humour is laced with half-hidden barbed asides (mostly directed at Katje and her suitor), but she lacks the capacity to be self-satirical. She is indeed satirized, but this function is fulfilled by Katje and the Englishman. They see to it that her shortcomings do not go unnoticed.

The narrative structure of Blignaut's stories is more economical, and here he anticipates Bosman very precisely. His stories typically begin with an apparently inconsequential remark – like: "This is another story I don't like to tell" ("Magersfontein"); or: "It's a mistake to let your enemy know you're thirsting for revenge" ("A Coffin in the Loft") – followed invariably by "(Hottentot Ruiter said)," a trademark also of the Oom Schalk sequence (and pioneered, it seems, by Slater). The 'audience' is introduced in a similarly economical way. The opening to "Magersfontein," for example, continues: "but I'm going to let you hear it now so that you can see that I speak the truth" (20). As with Bosman, the "you" here refers to an internal audience (perhaps even a single person) that usually goes unidentified and is not further represented textually.

What Blignaut achieved, in other words, was a method of reducing the narrative frame typical to the oral-style story to the point where it almost disappears altogether. A tendency to minimize the narrative frame progressively is evident in the sequence of oral-style stories examined in this study. Drayson's frame is so ponderous that it threatens to crowd out the embedded narratives; Scully and FitzPatrick are similarly uneconomical, the latter particularly being so leisurely about framing the embedded story in "The Outspan" that the reader's attention is fruitlessly diverted in several other directions; Glanville's frame is more concise but becomes tedious, with the young frame narrator having to ride out to Abe Pike's homestead on each occasion in order for a story to be told; Gibbon establishes his frame at the beginning of his sequence and the remaining stories can therefore unfold without delay; Slater uses the deft "Oom Mias said" to establish his narrative frame, while Smith contracts this still further, with Koenraad's tales being relayed by an unidentified and unobtrusive narrating agency. Blignaut and Bosman adopt the narrative structure Smith uses and are able to establish speaker, audience and setting in the space of the opening sentence.

The clearest break Blignaut makes with tradition is achieved by two major innovations: the creation of a complex, unreliable narrator and (perhaps as a consequence) the introduction of a metafictional dimension to the oral-style story. Both of these key features of the late, sophisticated oral-style story were taken over by Bosman and are worth considering in some detail.

In the previous chapter it was argued that Smith concentrated the narrative function in a single figure, Koenraad, but did not exploit the possibility of this figure being complex or fallible. The consequence of this was that her Koenraad tales are in many ways less sophisticated variants of the oral-style story than are those of Gibbon. In Hottentot Ruiter, Blignaut has created a character who is complex and dissembling, who seldom reveals the full extent of what he knows, and who leads the reader along by inference and suggestion rather than by direct 'telling.'

The creation of such a character, who is also an intradiegetic narrator (a participant in the stories he relates), enables the author to 'withdraw' and manipulate him from a distance. Whereas Gibbon had to resort to the use of a frame narrator in order to offer an alternative perspective on events described by the internal narrator, Blignaut is able to offer a range of perspectives through a single narrator by permitting him to speak in different voices. We encounter in Ruiter a person who is apparently 'simple' – who is duped into serving six months of indentured labour on the mines ("All that Glitters"), who is repeatedly defrauded by a corrupt lawyer ("Jackal in my Kraal"), and who is forced through his own ignorance to fit Biblical scriptures into his own limited frame of reference ("The Hottentot's God"; "Camp-fires") – but who has the ability to understand deeply buried human motives and to reveal the narrow-mindedness and injustice of the Afrikaner characters he describes. Concentrated in this character, then, is enough complexity to allow the author to convey through him attitudes and perceptions that alternate between naïveté and wisdom, obtuseness and perspicacity, ignorance and discernment – that, in other words, make of him a 'multivoiced,' composite persona.

Some disjunctures and incongruities result from this, however. One obvious failing in the presentation of this character is that he seldom sounds like, or comes across as, a "Hottentot." This problem is compounded by Blignaut's propensity for poetic and sometimes abstruse language. In "The Hottentot's God," for example, Ruiter describes some of the problems he experiences in the process of cadging brandy from Frans Celliers in exchange for stories:

> Then the story stuttered and brought Frans back to earth and our un-spoken bargain. And the unwilling word slid smartly into the tippling gap and he was back with me again on the tree gallows. And, as we shinned up it, kicking off scruffy bark, the dangling rope became as jittery once more as it had been on that terrible day, a nightmare memory. (54)

Here Ruiter is obliquely alluding to the day that he was almost hanged, and this passage therefore serves to foreshadow the main feature of the story that has yet to unfold. However, the style of speech is laconic to the point of opacity, and the illusion of the spoken word evaporates before the reader's eyes. The words used also sound incongruous in the mouth of an uneducated "Hottentot" farm-labourer, and the image of this wizened, sly, simple-seeming narrator is temporarily disrupted. This occurs frequently in the Ruiter stories, and the reader is left with an after-impression of a fractured, ill-defined miscellany rather than of a series of episodes that resolve themselves into a composite picture.

To be fair, this impression must be attributed partly to the fact that the original sequence of Hottentot Ruiter stories has not survived and that what *Dead End Road* constitutes is a kind of makeshift alternative. However, even within a single story such disjunctures and incongruities exist. In "Fire in the Reeds," for example, the homely opening –

"People often say to me (Hottentot Ruiter said), 'You are old and have seen much of the strange workings of things, so tell us what you reckon is the greatest lesson you've learnt between gathering wrinkles for your face'" – is followed by: "Now, no one can do anything about the plowing of time on his brow, but everybody can take a hand in stacking the stooks of experiences, good and bad sheaves, under a bright or dim harvest moon" (37). Juxtaposing such ill-matched paragraphs not only produces stylistic infelicities, but strains the reader's credulity. This is not a rustic "Hottentot" speaking, the reader subconsciously registers, but an intrusive author trying (not altogether successfully) to be poetic.

Blignaut's use of metafictional play is more successful. The adroit opening passages of "Dead End Road" have already been commented upon in this regard. Other examples include "A Coffin in the Loft," in which Ruiter's storytelling feats bring about a beating, and "The Hottentot's God," which plays upon the relationship between cadging brandy and being able to tell good stories. But perhaps the best example is "Campfires," in which Schalk Lourens makes an appearance:

> Schalk Lourens? Yes, I know him (Hottentot Ruiter said). He has blue eyes and a long beard, but I don't think the old song, "Die vaal hare en die blou oë" was made up about him; though he's gay when it's played on the concertina at a vastrap [folk dance]. He strokes his beard with his free hand then with the knuckles of the one holding the brandy; and when he has breathed in the fumes, he grows jollier still and sings, his beard beating time.
>
> It's a good beard, but mealies sprout things like that everywhere in the Marico, if the rust hasn't got at the early sowings; and he's the best teller of stories in the district, after me. I often wonder when he's going to trek to a district where he won't have to compete with me. (94)

A little further on, having commented on Schalk's practice of stealing his stories in order to impress the father of Sannie, the girl he is courting, and to "put a sparkle in Sannie's lovely eyes" (94), Ruiter claims that he did not really mind this, "but when he started selling them for money, I reckoned he should talk less about ruspes [caterpillars] and more about my share of what they left behind to go into the bottle" (95). (The last remark is a reference to Schalk's purported ploy of complaining about the damage done to his peach trees by ruspes – and hence to the supply of peach brandy he can offer to Ruiter.)

This textual encounter between the rival bushveld raconteurs was prompted by Bosman's writing of "Makapan's Caves," which, remarks Abrahams, was "produced [...] within days of its author's happy encounter with Ruiter and his tales – and in its turn inspired the writing of 'Campfires'" (Abrahams 1980: 10).

The echo in "Campfires" of the opening lines of "Makapan's Caves" – "Kafirs? (said Oom Schalk Lourens). Yes I know them" – is unmistakable, and amounts to what appears to be a return salvo across the 'racial' divide, Oom Schalk's insult to "kafirs" being returned with interest by Ruiter. Neither narrator must be taken at face value, however. Oom Schalk's racism is clearly not shared by the author, and as the story "Makapan's Caves" unfolds it becomes clear that the story's principal theme (that bonds of friendship can transcend racial boundaries) subverts Oom Schalk's bald opening assertion. And Ruiter's retort, for its part, is merely a front for Blignaut's playful and good-humoured acknowledgement of the mutual influence of the two writers.

The ludic nature of these exchanges, and of the earlier examples of metafictional play in Blignaut, however, are important signals of a decisive shift in the later oral-style story. The artless and ingenuous nature of the early oral-style story has progressively given way to a greater emphasis on fictionality, on artful inventiveness. The constitutive elements of the genre thus become merely conventional, a set of devices to manipulate for ironic effect. Blignaut's achievement was to have attained this degree of artfulness although, as has been argued, his narrator was not always equal to the task. It will be seen in the next chapter how Bosman was to take over Blignaut's innovations without inheriting his infelicities.

❦ ❧

9 The Oral Stylist *par excellence*
Herman Charles Bosman

I
N 1930 BOSMAN'S FIRST MAJOR STORY, "Makapan's Caves,"
appeared under the pseudonym Herman Malan. The story introduced the reading public to what would become South Africa's
most famous fictional narrator, who memorably begins: "Kafirs? [...]
Yes, I know them. And they're all the same. I fear the Almighty, and I
respect His works, but I could never understand why He made the
kafir and the rinderpest" (Bosman 1949: 65). From the very outset, then,
Bosman was to make use of his very distinctive brand of irony, and the
'artful' oral-style story had come into its own.

Bosman's stories have been treated extensively in criticism (Dickson
1975; Siebert 1977, 1986; Gray 1977, 1980, 1986; Abrahams 1980, 1988;
Pereira 1986b; Trump 1986; Titlestad 1987) and it is not my purpose to
add to the general discussion here. The purpose of this chapter, rather,
is to advance the main argument of this study by considering Bosman's
stories in relation to the earlier examples of the oral-style story already
examined. The chapter is divided into three parts. First, there will be an
analysis of certain aspects of the Schalk Lourens sequence, focusing
particularly on the differences between Bosman's use of the oral-style
story and that of its earlier practitioners. Then I shall look briefly at
Bosman's later "Voorkamer" conversation pieces and, lastly, at the
overtly metafictional stories which employ an authorial narrator. In this
last section I shall also speculate about the demise of the storyteller
figure in 'white' South African literature. These concluding remarks
anticipate the closing chapter of this study, which looks at the re-
discovery of oral forms in the black South African short story.

The Schalk Lourens Sequence

Bosman produced over 140 stories which are set in a rural milieu and which are often referred to as his "bushveld stories." The Oom Schalk sequence accounts for over fifty of these, and the "Voorkamer" sequence eighty.[1] The remaining stories fit into neither sequence but use a bushveld setting and characters appropriate to this milieu.

Typically, a chapter of this sort (a discussion of a group of stories by a particular writer) would consider the sequence of stories chronologically, then attempt to detect a development, or growing sophistication, in the writer's oeuvre. However, it is difficult to discern such a development in Bosman, whether in his stories or in his oeuvre generally.

Identifying three modes in Bosman's writing – "romantic, psychosexual 'Lawrentian' rhapsodising," "frank, gritty daily reportage," and "ironic comedy" (1986: 25) – Stephen Gray has pointed to the futility of trying to trace any coherent development in Bosman's oeuvre:

> It is almost unbelievable that one of his most fully-worked short stories, "Makapan's Caves" (the first of the Oom Schalk series, and one of his greatest achievements in the ironic mode), should first appear in the same year (1930) as his jejune exercise in the rhapsodic mode ("In the Beginning" by Ben Africa) and his asinine polemic in the mode of reportage, "Ex-student Attacks University Professors." (1986: 26)

There is a general movement from the Oom Schalk series to the Voorkamer sequence.[2] There is also, as we shall see, a gradual increase in self-reflexive narratives foregrounding the storytelling craft itself. However, such developments are only discernible very broadly. In fact, Bosman throughout his oeuvre continually switched between these different modes. The unevenness in the Bosman corpus that Gray points out is also evident in Oom Schalk stories produced in the same period.[3]

---

[1] I am indebted here to Stephen Gray's comprehensive and accurate bibliographic record of Bosman's work in his *Herman Charles Bosman* (1986: 181–97).

[2] All of the latter, and eight of the Oom Schalk stories, appeared in 1950 and 1951 (the last eighteen months of Bosman's life).

[3] Of the six such stories that appeared before Bosman's departure for London in 1934, for instance, Bosman saw fit to select only three for *Mafeking Road*. The other three were also excluded by Abrahams from his various Bosman collections, and were collected as miscellanea only much later in Valerie Rosenberg's *Almost Forgotten Stories* (1979) and her *Ramoutsa Road and Other Re-Collected Stories* (1987).

In his *Selected Stories* (1980) edition of Bosman's work, Gray arranged the stories in an attempt to trace a progression in the oeuvre, arguing in his Introduction that this selection reflects Bosman "working his way through his early attempts to retell folk tales [...] to the more formal short story which encapsulates the spoken episode, through to his later form, the conversation piece" (1980: 13).

The problem with this chronology is that the first two stories, "A Tale Writ in Water" and "The Affair at Ysterspruit," which Gray has chosen to represent Bosman's early "retelling of folk tales" period, were actually published after many of the supposedly later-period Oom Schalk pieces.[4] Thus, in order to achieve some sense of the progression he speaks of, Gray has actually rearranged the chronology of Bosman's work. Even then, a sense of progression is difficult to discern, aside from the indisputable general progression from the story arranged around a central narrator (the Oom Schalk sequence) to that employing multiple narrators (the Voorkamer conversation pieces).

From the above one must conclude that Bosman's Oom Schalk series is not characterized by tentative, rough beginnings, proceeding steadily towards ever greater sophistication and technical accomplishment. The first two stories in the sequence – "Makapan's Caves" and "The Rooinek" – are as carefully crafted as any Bosman later wrote, and the narrative structure, the humour, irony and pathos, which are the hallmarks of Bosman's style, are already impressively present. Indeed, the gentle pathos at the conclusion of "The Rooinek" is arguably more skilfully achieved than anything that was to come later:

> [...] we agreed that the Englishman Webber must have passed through terrible things; he could not even have had any understanding left as to what the Steyns had done with their baby. He probably thought, up to the moment when he died, that he was carrying the child. For, when we lifted his body, we found, still clasped in his dead and rigid arms, a few old rags and a child's clothes.
>
> It seemed to us that the wind that always stirs in the Kalahari blew very quietly and softly that morning.
>
> Yes, the wind blew very gently. (1949: 166)

---

[4] "The Affair at Ysterpruit" first appeared in Afrikaans in 1948 and was translated by Abrahams for his *Unto Dust* collection (1963). "A Tale Writ in Water" may well have been an early tale, although it was first published only in 1969.

This parable about a bond of friendship that transcends racial boundaries strikes the most melancholy tone of all the stories in *Mafeking Road*, and is all the more powerful by virtue of this contrast. That the collection as a whole achieves a resonance beyond the confines of the Marico and touches on issues central to the human condition is largely due to the stark power of stories like this one.

Instead of pursuing a strictly chronological and exhaustive study of Bosman's stories, then, I wish to focus rather on those aspects of the stories which bear upon a discussion of the development of the South African oral-style story. The movement from a single narrator (Oom Schalk) to multiple narrators (the Voorkamer sequence) will, of course, be brought into the discussion as it signals a broad shift in Bosman's oeuvre and also in the postwar South African short story in general. In addition, Bosman's later tendency to move away from internal narrators altogether and towards a self-reflexive authorial narrator will also be examined as it too suggests a great deal about the general trajectory of the South African short story.

Vivienne Dickson's study (1975) of Bosman's stories is a good place to begin: it is thorough and incisive and, indeed, raises issues central to the concerns of this study.

Dickson discusses the question of audience in Bosman's Oom Schalk tales, remarking that "the narrator frequently refers to places without describing them, which suggests to the reader that the narrator and presumed audience are equally familiar with the geography of the area" (1975: 26) and also that "historical references are never explained – it is enough for the narrator to refer to Mafeking or General de Wet for the readers to know what he is talking about" (26). "The presence of the narrator's peers," she goes on, "can also be inferred from those stories where an audience appears in the tale itself" (27). She concludes:

> In the "Marico" stories Bosman has thus been able to retain an essential element of the fireside tale, the audience, but without having to use clumsy devices to establish its presence. Schalk can go directly into his tale without a preamble to set the scene, and can complete his tale (which is always short) without interruptions which inevitably disturb the reader. Furthermore, the absence of the audience's comments allows the reader to make his own judgements – which is important in a writer who works by implication rather than direct statement. (27–28)

Dickson's implied comparison here is between writers who use the fire-side tale form clumsily and those, like Bosman, who use it skilfully. I have earlier discussed numerous examples of unsuccessful fireside tales (the 'artless' oral-style stories), which irritate the reader and in-duce ennui for precisely the reasons Dickson identifies. The narrative frame is usually established in a ponderous and predictable manner, and there are distracting interpolations by the narrator's interlocutors (FitzPatrick's "The Outspan" being the outstanding example). Bosman, on the other hand, with his customary deft interpolation "(Oom Schalk Lourens said)," sets the scene instantly and the tale proceeds with the minimum of obvious authorial interference.

Dickson's central argument is that "the fireside tale had few com-petent exponents in English" – FitzPatrick, Slater, Prance and Scully produced some examples of the genre, she notes – but it took Bosman "to raise the South African fireside tale to the standard achieved in other parts of the English-speaking world" (17–18). By the time Bos-man published his first fireside tale ("Makapan's Caves," in 1930), "there were few short story writers who had not abandoned the genre." One of the special demands on a modern writer working in an old form was that of "moulding the fireside tale to fit the pattern of the more stringently constructed literary short story." The attempts of Kipling and Conrad to achieve such a union usually sacrificed the qualities of one form for the sake of the other, while "Bosman's stories are rather more successful at keeping a balance between the require-ments of the fireside tale and those of the literary short story" (18–19).

Dickson's argument is a convincing one. Bosman's stories have the outward appearance of simplicity and artlessness and, indeed, as we shall shortly see, have been interpreted in this way; but artfulness and a thoroughly modern economy permeate every aspect of his tales. To turn first, though, to critical misapprehension of Bosman's art, of which there are at least two examples. One is an anonymous review of *Unto Dust* in the *Times Literary Supplement*:

> *Unto Dust* is a further collection of tales by the popular Afrikaner story-teller, Herman Charles Bosman. Bosman died in 1951 at the age of 46. He was once sentenced to death for murder, spent nine years in Europe in the 1930s, and worked as a journalist in South Africa. It is odd and ana-chronistic in the circumstances that he should have been able to make a

reputation for himself by telling old tales of the Boer war, and that, considering his undoubted gifts, he should have wished to.

The tales themselves seem authentic, old men's yarns that are likely enough to be told in an isolated, pioneering, bookless community: they serve an obvious purpose of whiling away the time. Yet in fact their appeal is to the deluded nostalgia of a very different community, and their seeming authenticity dissolves into pastiche. Bosman was an uncompromisingly backward writer, a poor Boer's, mid-twentieth-century Kipling. [cited by Gray, 1986: 28–29]

Oddly enough, this "infuriatingly inaccurate and demeaning review" (Gray 1986: 28), is partly echoed by another appraisal closer to home. In a contemporaneous review, Joseph Sachs, having favourably reviewed the stories of Gordimer and Lessing, says of *Mafeking Road* that Bosman's "simple unvarnished tales are more truly South African, than the intense and sophisticated writings of our other young writers." He then applauds Bosman for his "almost impersonal style" and his lack of "ideological luggage," remarking that there "is all of South Africa in that little book" (1951: 16).

Sachs's appreciation of Bosman's stories is sincere, and much of what he says in his review is well judged and accurate, but his tell-tale opening description of "simple unvarnished tales" in relation to the "intense and sophisticated" work of Gordimer and Lessing reveals his misapprehension of the sophistication and complexity of Bosman's art.

The judgement of both critics, in fact, applies far better to the work of earlier South African pioneers of the oral-style form. Ironically, they support Dickson's argument that Bosman used elements belonging to the two distinct genres of the fireside tale and the modern short story in fashioning his bushveld stories. Fixing on the outward appearance of the stories ("authenticity," "old men's yarns," "deluded nostalgia" and "backwardness"; "simple unvarnished tales"), these critics fail to see that Bosman has infused an older art form with a modern sensibility; yet their misconstruction of his art paradoxically reveals its true nature.

The issue which is at the centre of my own discussion of Bosman's bushveld tales is precisely that of the marriage of genres: Bosman took over the older genre of the fireside tale – for its qualities of intimacy and familiarity and its congruency with the milieu he wished to describe – but introduced into this familiar genre the new requirements of economy and trenchant social commentary.

By 1930 the fireside tale had outlived its usefulness as an 'authentic' mode of representing South African life and was capable only of yielding the "deluded nostalgia" spoken of by the *TLS* critic or of offering a conventional foil for the operation of unconventional, disruptive devices. It is, of course, the latter possibility that is exploited so richly by Bosman: he takes over many of the features of the oral tale – a narrator, a conversational narrative style, an appropriate milieu, and an implied audience – but introduces elements that are among the hallmarks of the modern short story – economy, irony, structural tautness, social critique. The disparate influences can now be seen to reassemble into a configuration which makes sense of Bosman's style. From pioneers like Scully and Smith, Bosman could see the virtue of taking South Africa as his subject-matter. The American humorous tradition – Twain, Harte, Leacock – would have offered compelling examples of the dissembling raconteur and his 'tall tale.' And 'moderns' like Poe and O. Henry would have suggested economy, focus on a single incident, psychological exploration and the powerful effect of the concealed ending.[5]

— Ω —

[5] The question of influences has preoccupied many critics. Vivienne Dickson's discussion of influences is the most wide-ranging. Having cited as possible local influences Scully, FitzPatrick, Blackburn, Slater and Prance, she goes on to remark that Bosman's fireside tales "owe much to the gentle sea-story teller [sic] W.W. Jacobs" (1975: 20). Edgar Allan Poe is also indubitably a major influence on Bosman, but it is the "American humorous tradition," she argues (citing at various points Twain, Josh Billings, Artemus Ward, Bret Harte, O. Henry and Stephen Leacock) "to which his writing ultimately belongs" (50). Dickson also notes various specific examples of direct influences on Bosman, including Poe's "The Tell-Tale Heart" (cf "Old Transvaal Story"), Washington Irving's "Rip van Winkle" (cf "A Boer Rip van Winkel") and Harte's "The Society upon the Stanislow," which "probably inspired" "Marico Man" and "Anxious to Hear" (42–43).

Bosman has himself acknowledged his indebtedness to the American pioneers of the short story. Poe, Ambrose Bierce, O. Henry, Twain and Leacock are some of the writers Bosman admired and emulated, and these luminaries he acknowledges directly in his essays (Bosman 1936; 1971a [1944]; 1971b [1946]; 1980 [1948]).

Poe's influence has been considered in detail by Irmgard Titlestad (1987). She argues that the writer was to exercise a lifelong influence on Bosman that verged on an obsession. This is so despite the profound differences that can be observed in the work of the two writers. In this regard, Lionel Abrahams notes: "The American's love of logical analysis and interest in science and mechanical devices are

I began by examining early examples of what I have called the 'oral-style' story and traced in this nascent tradition a growing sophistication in the use of its central devices. The introduction of irony and a critical distance between author and narrator in Gibbon I identified as the turning-point in the genre. The oral-style story had now achieved a level of complexity that gave it purchase on the increasingly complex social situation of twentieth-century South Africa.

In Bosman the South African oral-style story reaches its apogee, as can be variously demonstrated. Most importantly, the potential for subversion and irony in this style of story that lay dormant in the work of Drayson, Boyle, Ingram, Scully, and FitzPatrick is fully exploited by Bosman. This he achieved by creating a complex set of relationships between author, narrator, internal audience, and readership.

The famous opening lines of "Makapan's Caves" are worth revisiting to demonstrate this point:

> Kafirs? (said Oom Schalk Lourens). Yes, I know them. And they're all the same. I fear the Almighty, and I respect His works, but I could never understand why He made the kafir and the rinderpest. The Hottentot is a little better. The Hottentot will only steal the biltong hanging out on the line to dry. He won't steal the line as well. That is where the kafir is different. (1949: 65)

---

qualities for which Bosman had no scope whatsoever. And what could be more different than the polished solidity of Poe's high-flown prose and the open weave of Bosman's rough-textured language which even in its most purple passages never gets far from a certain self-mocking colloquial clumsiness?" (1988: 5). There is certainly more evidence of Twain, Harte and O. Henry in Bosman's ribald, yarn-spinning style, yet it perhaps attests to the catholic nature of his literary taste that Bosman can profess affinities with writers as diverse as Poe, Twain and Baudelaire.

Stephen Gray (1986: 4) drew attention to Bosman's early interest in Chaucer, a potential influence that has not been discussed in any detail. In 1925, the twenty-year-old Bosman wrote an article on *The Canterbury Tales* which appeared in *The University of the Witwatersrand Student Magazine*. Bosman was clearly struck by the ingenuity of the narrative frame which Chaucer employs to contain his tales, and the vitality of the characters he describes (Bosman 1925).

The above indicates that Bosman (like most writers) was subject to a wide range of literary influences, and that speculation and argumentation in this regard is potentially limitless. I do not wish to be drawn into a long excursus in this regard. The purpose of this note on influences on Bosman is to forestall any notion that my analysis of the development of the oral-style story – or of Bosman's role in this development – precludes recognition of the role of non-South African sources.

In the space of a few short sentences, Bosman established a narrative structure which set the pattern for the rest of the Oom Schalk sequence.

To begin with, we are alerted to the fact that the story to be narrated emanates (ostensibly) from the mouth of a fictional character and not from an authorial narrative voice. Immediately the possibility of a discrepancy between the narrator's attitude and that of the implied author is established. The narrator may or may not be speaking for the author: his presence allows the author to remove himself from the narrative. The author can then choose to speak through his fictional narrator, or, on the other hand, perhaps manipulate him for ironic effect. We should immediately be aware, therefore, of the possibility that the fictional narrator is fallible – that he is, in other words, an un-reliable narrator. The relationship between author and narrator is thus a complex one. The bland manner in which Schalk's unabashed racism is presented suggests that the author does not share his views.

Secondly, Oom Schalk's verbal style implies one or more inter-locutors. The subject of "kafirs" has evidently come up in conversation, and the raconteur is clearly going to air his opinions on the matter. An internal audience is therefore implicitly invoked; and the economy with which this is achieved is remarkable.

In the third place, the reader's relationship with the narrator is also a complex one. The collocation of religion and a dehumanizing racism is clearly meant to strike the reader as both hypocritical and comical, as is the association of the "kafir" with the rinderpest. The reader is thus constructed by the text as someone who is, unlike Schalk (apparently), aware of the irony of what he says.

There is another noteworthy feature in this opening passage: Schalk's reference to "the Hottentot," which is clearly a gesture of ac-knowledgement towards his fictional predecessor, Hottentot Ruiter. That this gesture takes the form of a humorous insult is typical of Bosman and also characterizes the nature of the relationship between Bosman and Blignaut. But the reference also alerts us to the presence of a metafictional dimension in Bosman's work, a feature that would become more pronounced as his oeuvre developed.

The complex set of relationships between implied author, narrator, and reader is further complicated by the variability in Oom Schalk's character. As the story "Makapan's Caves" unfolds, for example, it becomes clear that Oom Schalk's racist attitudes are not simply to be taken at face value. We begin to see that, in uttering apparently simple-minded racial slurs, Schalk is using merely one of the voices in which he speaks.

In the story, Schalk and his brother Hendrik join a commando which is formed to revenge the killings of Hermanus Potgieter and his family by a tribe under the leadership of Makapan. Schalk remarks:

> They also said that after killing him, the kafirs stripped off old Potgieter's skin and made wallets out of it in which to carry their dagga. It was very wicked of the kafirs to have done that, especially as dagga makes you mad and it is a sin to smoke it. (67)

After this remark, Schalk's apparent artlessness must surely already be called into question. Soon thereafter, the boys' father offers them some "good advice": "'Don't forget to read your Bible, my sons,' he called out as we rode away. 'Pray the Lord to help you, and when you shoot always aim for the stomach'" (68). Schalk's comment on this – "These remarks were typical of my father's deeply religious nature and he also knew that it was easier to hit a man in the stomach than in the head" (68) – can only be interpreted as selfconsciously ironic.

These are early signals that Schalk Lourens's simplicity is only apparent, that he is aware of the hypocritical nature of the society he is describing, and that he is offering veiled indications of this to the reader. The story's denouement describes how a faithful family servant, Nongaas, is unintentionally killed by Schalk when he bravely attempts to rescue Schalk's brother, wounded in the skirmish with Makapan's tribesmen. Hendrik is later found by Schalk, and the story ends thus:

> "You know," he [Hendrik] whispered, "Nongaas was crying when he found me. He thought I was dead. He has been very good to me – so very good. Do you remember that day when he followed behind our wagons? He looked so very trustful and so little, and yet I – I threw stones at him. I wish I did not do that. I only hope that he comes back safe. He was crying and stroking my hair."
> As I said, my brother Hendrik was feverish.
> "Of course he will come back," I answered him. But this time I knew that I lied. For as I came through the mouth of the cave I kicked against the kafir I had shot there. The body sagged over to one side and I saw the face. (75)

The story thus begins deceptively, the opening racist slurs misleading the reader into believing that a lighthearted anecdote about the thieving nature of "kafirs" is to be expected. What it finally comes to deal with, however, is the manner in which racial boundaries are transcended by bonds of interracial friendship and trust. That this trust is then accidentally betrayed gives the story its special pathos. The act of betrayal is performed by Schalk, the teller of the tale, and the manner in which he tells the story leaves the reader with an after-impression of his sense of culpability.

The story's denouement thus subverts the racist pronouncements with which it begins. The shock concealed ending (another Bosman trademark) retrospectively casts a new light on the story as a whole.

Unlike Gibbon, Bosman does not use a narrative structure in which the narrator's sentiments are destabilized and subverted by the frame narrator, whose attitudes can be taken to approximate an authorial perspective. Instead, these competing voices are located within the single figure of the storyteller himself, and interpreting this character and his pronouncements therefore requires greater circumspection on the part of the reader.

"Veld Maiden," for instance, begins with the bluff Oom Schalk commenting on the propensity of people to romanticize the veld:

> I know what it is – Oom Schalk Lourens said – when you talk that way about the veld. I have known people who sit like you do and dream about the veld, and talk strange things, and start believing in what they call the soul of the veld, until in the end the veld means a different thing to them from what it does to me.
>
> I only know that the veld can be used for growing mealies on, and it isn't very good for that, either. Also, it means very hard work for me, growing mealies. There is the ploughing, for instance. I used to get aches in my back and shoulders from sitting on a stone all day long on the edge of the lands, watching the kafirs and the oxen and the plough going up and down, making furrows. (1949: 141)

Typically, Oom Schalk addresses these remarks to an unidentified interlocutor, and they preface a tale about the effect of the veld on certain people. Again, there is also the characteristic comic reversal of expectations in his last remark, an indication that comments like this are far from guileless.

That behind his bluff and naive exterior Schalk is in fact astute and perceptive is elliptically signalled by his remark (before the start of the tale proper) that it is not "good to think too much about" the veld: "For then it can lead you in strange ways. And sometimes – sometimes when the veld has led you very far – there comes into your eyes a look that God did not put there" (141).

The story of John de Swardt, the young artist who camps on Oom Schalk's farm and paints pictures of the veld, then unfolds. The narrative allows for a great deal of humour, which arises from the protagonists' comically disparate views. When Schalk proposes that De Swardt paint his dam and new cattle-dip instead of the barren veld, the young man demurs, claiming that he wanted "'only the veld. Its loneliness. Its mystery'" (142). He remarks that only then will he be proud to put his name to his painting, to which Schalk replies, "'Oh, well, that is different [...] as long as you don't put my name to it. Better still [...] put Frans Welman's name on it'," adding: "I said that because I still remembered that Frans Welman had voted against me at the last election of the Drogekop School Committee" (142).

This is the first mention of Frans Welman, a figure who will play a significant part in the story, and it is typical of Oom Schalk's style that he introduces Welman so casually. We discover that the artist has painted a nude which he calls "Veld Maiden" and about whom he has had a vision. Oom Schalk's rejoinder is that if "'the predikant saw it he'd call it by other names'," but that he is "'a broadminded man'" who has "'been once in the bar at Zeerust and twice in the bioscope when [he] should have been attending Nagmaal'" (143), but that the artist should not let anyone see the Veld Maiden unless he paints a "'few more clothes on her'" (143).

We then learn more about Frans Welman and his pretty young wife Sannie, whom Schalk and the artist visit on several successive Sundays:

> Frans Welman was in some respects what people might call a hard man.
> For instance, it was something of a mild scandal the way he treated his
> wife and the kafirs on his farm. But then, on the other hand, he looked
> very well after his cattle and pigs. And I have always believed that this is
> more important in a farmer than that he should be kind to his wife and
> kafirs. (144–45)

Again, we are led to believe that Schalk's true sentiments are being expressed here, only to discover that he has seen more deeply into the problem of Welman's treatment of his wife and is a lot more sympathetic than his comment above makes him appear. For, a little while later, he hears from the elated artist that his vision has again occurred. However, this time, Schalk remarks, he "knew everything by the look he [De Swardt] had in his eyes" (147). Schalk orders the artist to leave his farm immediately, but the young man pleads to be allowed to stay one more day and night:

> His voice trembled when he spoke, and his knees were very unsteady.
> But it was not for these reasons or for his sake that I relented. I spoke to
> him civilly for the sake of the look he had in his eyes. (147)

De Swardt is allowed to stay, and then is gone, leaving his tent and the picture of the Veld Maiden, presumably, Schalk remarks, because "he had no more need for it" (147). "As for Frans Welman," Schalk concludes, "it was quite a long time before he gave up searching the Marico for his young wife, Sannie" (147).

The reader is clearly meant to infer that Sannie has left the district with the young artist – and has done so, significantly, with Schalk's blessing. As with "Makapan's Caves," the story's surprise ending casts new light not only on the events related in the story but also on Schalk's apparently simpleminded prejudices (this time against women).

This is a pattern that can be traced in virtually all of the other stories: the juxtaposition of humour and pathos, the deceptive approach to the main subject of the story, the skilful interweaving of seemingly irrelevant details, and – importantly for my argument about the complexity of Bosman's narrator – the self-subversion of Oom Schalk are all indications of Bosman's highly sophisticated deployment of the oral-style story genre.

We saw that Jean Blignaut used his Hottentot Ruiter character to reflect on matters far more immediate and pressing to modern South African society than the apparent backwardness of his narrator would lead us to believe, but that this introduced certain incongruities and infelicities. Oom Schalk is deceptive in the same way: his simple-mindedness and prejudice are only apparent, an effective guise behind which his deeper understanding of the foibles and fallibilities of humankind is free to range. However, where Oom Schalk is a distinct advance upon his predecessor is in his congruity with his milieu. By employing Oom Schalk as his mouthpiece, Bosman can locate the narrative within the community: the subject-matter, the verbal style, the humour and the pathos are all consonant with Schalk's ambience.

A little-known Oom Schalk story, "Die Storie van die 'Rooibaadjie'," first published in Afrikaans less than two years before Bosman's death, is a very good demonstration of the benefits that accrue to this congruity of narrator and milieu. "The Red Coat," an English version of the story, was first published in Valerie Rosenberg's collection of Bosman's tales *Ramoutsa Road* (1987), and it is to this version that I refer.[6]

In "The Red Coat," Oom Schalk recounts the story of Andries Visagie's rescue by Piet Niemand at the Battle of Bronkhorst Spruit during the second Anglo-Boer war. He first recounts Piet Niemand's version of the event. Piet claims to have been "advancing" against the enemy when he came across a donga and he thought to light his pipe there, as it was too windy on the open veld. In the donga he sees what he takes at first to be an English soldier lying on the ground – the man appears to be wearing a red coat. Then he observes that the man cannot be an Englishman because his neck is not red enough. He has just concluded that the man must be a Boer in an English uniform, and has raised his rifle to shoot the traitor, when he sees that the man's jacket is red because it is stained with blood from a wound. Trembling with the thought of what he had almost done, he revives the man with brandy.

Andries Visagie, who has a high fever as a result of his wound, recovers in hospital, and the two men become close friends. After Niemand's first visit, Visagie offers him a highly decorative gold watch as a gesture of gratitude. Niemand almost accepts the gift, but thinks better of it.

After the war, the two men accept neighbouring government farms in the Waterberg district. A few years pass, and then Visagie has

---

6 In her notes on the stories in *Ramoutsa Road*, Rosenberg remarks that the story was found "among the Bosman papers lodged at the Humanities Research Centre, Austin, Texas" and speculates that its reference to the decline of malaria in the Waterberg district dates it to the years after the Second World War, when malaria was brought under control. This makes it, argues Rosenberg, "one of the last Schalk Lourens stories Bosman wrote" (1987: 164).

another bout of malaria, which, he claims, allows him to remember the Bronkhorst Spruit incident clearly. He then remembers that when Piet Niemand was bending over him in the donga, Niemand was wearing a red coat.

The story is structured as a series of recollections by Marico people, those of the two men concerned being central. Interspersed among these recollections, which are then fashioned into a story by Oom Schalk, are remarks made by other observers, remarks which are used to foreshadow the narrative climax, add humour, and supply the story with historical and social background. In all of this, Schalk's compatibility with his setting is crucial. The general details of the story would be common community knowledge and would therefore conceivably be available to him. Bosman does not therefore have to resort to unlikely contrivances to place Oom Schalk in a position to observe incidents crucial to the story. For example, when he has to describe Niemand's visit to the hospital and the offer of the watch, Oom Schalk cannot adopt an omniscient, God's-eye view, but says instead: "Those who were present at this incident in the temporary hospital at Bronkhorst Spruit said that Piet Niemand reached over to receive the gift. He almost had his hand on the watch, they say. And then he changed his mind and stood up straight" (Bosman 1987: 111). When it comes to this kind of close detail, Schalk can rely on conveniently placed informants to sustain the story's credibility.

Thus, in the process of bringing the tale before the reader, several levels of narrative are activated and deployed by Oom Schalk: the men who experience the central event (the 'rescue' at Bronkhorst Spruit) tell their story; this is digested and commented on by other members of the community; these remarks are often the filter through which Oom Schalk tells his tale, although he for the most part has been a listener with the others – Jurie Bekker, Hannes Potgieter, others by implication ("I can still remember how annoyed *we* all were" 108; "*we* all laughed" 109; "What Hannes Potgieter meant *us* to understand" 109; my emphases) – and therefore tells most of the story from the information directly relayed to him.

The employment of a narrator who is privy to all local gossip, who is appropriately situated in his setting, means that not only is the story more credible (if this is the right word), but the entire social milieu of the storyteller's community is evoked. The story is told, in other words, from within the community, and the effect of this is to allow the reader a privileged view into the inner life of the community. The reader becomes, by virtue of this technique, a bystander at local events, a member of an intimate circle discussing community happenings.

This skilful evocation of a specific community and setting notwithstanding, it very soon becomes clear that Bosman's artistic concerns in his bushveld stories do not begin and end with a portrayal of South African backveld life. Critics have over the years argued convincingly that Bosman insistently allegorizes about broader issues touching the entire South African population and, indeed, the world beyond.

As Martin Trump (1986) has observed, if one takes Bosman's stories as a purely realistic evocation of rural life, a number of serious misrepresentations of his work could result. Militant black critics, for example, could object to his flat portrayal of the blacks of the region, without perceiving how his work is in fact a severe indictment of racist practices in South Africa. And, from the other side of the political spectrum, reactionary whites could see in his work a lighthearted but realistic rendering of a life-style which vindicates the former South African regime's dismissive attitude to the black population.

The complexity of Bosman's artistic vision is accompanied by the deployment of technical devices which represent an advanced use of the oral-style narrative mode. The complex set of relationships between implied author, narrator, and reader has already been discussed. Another important aspect of Bosman's sophisticated deployment of the oral-style story form is his artful foregrounding of narrative technique. The well-known opening to "Mafeking Road" is a good example: "When people ask me – as they often do, how it is that I can tell the best stories of anybody in the Transvaal (Oom Schalk Lourens said, modestly), then I explain to them that I just learn through observing the way that the world has with men and women" (1949: 50). He then punctures this spurious piece of philosophizing by conceding that it is a lie:

> For it is not the story that counts. What matters is the way you tell it. The important thing is to know just at what moment you must knock out your pipe on your veldskoen, and at what stage of the story you must start talking about the School Committee at Drogevlei. Another necessary thing is to know what part of the story to leave out. (50)

This kind of direct intratextual reference to the mechanics of fictional-izing is indicative of a selfconsciousness in the way Bosman crafts his stories – a selfconsciousness absent in the ingenuous oral-style stories of the nineteenth-century practitioners of the form.

However, in a manner so characteristic of Bosman, this playful opening to "Mafeking Road" is deceptively employed to begin a story which actually has a tragic theme: the betrayal of a father's values by his son, the father's act of retribution (in shooting his son), and his consequent deep, inexpungible sense of loss and regret. After the opening lines quoted above, Schalk remarks with regard to the art of storytelling that "you can never learn these things" (50):

> Look at Floris, the last of the Van Barnevelts. There is no doubt that he had a good story, and he should have been able to get people to listen to it. And yet nobody took any notice of him or of the things he had to say. Just because he couldn't tell the story properly.
>
> Accordingly, it made me sad whenever I listened to him talk. For I could tell just where he went wrong. He never knew the moment at which to knock the ash out of his pipe. He always mentioned his opin-ion of the Drogevlei School Committee in the wrong place. And, what was still worse, he didn't know what part of the story to leave out. (50)

The dissembling old raconteur does not let on at this stage why it is that Floris van Barnevelt's story fails: that it actually has nothing to do with the way he tells it, but, rather, that it is a story too tragic to be told.

Floris and his only son Stephanus are part of the commando that took part in the siege of Mafeking and was forced to flee when the town was relieved by the English. Stephanus's cowardice now surfaces, and the sounds of the rifles of the pursuing English panic him into turning back in surrender. Schalk remarks:

> Floris did not speak about what happened that night, when we saw him riding out under the star-light, following after his son and shouting to him to be a man and to fight for his country. Also, Floris did not mention Stephanus again, his son who was not worthy to be a Van Barnevelt. (55)

It is only long afterwards, Schalk reports, that Floris van Barnevelt started telling his story:

And then they took no notice of him. And they wouldn't allow him to be nominated for the Drogevlei School Committee on the grounds that a man must be wrong in the head to talk in such an irresponsible fashion.

But I knew that Floris had a good story, and that its only fault was that he told it badly. He mentioned the Drogevlei School Committee too soon. And he knocked the ash out of his pipe in the wrong place. And he always insisted on telling that part of the story that he should have left out. (56)

Schalk's last remark is a near-repetition of his statement at the beginning of the story, only it is now invested with an entirely different meaning. Again, the pattern is familiar: the concealed ending prompts the reader to return and reinterpret the events of the story. Each seemingly stray remark now fits into place and the story as a whole takes on a different, more poignant hue.

— Ω —

From the discussion so far it should be clear that Bosman's achievement was to have taken over a familiar, well-worn genre and to charge all of its elements with a new vitality, to redeploy a genre in a way which is at once more complex and also more simple-seeming.

Perhaps the best way of demonstrating the new use to which Bosman puts an old form is by comparing stories by Drayson and Bosman in order to show how the similar subject-matter is put to very different purposes by the two authors.

Drayson's "The Crafty Leopard" (alluded to in an earlier chapter) is narrated by someone simply identified as "a Boer" (who is among the company around the campfire at the outspan) and concerns the man's encounter with a leopard. A leopard's spoor is discovered on the Boer's farm and some of his chickens go missing. The Boer is mystified as to how the leopard is able to enter and leave the fortified enclosure in which the chickens are kept, until one day he goes into the loft of a hut near the hen-house to fetch some corn. He notices that the trapdoor, which is usually kept closed, is in fact open. He enters the loft and closes the trapdoor "to see if it closed all right" (1862: 72):

As I stooped to shovel the corn into one of the sacks I heard a rustling noise behind me, and upon turning round I saw, amidst a bundle of long Tambookie grass that lay just close to the ladder, a head and two glittering eyes, and in another instant I was aware that a large leopard was within five yards of me, and that I, unarmed, was shut up in a close room with the brute of which I had been in search. (73)

The Boer is transfixed for some time until he eventually musters the courage to contrive an escape by forcing his way through the thatched roof of the hut. By this time it is dark, and he decides to attempt to capture the animal the next day (his original plan to shoot it being supplanted by the notion of selling it for profit). However, the following morning he discovers that the cunning beast has also effected its escape through the hole in the thatch. He concludes:

I never saw any more of that animal, for if I had I should have been sure to remember his face, as he had a peculiarly crafty expression of countenance, which I had every opportunity of observing and examining during the half-hour that I was shut up with him in that confined loft. (79)

Bosman's "In the Withaak's Shade" needs little introduction, but a brief run through parts of the story will quickly reveal the ironic and satirical dimensions of his treatment of an encounter with a leopard.

Oom Schalk is out one day looking for strayed cattle. True to character, his search takes the form of lying under the shade of a withaak tree. "I could go on lying there under the withaak and looking for the cattle like that all day, if necessary," he observes: "As you know, I am not the sort of farmer to loaf about the house when there is a man's work to be done" (1949: 25). To Oom Schalk's horror, a leopard appears, inspects him closely, and then goes to sleep next to him.

Of course, Oom Schalk's attempts to convince the local farmers of the truth of this the next day render him the laughing stock of the area: "I could see that they listened to me in the same way that they listened when Krisjan Lemmer talked. And everybody knew that Krisjan Lemmer was the biggest liar in the Bushveld" (28). In typical Bosman style, satire is subtly interwoven into Oom Schalk's narrative. Oom Schalk is partly vindicated when a leopard's spoor is discovered in the neighbourhood, and great excitement ensues. There is, we hear, "a great deal of shooting at the leopard and a great deal of running away from him" (29). Says Oom Schalk: "The amount of Martini and Mauser fire I heard in the krantzes reminded me of nothing so much as the First Boer War.

And the amount of running away reminded me of nothing so much as the Second Boer War" (29).

The story ends poignantly when, some time later, Oom Schalk chances upon the leopard once again lying under the withaak tree: "But he lay very still. And even from the distance where I stood I could see the red splash on his breast where a Mauser bullet had gone" (30).

It is immediately obvious that whereas in Bosman's hands an encounter with a leopard becomes the occasion for humour and pathos, irony and satire, Drayson does not attempt to exploit the ironic potential of the tall tale in the same way, and his story as a consequence is little more than an attempt to evoke Africa in the minds of his metropolitan readers by way of a simple tale of adventure. Beyond the transient appeal of the confrontation between man and beast, the tale is superficial and ephemeral. And, as was argued in the chapter on Drayson, no attempt is made by the author to satirize or subvert his narrator's tale.

The qualitative difference between the two stories is also reflected in the different linguistic styles employed by the two authors. In the telling, Drayson's tale is ponderous and inert: he makes no attempt to capture the unique inflection of English in the mouth of a Dutch speaker, and the flat neutrality of the Boer's standard English is both incongruous and singularly unappealing.[7]

Like Drayson, Bosman also adopts the convention of spoken narrative, out he is not content merely to signal the use of this convention. The contours and inflections of the spoken word are a palpable presence here and in all of the Oom Schalk stories. Dickson sums up this technique succinctly as follows:

> Schalk is a farmer with little formal education. He is a storyteller, not a philosopher dealing in abstractions. Consequently his vocabulary is

---

[7] It is interesting in this connection to note that, in another tale, Drayson attempts to capture the accent of the English teller of the tale. The story begins:

> Well, I fear as how my tale about what happened to me once ain't half as spirited like as what you coves tell about lions, elephants, and savages, and them like creatures, but I knows what I always remembers as the nerversest night as ever I passed [...] ("The Emigrant's Story," Drayson 1862: 161)

It is possible (judging by his poor attempts to capture spoken Dutch) that Drayson was simply too unfamiliar with the language spoken by the Dutch settlers to simulate this in print.

limited, with a high proportion of monosyllabic words (about 80%) and a preference for concrete over abstract words. The sentences vary in length, but are broken by punctuation into phrases of about 10 words each, which can be said comfortably in a single breath. (1975: 33)

In an appendix to her study (1975: 202–15), Dickson examines in detail the revisions Bosman made to "The Selons-Rose" in order to achieve various 'artful' effects. Among these are revisions made in order to achieve a greater "unity of effect," sharper delineation of character and setting, and – most significantly – the illusion that oral rather then written language is being used (1975: 99–105).

Dickson's argument about Bosman's consciously employing techniques to create the illusion of oral speech is borne out by the fact that his stories have, with few alterations, been staged extremely successfully. The appeal of the Oom Schalk stories therefore lies partly in Bosman's skill in fostering the illusion that the medium of real, spoken language is being used.[8]

It is in this regard, too, that Bosman makes a major advance upon Blignaut. I demonstrated earlier that the illusion of oral speech, so successfully sustained by Bosman's Oom Schalk, is seldom attained with any consistency in Blignaut's Hottentot Ruiter sequence. Blignaut places in Ruiter's mouth an unlikely range of linguistic registers, and this interferes with the reader's sense of a coherent, wholly conceived storyteller figure. No such interference occurs in Bosman's Oom Schalk stories: the image of the dissembling old raconteur, pipe in hand, holding forth to an implied audience is carefully sustained throughout.

— Ω —

It would be misleading to conclude this discussion of Bosman's use of the oral-style story in his Schalk Lourens sequence without noting that, while I have chosen to locate the differences between his use of the form and that of his predecessors mainly at the level of narrative technique (in keeping with the themes of this study), the success of the

---

[8] In his record-breaking dramatizations of Bosman's stories, Patrick Mynhardt was able to use the full texts of the originals with very few alterations. The recordings made by Mynhardt also demonstrate this point. I have also found that it is very effective to read long extracts of Bosman's stories during lectures. The humour and irony are immediately conveyed to the students.

Schalk Lourens stories is surely also to be attributed to other crucial factors like thematic range and artistic vision.

Whereas the yarns of earlier oral stylists were dominated by hunting and African adventure, and dealt superficially with curiosities and arcana, Schalk tells stories in which humour, irony, tragedy and pathos are the key constituents, and these dimensions typically coexist in a single story.

Bosman's achievement is thus to have taken over an old and ailing genre and to re-equip it with a new purpose in order for it to engage meaningfully with the growing complexities of mid-twentieth-century South African life.

The Voorkamer Conversation Pieces

After Bosman's death in 1951, the centre of gravity of the South African short story shifts decisively. The style of the postwar short story (dominated by Paton, Gordimer, La Guma, Matthews, Rive and others) is overwhelmingly social realist in nature, and the setting is invariably an urban one. As was pointed out in the introduction to this study, this broad shift in the style and setting of the South African short story was largely a consequence of the increasing pace of industrialization and urbanization in the first half of the present century. Attendant upon these developments was the advent of race-based legislation in the 1950s, and this gave a new sense of urgency to South African literature. 'Serious' writing, it was felt, would now have to engage with these new, morally offensive realities.

Interestingly, this shift of literary focus, triggered by the steady movement of people from the outlying areas to the towns and cities, finds a resonance in Bosman's own oeuvre. In her review of the posthumously published *Jurie Steyn's Post Office* and *A Bekkersdal Marathon* (both edited by Lionel Abrahams and published in 1971) Gillian Siebert notes the distance between these two works and the earlier collections of stories, and argues that "in the gap between the world of Oom Schalk and Jurie Steyn's post office Bosman shows, as no other South African writer has done, the passage of twenty-five years on his people and his country" (1986: 74).

In Bosman's own lifetime, in other words, the fictional locale of the Marico was in the process of disappearing. The legendary long grass of the Marico was giving way to patches of thorny scrub and the young men and women of the district, daunted by the task of wresting a living from the semi-desert soil, had long since begun their trek to the cities. As early as 1965, David Goldblatt had recorded this demise (Goldblatt 1986: 53–54). Stephen Gray has also noted that "the Voorkamer Marico exists almost a generation later, and it features farmers deracinated from the past, and detached from the present which they are ill-equipped to handle. And they are now imprisoned, impotently, within the four walls of the Drogevlei Post Office, cut off from the veld outside" (1977: 85).

This change is reflected in interesting ways in Bosman's short story oeuvre: the stable fictional narrator is replaced by the 'conversation forum' that is Jurie Steyn's voorkamer. A satisfactory resolution of issues raised is seldom achieved, and the unified and essentially optimistic vision of Oom Schalk is replaced by the desultory to-and-fro of discussion between the disgruntled characters in the voorkamer.

Bosman wrote eighty Voorkamer pieces to a weekly deadline for the *Forum* between April 1950 and October 1951 (the month in which he died). The pieces are more accurately described as 'conversation pieces' than as 'stories,' in that they seldom have a strong narrative line. In his Foreword to *Jurie Steyn's Post Office*, Abrahams makes this point:

> 'Stories' may be a misleading description of the eighty pieces in this series – if 'story' suggests a narrative in which characters appear in order to enact an *event* and their dialogue, if any, is the form of their participation in the event. What takes place week by week in Jurie Steyn's voorkamer, which serves as the Drogevlei post office, is essentially not an event, but a conversation. (1971: 7)

Abrahams's remark foregrounds an aspect of the pieces very central to the themes of the present study: their rootedness in the medium of the spoken word. The Voorkamer sequence can in fact be seen to be a further development of Bosman's preoccupation with oral narrative modes, his fascination with telling stories.

This time, however, in the place of a single storyteller figure through whom the entire narrative is filtered, we have a set of speakers – the habitués of Jurie Steyn's voorkamer. Apart from Steyn himself, we usually encounter Gysbert van Tonder, the biggest cattle-smuggler in the district, Chris Welman, who is usually aggressively at odds with Jurie, At Naudé, avid radio-listener and the chief purveyor of news, young "Meneer" Vermaak, the earnest schoolmaster who is remorselessly baited by the others, Johnny Coen, the most romantically inclined of the backveld rustics, and Oupa Sarel Bekker, the elder statesman among the raconteurs, who bears a distinct resemblance to Schalk Lourens. Conveying all of this to the reader is an anonymous narrator, memorably described by Gillian Siebert as "a transparent minutes secretary of the eternal, inconclusive voorkamer debates" (1986: 74).

The pattern of the pieces is typically a desultory, meandering conversation sparked off by an item of news (marathon dancing, atomic warfare, race classification mix-ups, lost cities), an event in the district (the return of a pretty girl from finishing school in the Cape, the arrival of a new border police officer) or a perennial theme (mothers-in-law, white ants, and bank managers). Various voices take up the thread of conversation, usually turning it in a different direction and often trying to needle or dupe one of the present company.

While many of the pieces are random and inconclusive, some have a strong narrative thread and a degree of coherence. These usually feature Oupa Bekker as the main narrator and come to a conclusion rather than taper off. Some examples are: "News Story," "Easy Circumstances," "The Terror of the Malopo," "Feat of Memory," and "Potchefstroom Willow." The first of these, for example, begins with At Naudé exclaiming and shaking his head about the "way the world is today" (Bosman 1971b: 14). This prompts Oupa Bekker to relate how they got the news "in the old days" – which in turn leads to a series of seemingly random remarks about a man called Du Plessis and a veldkornet:

> "Well, you would be standing in the lands, say, and then one of the Bechuanas would point to a small cloud of dust in the poort, and you would walk across to the big tree by the dam, where the road bends, and the traveller would come past there, with two *vos* [bay] horses in front of his Cape-cart, and he would get off from the cart and shake hands and say he was Du Plessis. And you would say you were Bekker, and he would say, afterwards, that he couldn't stay the night on your farm,

because he had to get to Tsalala's Kop. Well, there was *news*. You could talk about it for days." (16)

In his typically meandering style, Oupa Bekker, of course, neglects to mention why Du Plessis couldn't stay, and his remarks are then interrupted by impatient and dismissive comments by the others. A little later on, after several digressions by the others, he comes back to relating what news was like in the old days:

"Or another day," Oupa Bekker continued, "you would again be standing in your lands, say, or sitting, even, if there was a long day of ploughing ahead, and you did not want to tire yourself out unnecessarily. You would be sitting on a stone in the shade of a tree, say, and you would think to yourself how lazy those Bechuana look, going backwards and forwards, backwards and forwards, with the plough and the oxen, and you would get quite sleepy, say, thinking to yourself how lazy those Bechuanas are. If it wasn't for the oxen to keep them going, they wouldn't do any work at all, you might perhaps think.

"And then, without your in the least expecting it, you would again have news. And the news would find a stone for himself and come along and sit down right next to you. It would be the new veldkornet, say. And why nobody saw any dust in the poort, that time, was because the veldkornet didn't come along the road. And you would make a joke with him and say: 'I suppose that's why they call you a *veld*-kornet [field cornet], because you don't travel along the road, but you come by the veld-*langes* [you come through the fields]'." (17–18)

At this point At Naudé begins to show impatience at Oupa Bekker's leisurely loquacity, accusing him of talking "'second-childhood drivel'" (18). However, after a few more interruptions, Oupa Bekker brings his narrative (for this is how it is turning out) to a close:

"On another day, say," Oupa Bekker would go on, "you would not be in your lands at all, but you would be sitting on your front stoep, drinking coffee, say. And the Cape-cart with the two *vos* horses in front would be coming down the road again, but in the opposite direction, going *towards* the poort, this time. And you would not see much of Du Plessis's face, because his hat would be pulled over his eyes. And the veldkornet would be sitting on the Cape-cart next to him, say."

Oupa Bekker paused. He paused for a while, too, holding a lighted match cupped over his pipe as though he was out in the veld where there was wind, and puffing vigorously.

"And my wife and I would go on talking about it for years afterwards, say," Oupa Bekker went on. "For years after Du Plessis was hanged, I mean." (19)

So Oupa Bekker's exasperatingly slow and seemingly pointless set of remarks, punctuated by the increasingly ironic "say," turn out to have a point, after all – in fact, constitute a *story*. Oom Schalk's characteristic leisureliness, his propensity for apparently pointless digressions, his poker-faced ironies, all re-surface in Oupa Bekker, fighting this time against the interruptions of his unwitting collocutors.

"The Terror of the Malopo" is even closer to the Oom Schalk formula, with Oupa Bekker talking for the entire duration of the piece about his encounter with Hubrecht Willemse, an escaped convict who once terrorized the district. The same distinctive humour is there, the throwaway remarks delivered with deadpan irony, the characteristic concealed ending and the tacit commentary on human weaknesses.

In other stories the anonymous narrator takes a bigger hand, weaving a coherent story around the occasional interpolations of the others. The best-known example of this is "A Bekkersdal Marathon," which is prompted by At Naudé's comment about marathon dancing, "the newest thing in Europe" (Bosman 1971b: 7). The anonymous narrator then remarks: "We listened for a while to what At Naudé had to say, and then we suddenly remembered a marathon event that had taken place in the little dorp of Bekkersdal – almost in our midst, you could say" (7).

The story that then unfolds concerns the local preacher, Dominee Welthagen, who at one Sunday morning service goes into a trance, having announced the psalm to be sung without indicating how many verses the congregation should sing. The psalm in question has 176 verses, and the staunch, duty-bound congregation eventually sings all of them. Of course, the story abounds in opportunities for humour. The organist requires a regular topping up of his "medicine" in order to continue playing, and the elders who dutifully get him the Nagmaal wine begin to linger in the "Konsistorie" on each occasion, and re-emerge considerably less stable on their toes. The three local black convicts who are press-ganged into turning the handle of the organ when the regulars collapse from exhaustion also threaten mutiny towards the end of the marathon. When the last verse is eventually sung and a sudden silence follows, the Dominee is brought out of his trance and looks outside to see that night has now fallen. Believing himself now to be leading the evening service, and just before he lapses into another trance, he addresses the congregation: "'We will,' Dominee Welthagen announced, 'sing Psalm 119'" (13).

The unidentified narrator relates the entire story to the reader without any direct interventions by the other voorkamer characters. In between these two extremes (narration by one of the characters, and narration by the anonymous narrator) lie the bulk of the Voorkamer pieces. Typically, the Voorkamer pieces are colloquies: several characters contribute (sometimes simultaneously) to the topic of discussion, mislead each other (intentionally and unintentionally), needle and attempt to score points off each other. Abrahams sums up the nature of the Voorkamer pieces well:

> The point is that, despite the pressure under which it was produced, the Voorkamer series provided an apt vehicle for some of Bosman's special gifts and concerns – his concern, for example, with different kinds of knowledge and different kinds of innocence, his concern with the pressure of change in the world and its effects both on the aesthetic values in our experience and on conduct, his perpetual, fascinated concern with the desires and susceptibilities that motivate people and make them *more* or *less* 'human.' (Abrahams 1971: 9)

The discussion so far has been concerned to describe the pieces generally and to classify them into three broad groupings. Stories belonging to the first group usually feature Oupa Bekker as narrator and have strong narrative lines ("News Story" and "The Terror of the Malopo" were cited as examples). The second grouping contains stories narrated by the "transparent minutes secretary" ("A Bekkersdal Marathon" is the best example of this group). Most of the stories belong to the third group, which contains stories poised somewhere between the first two groupings. The term 'conversation pieces' applies most accurately to these stories: several narrators are used, the narrative pace is desultory, and seldom is there any telling denouement or thematic impact.

The purpose of the remainder of this discussion is to assess the place of the Voorkamer sequence in Bosman's oeuvre in particular and in the South African oral-style story genre in general.

With few exceptions ("A Bekkersdal Marathon" is one), the Voorkamer pieces are predominantly narratives in which the spoken word is foregrounded; in which direct speech is the dominant mode. The pieces thus employ fictional characters from whose mouths these narratives ostensibly proceed, and the setting of the pieces (almost exclusively Jurie Steyn's voorkamer) is also typical of the oral-style story. In form, then, the pieces resemble earlier examples of oral style.

Indeed, a fairly striking structural similarity exists between the typical Voorkamer piece and a tale like FitzPatrick's "The Outspan." In both cases, multiple narrators are employed, several digressions occur, and the narrative proceeds in a leisurely meander, apparently without direction. In "The Outspan," as we saw earlier, two principal narrators unwittingly tell two parts of the same story, and their narratives intersect only when the first narrator, having heard the second narrator's story, realizes that they have both spoken about the same subject, a man called Oliver Raymond Rivers. These main narratives, along with several other anecdotes related by other speakers, are conveyed by an unidentified frame narrator, whose overarching theme is that of remarkable coincidences.

The structural resemblance to Bosman's Voorkamer pieces is clear. The oral-style story setting – a company of congenial interlocutors, time to fill and the desire to hear a story, preferably a 'true' one – is merely the most obvious resemblance. As with FitzPatrick's story, a typical Voorkamer piece is prompted by a stray remark or item of news, and the various speakers take turns offering their understanding or experience of the topic at hand. More importantly, there are also distinct narrational resemblances. In the case of both "The Outspan" and the Voorkamer sequences, there is an anonymous frame narrator who relays the collection of embedded narratives to the reader.

These resemblances suggest a great deal about the timeless nature of the oral tale: given a congenial setting and audience, and time to fill, a storyteller will emerge to entertain and instruct his or her audience, and this pattern knows no temporal or spatial boundaries. It should not be surprising, therefore, to find these sorts of resemblance between writers who were, after all, part-contemporaries, who lived in and wrote about the same country, and whose stories reveal a shared interest in the veld and the kind of human discourse that unfolds around a campfire or on a farm stoep.

My earlier distinction between 'artless' and 'artful' oral-style stories also holds for this comparison, however. The above surface similarities notwithstanding, a more important difference between FitzPatrick's tale and those told in Jurie Steyn's voorkamer lies in the nature of the interaction between the various internal narrators and also in the relationship between frame narrator (and hence, implied author) and reader.

As was observed in an earlier chapter, the relationship between the various speakers around FitzPatrick's campfire is one of bonhomie and comradely equality. Their voices and the tales they tell may take on individual tones and hues, but they are not placed in ironic juxta-position by the author. Moreover, the tale as a whole is relayed without any indication of an ironic intention on the author's part.

In the case of the Voorkamer pieces, not only is there a conspicuous degree of rivalry, upstaging, and dissonance between the various speakers, but the anonymous frame narrator also interpolates remarks that are clearly meant to reflect ironically on what is being said by the voorkamer characters.

For example, in "White Ant" Oupa Bekker tries to upstage everyone else by telling a story of how bad the white ants were in the old days. As a transport rider, he recounts, he was travelling through a region of the Marico with a companion who had a wooden leg. This man wakes up one morning remarking how light he felt that day. They inspan the oxen and continue on their journey, noting also how light the wagon felt that day. They later encounter a stiff breeze, and the explanation for these odd experiences is suddenly revealed to them. The wagon and its load of planed oregon pine, says Oupa Bekker, were carried away in a cloud of dust, leaving the oxen pulling only the trek-chain and his com-panion standing on one leg.

The frame narrator then remarks: "Thus, Oupa Bekker's factual account of a straightforward Marico incident of long ago, presenting the ways and characteristics of the termite in a positive light, restored us to a sense of current realities" (Bosman 1971a: 35). The humour in this piece is light, but it does reveal a deeper ironic scepticism on Bosman's part that would refuse to take seriously tall tales purporting (like FitzPatrick's story) to tell "plain truth just as it happened" (Fitz-Patrick 1897: 3). Oupa Bekker's fantastic tale is immediately followed by the frame narrator's deeply ironic comment, suggesting that the former's tale is merely there to elicit incredulous laughter. Thus, as with his Schalk Lourens stories, Bosman in his Voorkamer sequence employs the familiar constitutive elements of the fireside yarn, but does so in order to poke fun at his characters and to reflect ironically on aspects of human nature.

It can readily be seen that, in comparison with earlier writers like FitzPatrick, Bosman handles the 'conversation piece' very artfully and with a good deal of ironic intent. But how do the Voorkamer pieces fit into Bosman's oeuvre itself? Their immediate context (the *Forum's* "In die voorkamer" column of the early 1950s) must not be overlooked in answering this question. Gillian Siebert correctly suggests that, on one level, they are meant to reflect ironically on the *Forum* itself:

> *Forum* was a voice of the times, and Jurie Steyn's voorkamer becomes in effect a forum for Bushveld opinion on a variety of topical subjects: a go-slow strike, a dancing marathon, race classification ... all things to which Oom Schalk Lourens, not having At Naudé and his wireless to supply up-to-date and extra-Marico news, doesn't hear of. (1986: 72)

As the title of her review suggests ("A More Sophisticated Bosman"), Siebert regards the voorkamer pieces to be a formal advance on the earlier Schalk Lourens formula. This, she argues, is in keeping with the more demanding times which the voorkamer characters inhabit:

> In Oom Schalk's stories the Marico is a universe complete within itself, capable of supporting universal conclusions. The Marico in which the Drogevlei Post Office stands, however, is criss-crossed with the ambiguities of modern life, which Bosman accommodates in the elastic voorkamer conversations where the past, the present, the Marico and the outside world are thrown into conflict as the various characters express their opinions; and if no conclusion is reached, it doesn't matter, for the whole point of the voorkamer pieces is their interplay of personality, level and mood, which the conversation form allows. (73–74)

She goes on to remark that the conversation form gives Bosman's "imagination full play" (74) and that the pieces are "more sophisticated in intention" than any of his earlier writing.

Stephen Gray supports this contention, arguing that the conversation pieces "show Bosman innovating within the short story form" (1980: 13). They are, he contends, "more sophisticated, more virtuoso performances on Bosman's part, because the idea of shaping a freewheeling conversation into a balanced whole is more of a juggling act for a writer to hold together than the old monologue" (13).

That the Voorkamer pieces are markedly more uneven in quality than the Schalk Lourens stories is conceded by both Siebert and Gray, but they put this down in part to Bosman's ill-health and his crushing weekly deadline. Gray also implies that the greater formal experimentation required by the pieces brings with it a greater chance of failure.

However, the question that is of importance here and that remains to be answered is how this form of oral-style story fits into the pattern of increasing sophistication and economy traced in the stories selected for this study. For it has been argued that several simultaneous developments can be discerned in this selection of stories that point to an increasingly sophisticated use of the oral-style story genre: a steady movement away from 'factuality' and towards 'fictionality'; a concomitant movement away from the stock declarations of 'faithfulness' and 'authenticity' and towards selfconscious artfulness and ironic deception; and the introduction, accordingly, of a more ironic and satirical relationship between internal narrator and frame narrator.

In some ways, the fragmentation of the unified storyteller figure into a collection of competing voices may appear to be a regression. Having created a complex fictional narrator, Bosman was able to locate the competing voices of Gibbon's narrator and frame narrator, for instance, in the figure of a single character. This character, as a consequence, became a good deal more interesting, and presented the reader with an interpretative challenge. (A large part of the appeal of the Schalk Lourens stories is surely to be ascribed to the character and verbal style of the wily, simple-seeming old raconteur.) Assigning the narrative function to a single character also, as we saw, introduced greater economy into the formerly rambling, digressive oral-style tale. Bosman was able, through Oom Schalk, to introduce economy and Poeian unity of effect into the old, characteristically diffuse narrative form.

Certainly, most of the conversation pieces are a great deal less focused, and one cannot help feeling that Bosman was often merely fulfilling the 1500-word requirement by fleshing out the skeleton of an anecdote with distracting and unnecessary digressions. It is significant, for instance, that the best-known piece, "A Bekkersdal Marathon," is also the least typical of the sequence as a whole. As we saw, it employs a single narrator (the "minutes secretary") and focuses sharply on what is essentially a single incident. With few exceptions, therefore, the Voorkamer pieces are not nearly as effective as examples of short fiction forms. They lack strong narrative lines, often end weakly, and seldom possess much thematic impact. They may foreground (perhaps even more prominently than earlier oral-style stories) the discordant voices heard in spoken narratives, but the grounds for disagreement are increasingly petty and ephemeral.

In short, these later stories fail precisely because their narrators do not observe the economies and devices urged by Oom Schalk in "Mafeking Road." As Oom Schalk knows, the way you tell a story is crucial: you must know which devices enhance narrative tension (when to knock your pipe out on your veldskoen), how apparent digressions can be structurally and thematically important (when to talk about the School Committee at Drogevlei), and, most importantly, what part of the story to leave out. The better of the Voorkamer pieces ("News Story" and "A Bekkersdal Marathon," for example) are those which narratologically most closely resemble the Oom Schalk tales (in other words, those which use a principal narrator rather than a disorderly collection of voices) and which also adhere most closely to the above injunctions. They are also – significantly – the least typical of the sequence as a whole.

The conversation pieces thus do not represent an advance upon the late, sophisticated oral-style story exemplified by the Schalk Lourens sequence. The increasingly economical, focused, complex form that we find in the latter stories brings with it a capacity to reflect more profoundly on themes pertinent to South African life, and this has ensured the durability of the best Oom Schalk stories.

The fragmentation of the storyteller figure into a collection of discordant voices seems to suggest, rather, both a broad movement in Bosman's oeuvre and a decisive shift in the nature of the South African short story: in postwar South Africa, with apartheid practices soon to be codified by law, the art of storytelling, and the use of a storyteller figure possessing the wisdom distilled by years of experience, had become an anachronism. "The resources of satire and fantasy," Ernest Pereira remarks, "can seem pitifully inadequate, if not irrelevant, in a world where the absurd and unthinkable have become painful realities" (1986: 106).

The Later Metafictional Stories

That the South African oral-style story had run its course by the late 1940s is thus signalled by Bosman's move away from a single narrator in the Voorkamer stories. However, there is another, simultaneous, tendency towards an increasingly reflexive, self-ironic meditation on the craft of storytelling itself. To be sure, a degree of reflexiveness is evident even in the early Oom Schalk stories. As the above discussion shows, "Mafeking Road," which first appeared in 1935, is the outstanding example in this regard.

However, there are a number of stories by Bosman, set in the bushveld but without Oom Schalk as a narrator, which manifest an even greater degree of reflexiveness. These include "Old Transvaal Story," which first appeared in 1948 as "The Transvaal Murder Story," "The Affair at Ysterspruit," first published as "Die Voorval by Ijzerspruit" and translated by Lionel Abrahams for his *Unto Dust* collection (1963) of Bosman's stories, and "The Clay-Pit" and "A Boer Rip van Winkel," both first published in *Unto Dust*.

In these stories, Bosman has dispensed with a fictional narrator and instead employs the voice of a story-writer reflecting on his craft. In "The Affair at Ysterspruit," for example, this narrator, speaking in the first person, makes the following remark:

> I was a school-teacher, many years ago, at a little school in the Marico bushveld, near the border of the Bechuanaland Protectorate. The Transvaal Education Department expected me to visit the parents of the school-children in the area at intervals. But even if this huisbesoek was not part of my after-school duties, I would have gone and visited the parents in any case. And when I discovered, after one or two casual calls, that the older parents were a fund of first-class story material, that they could hold the listener enthralled with tales of the past, with embroidered reminiscences of Transvaal life in the old days, then I became very conscientious about huisbesoek. (1963: 122–23)

This remark is inserted into the tale about Ouma Engelbrecht, who tells the story about her son, Johannes, and how he was shot in the Second Boer War. Ouma Engelbrecht "would talk very fast about people not being able to understand the feelings that went on in a mother's heart," the narrator remarks: "'People put the photograph away from them,' she would say, 'and they turn it face downwards on the rusbank [couch]'" (121). At the conclusion of the story, the narrator, having disarmed the reader with long discursive passages about his encounters with people in the Marico, their reminiscences of the war, and the circumstances in which he came to hear Ouma Engelbrecht's story, then draws the story to a climactic close:

> Anyway, it was well on towards evening when Ouma Engelbrecht, yielding at last to my cajoleries and entreaties, got up slowly from her chair and went into the adjoining room. She returned with a photograph enclosed in a heavy black frame [...]
>
> Flicking a few specks of dust from the portrait, Ouma Engelbrecht handed over the picture to me.
>
> And she was still talking about the things that went on in a mother's heart, things of pride and sorrow that the world did not understand, when, in an unconscious reaction, hardly aware of what I was doing, I placed beside me on the rusbank, face downwards, the photograph of a young man whose hatbrim was cocked on the right side, jauntily, and whose jacket with narrow lapels was buttoned up high. With a queer jumble of inarticulate feelings I realised that, in the affair at Ysterspruit, they were all Mauser bullets that had passed through the youthful body of Johannes Engelbrecht, National Scout. (126)

Although the familiar Oom Schalk parting shot, the irony and pathos are all present in the story, the metafictional elements in the Oom Schalk sequence (Schalk's musings on the craft of storytelling, his speculations as to why he is the best storyteller in the region, and so on) are more conspicuously foregrounded in this third group of stories. Having dispensed with a fictional narrator and replaced him with an authorial persona, the various reflections on the art of telling stories that occur now take on the form of a writer meditating on his work.

The effect of this is to make the metafictional dimension in the stories more immediate. The "you" that now appears no longer refers to an intradiegetic audience listening to Oom Schalk's yarns, but to the reader. The relationship between author and reader is thus no longer mediated by the device of the story frame. In "The Clay-Pit," for example, when the narrator remarks, "Anyway you can see from this that the incidents linking together the fortunes of the young bywoner, Diederik Uys, and of the girl, Johanna Greyling, and of the aging Bertus Pienaar made a good story," the "you" here refers to the reader, not an implied internal audience.

What makes this type of Bosman story distinctive is its disconcerting mixture of discursive modes. As we saw above, "The Affair at Ysterspruit" is at once a commentary on the nature of storytelling and a story in itself. Bosman lures the reader into thinking that a discursive essay on story-writing is to be expected, and then he shifts gears and tells a story instead. This reveals what Stephen Gray calls his "perpetual fascination with the techniques of story-telling":

> [...] perhaps Bosman's most interesting quality, one which is implicit in everything he wrote, lies in his own doubts and anxieties about the one thing which was important to him – the practice of his art. Bosman knew, as every fiction-writer knows, that the art of writing is based on creating an illusion which must appear, in the reader's eyes, as real. In this selection of stories [*Selected Stories*] the intention has been to stress this rather elusive side of Bosman. His on-going commentary on the practice of fiction intrudes quite frequently as you read along, as he explains himself, backtracks, apologises, insists that it is only a trick after all. Often he actually explains the trick to you, only to pull another one later. He was as interested in his medium as he ever was in the Marico, or in Johannesburg. And it is through his medium that he is able to reflect that all of life is, after all, only an illusion. (Gray 1980: 14)

"A Boer Rip van Winkel" is a good example of this process of writerly introspection. The story begins in the following way:

> Every writer has got, lying around somewhere in a suitcase or a trunk, various parts of a story that he has worked on from time to time and that he has never finished, because he hasn't been able to find out how the theme should be handled. Such a story – that I have had lying in a suitcase for many years – centres around the things that happened to Herklaas van Wyk. (1963: 154)

Claiming that the "plot of a story has no particular appeal," the narrator remarks that his own stories that he likes best "are those that have just grown" (154). Near the end of writing this kind of story, he then comments, he is often "surprised to find what a very old tale it was that kept [him] from the chimney-corner" (154). This he finds agreeable, he adds, for he has "a preference for old tales" (154).

These remarks preface the tale of Herklaas van Wyk, the Boer War veteran who was last seen still fighting towards the end of the war, and who then disappears and re-surfaces only in 1914, when the Boer rebellion breaks out. The problem with this story, says the narrator, is that, although the story "told itself quite all right" (154), he has been unable to "fill in that interval of a dozen years satisfactorily" (155).

Having thus presented the problem to the reader, the narrator goes on to provide background to the story: how Herklaas van Wyk was part of a commando that had penetrated deep into the Cape Colony, had joined up with a band of Cape rebels, and had pushed through to the Atlantic coast. Herklaas then realizes that the commando is doomed to failure. Up to this point, remarks the narrator, the story was "straightforward enough," and could be read in any "history-book dealing with that period" (156). From this point on, however, his story "quits the pages of printed history [...] and enters the realm of legend" (156).

Herklaas van Wyk's own story of what followed, the narrator relates, is that "he crept into a deserted rondavel at the foot of a koppie in the Upington district, and that he fell asleep there, with his Mauser beside him, and his horse tethered to a thorn-tree" (156–57). Other stories, we read, are provided to account for the twelve-year lapse. These are more pedestrian: that he worked on a farm in the Upington district as a bywoner until the outbreak of the rebellion; and that he suffered a loss of memory as a result of an old bullet-wound and was suddenly revitalized by the sound of warfare once again.

Confessing that he cares for neither of these versions, the narrator remarks that Herklaas van Wyk's own story is to be preferred by far:

> For one thing, if we accept Herklaas van Wyk's account of his long sleep in the abandoned rondavel at the foot of a koppie in the Upington district, we have the material for a South African legend as stirring as the one that Washington Irving chronicled. Van Wyk and Van Winkel. This is surely no idle coincidence. Above all, there is a Gothic quality in Herklaas van Wyk's own story – a gloomy magnificence that is never

absent from the interior of a rondavel at the foot of a koppie, if that koppie is composed of iron-stone. (158)

Bosman's preference for the "poet's embroidered lie" (Abrahams's phrase) over the quotidian is very much in evidence here, and the narrator then provides a full version of Herklaas van Wyk's own story.

The preoccupation with how to tell a story, the intertextual reference to Irving, and the mixing of modes (reflecting on the mechanics of fictionalizing and then, imperceptibly, switching over into actually telling a story) all illustrate Gray's comment about Bosman's "perpetual fascination with the techniques of story-telling."

"I have a preference for old tales," says the narrator in "A Boer Rip van Winkel," and this remark is especially significant in relation to "Old Transvaal Story." As the title indicates, the story that will be told does not purport to be a new one. Indeed, Scully's "Ukushwama" is acknowledged in its opening line, and there are other sources.

"Old Transvaal Story" is actually a rewriting of Bosman's earlier Oom Schalk story "The Gramophone," which first appeared in May 1931. In this story Schalk describes the troubled relationship between Krisjan Lemmer and his wife Susannah. Krisjan acquires a gramophone and this causes quite a stir in the neighbourhood. People come to listen to it, particularly Schalk, who begins to notice the deteriorating relations between Krisjan and Susannah. One day he goes to the house to borrow Krisjan's wagon-sail, and Susannah is not there. Krisjan claims that she has "gone back to her mother" (1949: 108), and they sit down and listen to the gramophone. Schalk then begins to realize that all is not right:

> Then an awful thought occurred to me.
>
> You know sometimes you get a thought like that and you know that it is true.
>
> I got up unsteadily and took my hat. I saw that all round the place where the gramophone stood the dung floor of the voorkamer had been loosened and then stamped down again. The candle threw flickering shadows over the floor and over the clods of loose earth that had not been stamped down properly.
>
> I drove back without the bucksail. (110)

This story apparently has its origins in Bosman's experiences in prison, where he encountered a fellow-prisoner who killed his wife and buried her under the dung floor of his dining-room. The man was then beset by a group of his friends who sprang a surprise party and he was forced to go through with his bizarre pretence that his wife had gone away. This tale is recounted in "Rosser," a story which first appeared in 1958 in the *Purple Renoster*, the literary magazine edited by Lionel Abrahams.[9]

A still earlier potential source, argues Vivienne Dickson, is Poe's "The Tell-Tale Heart" (first published in 1845), in which a clearly deranged first-person narrator recounts his minutely planned and executed murder of an old man who lives with him. Three officers of the law pay him a visit in the early hours of the morning on the night of the murder, saying that they had been alerted by neighbours who had heard a shriek. The narrator convinces the policemen that he knows nothing, and that the old man is away on a visit, but the "tell-tale heart" of the old man, buried beneath the floor-boards of his bedroom, begins to thump audibly – or so the narrator believes. His panic rises and he eventually shrieks out: "'I admit the deed! – tear up the planks! here, here! – it is the beating of his hideous heart'" (Poe 1953: 342).

It is very likely that Bosman had read Poe's story, given his enthusiasm for the author, and this influence may partly account for Bosman using a variation of the tale. However, as Bosman's own references to Scully's "Ukushwama" and the Transvaal's "only ghost story" suggest, the tale probably has variations in numerous folk-traditions in various parts of the world, and is therefore not 'original' to any one writer:

> As Scully, I think, knew – have you ever chanced upon his "Ukush-wama"? – the Transvaal seems to have had only one ghost story. It is a story that I have heard very often, told over and over again in voorkamer and by campfire, with the essential features always the same, and with only the details, in respect of characters and locale, differing with the mood and the personality – and the memory, perhaps – of each person that tells it. (1963: 107)

After this playful reference to Scully and the endless recycling of the ghost story that he used, the narrator in "Old Transvaal Story" then recounts the typical form that this story would take, remarking that he

---

[9] Valerie Rosenberg was the first to collect this story (in her *Ramoutsa Road*), and I am indebted to her for bringing it to my attention.

has heard so many variations of the story that he has become "blasé about the Transvaal's only ghost":

> The result is that, nowadays when a man says – lowering his voices and trying to make his tones sound sepulchral, "And so Oom Hannes Blignaut said to me that I would not be able to ride my horse through that poort in the full moon," I short-circuit him by asking, "But why didn't you go on a push-bike, instead?"
>
> I have not, to date, found an answer to that one. (1963: 108)

But "Old Transvaal Story" actually turns out to be a murder story, which, the narrator claims, he first heard as a child; "since then it has been related to me many times, as I am sure it has been to every South African who has spent some portion of his life on the Transvaal Platteland" (1963: 108):

> I suppose the story is based on historical fact: its salient features seem to relate to some murder that actually was committed long ago.
>
> This story, I should like to add in parenthesis, has never been told to me in the first person. No man has ever said to me, "And so after I hit my wife with the chopper I buried her under the mud floor of the voor-kamer and later on the police came." (108–109)[10]

The narrator then proceeds to outline the main features of the story, commenting that the story is only really made remarkable by the unexpected development of the surprise party: "This is the sensational development in the plot that distinguishes the Transvaal's only murder story from almost any other murder story I have ever lighted upon" (109). The idea of people dancing on the head of the dead woman, he remarks, "is a situation providing lots of blossomy openings for fragile irony and high drama" (110).

In another piece of reflexive commentary, the narrator remarks:

> Incidentally, I, too, have told that story before of the woman interred under the floor of the voorkamer. And I have always known that I

---

[10] In "Rosser," however, the convict tells the story in precisely these terms: "'I done my wife in with a chopper because she was sweet on another man,' Rosser explained, 'and I buried her under the floor and all'" (Bosman 1987: 94). It is possible that Bosman's rewriting of this story in this fashion was prompted by the thought conveyed in his remark in "Old Transvaal Story."

would have to dig her up again, some time. She was too useful a character to be left lying there, buried under four lines of prose. (110)

After this long, playful introduction to the infinite fictional possibilities inherent in relating the Transvaal's only ghost story and its only murder story, Bosman concludes tersely with what he calls the "love-story of Gideon Welman and Alie du Plessis" (111), but which turns out to be his own version of the story of the man who murdered his wife and buried her under the floor of his house.

The marriage of Gideon and Alie is idyllic until Alie mentions the name Rooi Jan Venter once too often, and things begin to take an ugly turn:

> For a while – as far as the outside world was concerned, at least – they lived together happily in their little house in the bushveld, with the newly-whitewashed walls and the roof thatched with what was still that year's grass. And then events slid into that afternoon on which Gideon Welman was working very fast, and in a half-daze. He had the queer feeling that he was living in another life, going through a thing that had happened before, to somebody else, long ago. It was quite dark by the time a knock came at the door.
>
> And when he got up from the floor quickly, dusting his knees, Gideon Welman knew what that old Transvaal story was, into whose pattern his own story had now fitted, also. For the door of the voorkamer opened. And out of the night came the laughter of girls. And Rooi Jan Venter and another young man entered the voorkamer, carrying bottles. (1963: 112)

What Bosman therefore does in this story is artfully merge a discussion of the Transvaal's "only ghost story," and its "only murder story," with a variation of his own on these 'many-told' tales. The passage of the fifty-odd years between Scully's story and Bosman's retelling has some interesting effects on the narrative texture of the tale. Where Scully's story is told as a fairly ingenuous piece of local colour, in Bosman's rendering the artifice of the tale is foregrounded. Bosman sends up the genre of the 'ghost story': his conversational, lighthearted tone runs directly counter to the atmosphere that traditionally envelops a rendering of the tale, and where the storyteller would normally attempt to conjure up suspense in the opening part of his tale, Bosman addresses the reader directly. He eschews the customary device of his raconteur Oom Schalk, and lures the reader into believing that a discursive rather than narrative piece will unfold. Of course, towards the end Bosman changes gears, and the story ends climactically.

Of interest, then, are the overtly metafictional aspects in Bosman's rendering of the tale. The merging of genres (discursive, fictional) is only one example of this. Bosman is also supremely conscious of the impossibility of being entirely original in the telling of a story: a story one tells is inevitably a reconstitution of the "always already written," to use the famous Derridean phrase, and Bosman implicitly acknowledges this here. What remains to the writer, therefore, is the self-conscious redeployment of preexisting materials, a process Bosman puts into practice with consummate mastery in this story.

I have devoted so much space to the piece because I believe it is suggestive of the fate of the oral-style story in South African literature. Although Bosman would go on to write twenty more Schalk Lourens stories (over a third of the total number in this sequence, in fact), 1948, the year in which "Old Transvaal Story" first appeared, seems portentous: not only was the old Marico as Bosman knew it in 1925 fast disappearing, but the election victory of the National Party, which was soon to be followed by the banning of political parties, the introduction of racist legislation and the suppression of freedom of expression, would begin to erode the basis for the humanistic and romantic vision of Oom Schalk Lourens. *Cry, the Beloved Country* (first published in 1948) more accurately reflected the tenor of the times. Its poignant lament for the breakdown of traditional rural communities and the consequences of this for South African society strikes a prophetic note, heralding both the irreversible degeneration of rural communities and the reflection of this in South African fiction from this point onwards.

— Ω —

The stories of Herman Charles Bosman can thus be seen to represent the apogee of the South African oral-style story and also to prefigure its demise. Although, as I have argued, there is no clear-cut technical 'progression' – that, in fact, Bosman tended to work in different modes at the same time – there is a broad movement from the rural tale told by a single narrator to one which features several discordant voices speaking on contemporary (1950s) topics. Stephen Gray offers a useful view of the broad sweep of history covered in Bosman's stories:

The Oom Schalk series covers the time from the Frontier wars before Majuba (1881), through the rinderpest and the Three Years' Anglo-Boer War of the turn-of-the-century, up to Union in 1910, to the Jazz Age of the Twenties and into the Depression of the Thirties [...] You feel the impact of history behind even the smallest details – the trek-boer gives way to commandos; the commandos to the settler, with his bywoners and konsessie farms; they in turn meet the outside world that arrives, first, by donkey-cart or ox-wagon, on horseback, then by motor-car, and finally on the railways. By the time the second series of stories begins [...] we have the weekly deliveries of the postal lorry, the radio, newspapers, even the Land Bank and the four-disc harrow. Grandparents who had home-made dolls and clay-oxen as toys give way to their grandchildren who want electric trains. (1980: 12)

Perhaps the most significant thing about Gray's historical panorama is its reminder that the temporal sweep of Bosman's stories takes in virtually the entire period setting of the South African oral-style story. Scully's tales about Frontier Wars and Xhosa rebellions, FitzPatrick's of the era of prospecting and transport-riding, Gibbon's settled Dutch farmstead and Smith's late nineteenth-century rural idyll all resonate in some way in Bosman's bushveld-story oeuvre. Even Drayson's era of the "Great Hunter," when Africa was seen as an empty and unspoilt hunting paradise, finds an echo in Oom Schalk's tales of pioneering ventures into the African hinterland.

Unlike his predecessors, however, Bosman's vantage point of the 1930s and after allows him to reflect ironically on the events in these three-quarters of a century of history – of encounters between Boer and African, Boer and Briton, and the arrival of modernity in the bushveld. In the seventy years separating Bosman's tales from those of Drayson, numerous wars between Dutch settlers and African tribesmen had taken place, two Anglo-Boer wars had been fought, South Africa had achieved Union and had participated in the Great War, and the depression following this war had begun to be experienced. As this chapter has shown, this temporal advantage Bosman translates into a highly sophisticated version of a genre pioneered in the middle to late nineteenth century.

——————— ᭡ ᭡ ———————

10 Postscript
The Oral-Style Story After Bosman

T HIS STUDY HAS TRACED THE DEVELOPMENT of the oral-style story from its '*ur*-form' in the middle of the nineteenth century to its apogee with Bosman in the 1930s, 1940s and 1950s. After Bosman, this style of story goes into sharp decline and surfaces only sporadically, and in substantially altered form, mainly in the work of black writers in the modern era. The postwar South African short story by whites – led by writers like Gordimer, Lessing, Jacobson, Cope, and Paton – is predominantly social-realist in nature, typically focuses on the inner consciousness of a single protagonist, and is highly compressed in form; it conforms, in other words, to the requirements of the modern short story. The broad development of the (overwhelmingly white) South African short story from its beginnings in the mid-nineteenth century to the stage it has reached in the present day, then, can be characterized as a steady and irreversible progression from fireside tale (or what I have called the oral-style story) to modern short story.

When one turns to stories by black South African writers, however, this progression from fireside tale to modern short story (which brings with it the decline of narratives written in an oral style) is to some extent reversed: from an initial reliance on Western modernist literary models in emergent black South African fiction in the late 1920s, many black writers sought increasingly to throw off Western influence and adopt African (largely oral) cultural modes. So, while short stories by white writers evince a marked decline in oral influence in the postwar period, in the same period black South African writers were just beginning to rediscover their cultural roots. Prior to this, the tendency to mix cultural traditions was already evident in black short fiction (in R.R.R.

Dhlomo, for instance), but this tendency gained impetus later, and is to be found chiefly in the writing of the 1970s and 1980s: short stories by Bessie Head, Mtutuzeli Matshoba, Mbulelo Mzamane, Mothobi Mutloatse, Joel Matlou, and Njabulo Ndebele all bear the traces of such cultural 'hybridity.'

The style of story whose lineaments have been explored in the present investigation possesses a determinate set of narrative conventions. These conventions cluster around the use of a narrative frame, an internal narrator (or set of narrators) recounting the 'embedded' tale, and the literary imitation of oral speech. The chief characteristics of the oral-style story, then, are the presence of a fictional narrator and his or her speaking voice. This 'voice' is assigned central narrational status: it is the *mode* in which the story is presented. As I argued in the introduction (following Eichenbaum), in the oral-style story, narrative *events* surrender pride of place to the *recounting* of such events. In other words, the *process of telling* is foregrounded.

As should be evident by now, the convention of the frame narrative and the use of an intradiegetic storyteller figure in the South African short story occur very seldom after Bosman. Instead, what we find in the work of those writers attempting to adopt an 'oral style' in the modern era is the assumption by the author of the role and function of the oral storyteller. Instead of employing the convention of the internal narrator and framed narrative, the writer him- or herself takes on this narrative voice. "The Writer as Storyteller?" is the title of Michael Vaughan's paper (1988) on Ndebele, and it captures well the nature of this phenomenon. In different ways, various black writers (Head, Matshoba, and Ndebele in particular) attempt to cast their stories in an oral style, and they do this by assuming the mantle of the traditional oral storyteller.

In very few cases, however, is an oral style adopted as the *mode* in which their stories are narrated – their stories, in other words, do not employ a storyteller figure and the cadences of oral speech – thus the link with the earlier oral-style tradition examined in this study is tenuous. More frequently (and most conspicuously in the case of Ndebele), oral cultural modes and values are merely *thematized*: as we shall see, they form a significant part of the subject-matter of the stories without significantly affecting the manner in which the stories are told.

However, it would be misleading to conclude a study on the 'oral-style' South African short story abruptly with Bosman in the 1950s – as if the interpenetration of oral and literary modes in the South African short story suddenly ceases with the last Oom Schalk tale. A number of stories by black South African writers manifest influence from oral cultural forms. As indicated above, these include stories by Dhlomo in the late 1920s and early 1930s and also those by contemporary writers. The purpose of this chapter, then, is to examine briefly the oral-influenced, modern South African short story by black writers, in order to illustrate the various forms that this influence can take. This study is primarily concerned with a particular kind of story whose chief distinguishing characteristic is the use of a fictional narrator, but, as we shall see, the interpenetration of oral and literary modes can take various other forms.

R.R.R. Dhlomo

Oral influences are evident in black fiction from the start. Sol Plaatje's *Mhudi* (1978 [1930]), as Stephen Gray (1976) and Tim Couzens (1978) have comprehensively documented, is an early example of the intermingling of indigenous and exogenous cultural influences. *Mhudi* reflects the stylistic inelegancies of this cultural eclecticism: Shakespearean iambic pentameters, biblical phraseology, and African oral idioms coexist awkwardly. The narrative style of the text also shows influences of a diverse nature: the epic-quest pattern of Bunyan's *Pilgrim's Progress* is broken by numerous tales drawn directly from Tswana oral lore (see Gray 1976).

The brothers H.I.E. and R.R.R. Dhlomo are two other early black writers whose work manifests a cultural mix. Herbert Dhlomo was a prolific writer, and his plays and poetry reflect his mixed cultural heritage: he was equally at home imaginatively reconstructing a praise-poet's eulogy to a king, as he did in his historical play *Cetshwayo* (1985a [c.1937]), or composing an elegant sonnet lamenting the lack of recognition accorded "Ndongeni," the guide who accompanied Dick King in 1842 on his epic journey to Grahamstown (1985b [1942]).

The first black writer of importance here, however, is Herbert Dhlomo's older brother Rolfes, who is best known for his 1928 novelette *An African Tragedy*, the first work of its kind by a black South

African. However, his stories, published in the late 1920s and early 1930s, are just as significant. Little known until their collection and republication by Tim Couzens in a special issue of *English in Africa* in 1975, they can be taken to represent the emergence of black South African short fiction.

R.R.R. Dhlomo was a prolific writer of journalistic sketches, stories, and feature articles. However, Dhlomo, like other early black writers, lacked outlets for his work, and many of his pieces originally appeared in the black newspapers *Ilanga Lase Natal* and *Bantu World*. Stephen Black's short-lived but important journal *The Sjambok* (which also published work by Bosman) was instrumental in bringing Dhlomo's English stories to the attention of a wider reading public. Most of the better stories collected by Couzens appeared in this journal, among them "The Death of Masaba," "The Sins of the Fathers," and "The Dog Killers."

While they often lack the technical accomplishment usually associated with the modern short story, Dhlomo's stories are of considerable literary and sociological importance. In them can be seen many of the elements that came to characterize the themes of later black South African writing: the drift to the cities, the breakdown of traditional life, and the often tragic consequences of old customs encountering new and unaccommodating social circumstances. Of particular interest to this study, however, is the evidence of the intermingling of cultural traditions in Dhlomo's stories. In the analysis that follows, various instances of this will be identified and briefly discussed. The significant point, however, is that this cultural mingling does not influence the narrative style employed by Dhlomo, and his stories are thus not part of the 'oral-style' tradition analyzed in this study.

The mission-educated Dhlomo was proficient in both Zulu and English and wrote prolifically in both languages. It is unsurprising, therefore, that his 'English' pieces are characterized by the free intermingling of both languages. And, as many of his pieces deal with life on the mines, *fanagalo* and township argot are also used abundantly.

The story "The Dog Killers" (1930) provides a number of examples of this. The story begins with the following exchange:

> "I say, Jama, did you hear?"
> "Did I hear? What?"

"About the dogs, man. It is said to-morrow they are going out to kill them again." (1975: 26)

Dhlomo's use of the peculiarly English form of opening a conversation ("I say") would immediately strike the modern reader as quaint ("The Death of Masaba" begins similarly: "'Fellows, what do you think of this business of Masaba?'"; 14). However, the following lines occur shortly afterwards:

"*Hau*, Muti!" exclaimed Jama, jumping to his feet. "Are you true? Tell me, man; are you true?" (26)

The Zulu exclamation, followed by the corruption of the English "Are you telling the truth?" ("Are you true?"), is evidence of the strongly indigenous grounding of the story. And, indeed, the verbal exchanges that follow are very strongly coloured by the vernacular.

But then one comes across the description of the selection of the men who will do the dog-killing:

Mlungu and his police boy then went round the rooms taking care to pick only those boys whose natures would glory in the impending butchery. Boys who knew how to hold their tongues. Boys who had ere now engaged in similar killings and had defied all efforts of the outsiders in getting inside information of the source of these killings. (27)

Once again one comes across several peculiarities in the text. One of the most obvious is the quaint and archaic use of the word "ere" ("before"), which reinforces the earlier impression of an imported (this time nineteenth-century) use of English (another example is "the devil take them"; 27). Upon closer inspection, other interesting features emerge. For instance, in the passage quoted above, Dhlomo uses the word "boys" to describe the mine workers throughout. And the description of the dog-killers abounds in words and phrases like: "night brawls," "drunken mirth," "savage joys," "bloodshed," "orgies," "butchery," "mad with the lust for blood" (27–28). Little care is taken to analyze the factors influencing this form of behaviour, and to the modern reader it is immediately obvious that the men are described from the outside, from the vantage point historically adopted by the white overseer.

It should immediately be pointed out, however, that Dhlomo was by no means an uncritical purveyor of this kind of paternalistic ideology. Most of the other stories (and "The Death of Masaba" and "A Mine Tragedy" in particular) very realistically and sympathetically evoke the plight of black mine-workers and township dwellers, portraying these people as victims of gross injustice. Indeed, when read as a whole, Dhlomo's 'mine'-pieces constitute a severe indictment of the mining practices at the time. Couzens's remark that there is "a great deal more to understand in these stories" and his warning that care needs to be taken "before snap judgements are made" (1975: 6) are well taken.

The point of noting these anomalies in Dhlomo is, rather, to suggest that he was subject to diverse literary and social influences and – given his time and context – that he was not able to articulate an entirely coherent perspective on contentious issues. Couzens himself draws attention to this:

> [...] amongst the welter of possible themes one could choose to comment on in order to indicate the complexity of Dhlomo's moral position, I would like to indicate briefly the ambiguity of that position as regards traditional custom, and in particular the role of the "witchdoctor" (the physician–priest). Whereas in "Zulu Christian Science" Dhlomo, himself at first a reasonably orthodox Presbyterian, tends to condemn traditional medicine, he makes little condemnatory comment in "Dumela Defies Lightning" and almost accepts the prophetic–historical role of the protagonist in "Death of Manembe." (6)

At the risk of oversimplifying, it might be argued that Dhlomo, as a pioneer black intellectual living in the dislocated mid-war years, did not have access to the more coherently articulated political ideologies that were to come with the rise of Africanism and Black Consciousness in the 1960s and 1970s. However, together with his better-known brother and other pioneer writer–politicians like Sol Plaatje, Rolfes Dhlomo was undoubtedly instrumental in laying the foundation for these later developments.[1]

The purpose of this brief discussion of Dhlomo's stories is to provide a point of reference for the more recent black South African short story. I have already noted the coexistence in Dhlomo's stories of

---

[1] By way of demonstrating his importance in this regard, Couzens (1975: 4) lists the dignitaries at his funeral in 1971, among them Selby Msimang and A.W.G. Champion.

formal, received English (which sounds quaint to the modern reader) and various vernacular styles. The same kind of hybridity cannot be said to characterize the mode in which the stories are conveyed, which is for the most part either that of the dramatized incident – journalistic copy with dialogue added – or otherwise that which uses the conventions of the Western realist tradition, with credible characterization, a conventional story line and exposition, and a third-person narrator.

The narrative style of Dhlomo's stories thus reflects very little of his mixed cultural inheritance. "Magic in a Zulu Name" (1933) is one possible exception to this. As its title suggests, the story concerns the consequences of choosing a name. Mlalazi has named his son Unyazi ("lightning") and reveals this to Zibi Sokela, the witch-doctor who has come to treat the boy, lying trembling in a corner of the hut after a fierce thunderstorm. Sokela reacts with horror at this disclosure and demands an explanation from the father. A brief tale-within-a-tale ensues in which Mlalazi describes the circumstances of his wife's death in childbirth. She was, he reveals, struck dead by lightning immediately after giving birth. Mlalazi claims that in this moment something caused him to forget himself and he named his son after the calamitous event. After witnessing the boy's distracted behaviour in the midst of another thunderstorm, Sokela proceeds to cure him by planting "'doctored' pegs" (47) around the hut and administering a powerful herbal antidote to the boy. Afterwards, in another short story-within-a-story, he provides Mlalazi with an explanation for the strange events surrounding his wife's death and for his son's behaviour. A jealous former lover, Sokela reveals, placed a curse on Mlalazi's wife by mixing the dust where her foot had trod with the dust of the site of a lightning strike, and concocting a potion into which he cast his evil spirit. Had she not died the night she gave birth, she would have been permanently afflicted with the psychological condition her son only displayed during thunderstorms. The story ends with Mlalazi interrogating the witch-doctor:

> "But what killed his mother?" asked Mlalazi. "Was it the lightning or
> the pains of labour?"
>   "She was killed by fear."
>   "What is it you say, Sokela?"

"She was killed by a great fear which when she actually saw her son born overpowered her and killed her."

"So she knew she was cursed by the spirit of Duma?"

"Yes, she knew her fate and she feared for her child who would be motherless while its mother lived. This thought came at a critical moment and killed her." (48)

The story ends with this climactic revelation, a feature shared by many of the other stories, and this again reveals something about the mixed mode in which Dhlomo worked. While it deals with the subject-matter typical of an African folktale, the story is compact and economical in style. In fact, it imparts the curious sense of being a Poe-ian detective story set in the heart of rural Zululand, and its tension owes as much to the dramatic events described as to Mlalazi's (and the reader's) desire to find an answer to the mystery. This suggests that Dhlomo's narrative style has more in common with the traditions of Western narrative realism than with African oral forms.

Thus, the double story-within-a-story structure notwithstanding, there is no sense that Dhlomo has attempted to capture the style of the oral tale in the written short story. As has been indicated above, evidence of the writer's African cultural inheritance manifests itself mainly in the subject-matter of his stories and the verbal style adopted by some of his characters. The manner in which the stories are told, on the other hand, is conventional in the received Western tradition.

— Ω —

Between Dhlomo in the 1930s and the heyday of *Drum* in the middle 1950s, only two short-story collections of note by black writers appeared, neither of them exhibiting significant oral influence. Peter Abrahams's *Dark Testament* (1942) and Es'kia Mphahlele's *Man Must Live and Other Stories* (1946) are both pioneering works in their own right, but neither attempts to negotiate the interstices of oral and written narrative modes, the theme of this study.

With few exceptions, the *Drum* period itself also yields little of interest to this study. Ernest Pereira (1986b: 106) observed that if one were to look to the post-Bosman period for a more contemporary yarnster, then Casey Motsisi would fit the bill. And indeed, in the way he flies in the face of white authority and resourcefully seeks the risible in the deadening encroachment of grand apartheid, he reveals the ebullience and irrepressibility of the 'tall teller of tales.' However, Motsisi's style, while owing something to the tall-tale tradition of the American mid-West, is far more influenced by writers like Damon Runyan and the American B-grade movies that were popular at the time.

The work of other *Drum* writers also reflects the tendency of the era to look to the West for inspiration. Can Themba, for example, delighted in the kind of sophisticated verbal play that recalls Oscar Wilde. In style, his stories are effusive and display a love of intricate phrases and unusual combinations of words – and, significantly, they reveal little influence from African oral narrative modes.

Es'kia Mphahlele's "Mrs Plum" (1967) is the one exception to this tendency. In this story, Mphahlele attempts to capture the idiom of English as spoken by unschooled black domestic servants. The story is narrated by Karabo, a domestic servant in a Johannesburg northern-suburbs home, and her narrative employs an African-idiomatic verbal inflection. However, there is no evidence that this story was part of a larger attempt on Mphahlele's part to re-situate the narrative voice in an African-oral context. None of the other stories of *In Corner B* (1967) employs such a narrative style and "Mrs Plum" therefore stands out as an isolated narrative experiment.

A.C. Jordan

It was only in 1973 with the appearance of A.C. Jordan's *Tales from Southern Africa*, a collection of Xhosa tales translated into English, that a sizeable portion of an African oral tradition emerged in print. These tales, "translated and retold" by Jordan, are the earliest examples of a sustained attempt by a black South African writer to render oral tales in the written form. Significantly, as Z. Pallo Jordan notes in his Foreword, this was done partly for political reasons:

> In colonial societies, where the majority of the people are, as a matter of policy, kept semi-literate, the 'folk' can be a revolutionary concept employed for the reaffirmation of a national identity. Jordan, therefore, chose the Southern African tale – with its oral tradition, and hence not limited to a reading public – as the medium through which to express his protest against the existing order. He sought to transform the tale into a

great collective symbol around which the African people could be mobilized for social and political change. (xxii)

As Njabulo Ndebele (1984) was later to argue, recourse to African cultural traditions (and the hybrid forms they take in an urban context) constitutes a way of developing a potent oppositional literary aesthetic. In other words, cultural colonization by the West can be countered by adapting autochthonous African cultural forms to new situations. According to Z. Pallo Jordan, this is precisely what A.C. Jordan does in his collection.

Tales from Southern Africa is a collection of thirteen Xhosa *iintsomi*, a genre, Z. Pallo Jordan notes, that "is understood to refer to the fictitious, mythological, and fantastic" (xvii). He remarks that A.C. Jordan collected these both in rural areas, where he sought old women who were renowned as storytellers, and in Cape Town's District Six, where people from the Tsolo and Qumbu districts lived.

In his Introduction to the collection, Harold Scheub discusses the aesthetic elements of Jordan's tales, and these remarks are fleshed out in the individual prefaces he has supplied for the different stories. "A basic aesthetic element of the *ntsomi* tradition is repetition," he observes. "The movement between the conflict and resolution takes place structurally through the continued repetition of the core-cliché" (3). This repetition of a song-like refrain is very much in evidence in the stories, and the oral origins of the tales are therefore very conspicuously foregrounded. Other distinctively oral characteristics are the coexistence of the fantastic and the real in the stories and the 'flat' characterization. On an ideological level, the stories are also conservative in nature: the performer of the *iintsomi*, Scheub remarks, has "much freedom to improvise and originate" and indeed is "often judged on the freshness which she brings to the externalisation of images"; however, "she is always guided by a broad theme that centres about the need for an ordered society, a stable and harmonious community" (9). This recalls Walter Ong's remarks about the conservative or traditionalistic nature of oral culture:

> Since in a primary oral culture conceptualized knowledge that is not repeated aloud soon vanishes, oral societies must invest great energy in saying over and over again what has been learned arduously over the ages.

> This need establishes a highly traditionalist or conservative set of mind
> that with good reason inhibits intellectual experimentation. (1982: 41)

All of Jordan's tales conform to this tendency. Invariably, their thematic
movement is towards the reinforcement of traditional mores and
societal taboos. In this respect, above all, the stories are more closely
akin to the oral tale than to the characteristically nonconformist modern
short story.

All of the above notwithstanding, Scheub goes on to argue that
Jordan's narratives are "based on ntsomi performances, but the narratives are not now *ntsomi* performances. They have not been retold by
A.C. Jordan so much as recast by him" (10). Declaring the stories therefore to be "hybrids," and noting that the physical presence of the
performer (and all that this figure introduces by way of dramatization,
verbal intonation, interaction with audience and the like) is entirely
missing in the written versions, Scheub concludes that

> the qualities of an oral language are untranslatable to the written page.
> The tensions that exist between artist and audience, and the performer's
> manipulation and exploitation of those tensions: how can these essential
> ingredients of a public performance be captured in the privacy and
> remoteness of a page in a book? (11)

One response to Scheub's rhetorical question is to refer him to
Bosman's stories, where the presence of a storyteller and his interaction
with a company of interlocutors is as tangible as it is possible to achieve
on the printed page. Flippant though such a rejoinder may sound, it
does raise an important point about the narrative structure of Jordan's
tales: nowhere in *Tales from Southern Africa* is there an attempt to evoke
the textual presence of a narrator and the possibility of ironic interplay
between this figure and frame narrator or audience. The tales all employ a conventional invisible third-person narrator, and eschew what I
have called an 'oral style.' In many respects (as the discussion above
attests) the tales are conspicuously oral-derived, especially regarding
thematic concerns, characterization, and setting; but they fail to carry
this oral-traditional content through into an oral style of narration.

It is interesting to observe in this regard that "The Turban," the best
known of Jordan's tales, is also possibly the most 'literary.' Of all the
stories in the collection, it most closely approximates the modern liter-

ary short story in terms of characterization, narrative tension, and focus on a single incident. It is shorter than most of the other stories (several of which run to forty or fifty pages, with very convoluted story lines) and traces, economically and with well-controlled dramatic tension, the fate of its central character, Nyengebule, who kills his favourite wife in a momentary fit of rage and is forced to submit to a ritual killing by members of her family. More so than in the other stories, the characterization of Nyengebule in "The Turban" borders on the complex. In accordance with the characterization typical of the oral tale, he is still described 'from without,' but the reader's identification with him and sympathy for his plight are elicited by descriptions of his actions and state of mind. In his prefatory commentary to the story, Scheub implicitly makes a similar point:

> It is his ability to continue with life, almost as if in a stupor, as if nothing had happened, that invests the story with much of its horror, and which simultaneously, strangely underscores the love that he had for his wife. The man has committed a crime, and does not know what to do. (16)

"The Turban" is therefore what might be called a 'successful' short story; it negotiates the gap between oral and written modes better than any of the others. However, the point is that it moves directly in mode from oral tale to written story without availing itself of the possibility of an oral style of narration; it thus forgoes the opportunity of harnessing the richness and cultural potency of Xhosa traditions in its narrative style. As with the other stories, it employs what Scheub terms a repetition of "core-clichés" or song-like refrains, which points to its distinctive oral origins; but it does not use a narrator or deploy the various levels of irony to which oral-style stories lend themselves.

The purpose of pointing this out is to demonstrate that Jordan, in adopting a conventional third-person narrator, has missed the opportunity of putting an old and venerable genre (the Xhosa *iintsomi*) to new and potentially powerful political use. I wish therefore to return to Z. Pallo Jordan's remarks that the 'folk' can be a "revolutionary concept employed for the reaffirmation of a national identity"; and that A.C. Jordan "chose the Southern African tale – with its oral tradition, and hence not limited to a reading public – as the medium through which to express his protest against the existing order" (xxii).

Clearly, the recuperation of cultural art forms is inevitably an act of opposition to a ruling order whose policy is to suppress both the society itself and the cultural artifacts it produces. However, when this process of recuperation does not involve an adaptation of such art forms to changed circumstances, there is little to distinguish this act from that of the anthropologist who collects such artifacts in order to preserve for posterity relics of a society threatened with extinction.

That Jordan was a product of the society whose culture he attempts to recuperate is a factor that must not be elided; his relationship with his subject is simultaneously organic and intellectually constructed. But he does not attempt to redirect the tales he garnered, to subvert the inherent conservatism of the artifacts he inherited and to infuse them with a new, more urgent purpose. Z. Pallo Jordan's argument that he "sought to transform the tale into a great collective symbol around which the African people could be mobilized for social and political change" (xxii) is therefore not altogether convincing. A.C. Jordan rescued artifacts of a dying tradition and in so doing performed a valuable service on behalf of future generations; but, on the evidence of his style of storytelling in *Tales from Southern Africa*, his intervention in the area of cultural contestation in the turbulent 1960s and 1970s is unlikely to have been very significant.[2]

Again, Bosman constitutes an instructive counterpoint. As argued in previous chapters, Bosman (and, to a lesser extent, Gibbon and Blignaut before him) took over a fundamentally nineteenth-century art form but infused it with new purpose, in the process making it responsive to new exigencies and artistic priorities.

At the risk of being fanciful, it is possible to imagine a black Oom Schalk Lourens, whom Jordan – with all of his insider's knowledge of Xhosa culture – could have manipulated to tell tales that may outwardly assume a traditional form but which are invested with irony and which are tacitly critical of contemporary forms of white oppression. Of course, Jean Blignaut's Hottentot Ruiter provides a model of a 'black' narrator who skilfully pokes fun at white assumptions of superiority and who also obliquely (but powerfully) exposes white-on-black bru-

---

[2] One indication of this is the fact that *Tales from Southern Africa* never achieved a wide circulation in South Africa. No publisher has taken up local rights, and the book has long been out of print.

tality. However, the dynamics here are different: Ruiter is a member of a marginalized and numerically minuscule race squeezed between the politically powerful whites and the numerically powerful Africans; and, as a member of the white race group, Blignaut as author stands in a different relation to his narrator than Jordan would to, say, a traditional Xhosa storyteller.

It is significant to note that, according to Z. Pallo Jordan, A.C. Jordan heard many of the tales he 'retells' here from a woman originally from Qumbu in the Transkei, but then living in Cape Town:

> She had an extensive repertoire of tales and was known as a great narrator. Together with the large audience that gathered for her sessions, she contributed quite a few tales to this collection. Though the atmosphere was perhaps contrived, it was the closest parallel to the traditional setting that could be recreated in the cities. (xxiii)

Surely here we have presented the possibility of a hybrid art form drawing on the ancient oral culture of rural Transkei, but directing its attention to complex and pressing new concerns of an urban nature. Such a strategy would indeed constitute a "protest against the existing order." Jordan chose instead to cast his tales in the timeless and politically neutral context of rural Transkei, where the devastation wrought by numerous Frontier Wars and later social upheavals never obtrudes.

By 1968 A.C. Jordan was dead, and his *Tales from Southern Africa* is therefore more of a literary tribute to the man's scholarship in preceding decades than a statement for the period of the 1970s. For it was in this politically turbulent decade that the black South African short story achieved greater political and aesthetic 'point.' In this period, and within the genre of the short story, Bessie Head's *The Collector of Treasures* stands out both as a work which makes much more trenchant points about various forms of political and gender oppression and as one that (importantly for this study) adopts aspects of an African oral culture in order to do so.

Bessie Head

Most of the stories in Bessie Head's *The Collector of Treasures* engage directly with the oral culture of the traditional African village of Serowe, the setting for her collection of tales. This tradition takes both ancient and modern forms: Serowe possesses venerable old "tribal historians," but it is also characterized by a contemporary ethos of village gossip and storytelling. The historical range of Head's stories attests to this multi-faceted nature of Serowan oral culture.

The first story in the collection, "The Deep River: A Story of Ancient Tribal Migration," deals, as the title suggests, with an important aspect of oral culture: traditional history. The story depicts the rift that occurs when the new chief of a tribe, Sebembele, breaks with tradition and is forced to leave the kingdom with his followers. A footnote to the story reads:

> The story is an entirely romanticized and fictionalized version of the history of the Botalaote tribe. Some historical data was given to me by the old men of the tribe, but it was unreliable as their memories had tended to fail them. A re-construction was made therefore in my own imagination; I am also partly indebted to the London Missionary Society's "*Livingstone Tswana Readers,*" *Padiso III*, school textbook, for those graphic paragraphs on the thanksgiving ceremony which appear in the story. (1977: 6)

Evidently this story arose from the interviews that Bessie Head was doing for her social history, *Serowe: Village of the Rain Wind* (1981).[3] She draws upon the recollections of the old men of the tribe, but recasts the whole story and, of course, arrives at a different conclusion from that of the old men, who say at the end that "women have always caused a lot of trouble in the world" (6). What the story achieves in the context of the collection is that it sketches a mythical map of the Botalaote tribe's origins and provides a historical introduction that places the stories that follow. In doing this, Head is assuming the role of tribal historian, although the story is narrated in the third person and cannot therefore be said to adopt an oral style.

The second story retains some sort of continuity with the first, in that it describes the recent history of a family and, by implication, that

---

[3] Head conducted a series of interviews with Serowe villagers in the mid-1970s. Using an interpreter, she spoke to a wide range of people, old and young, educated and illiterate. Although the fruits of the research are mainly to be found in her social history, *Serowe: Village of the Rain Wind* (1981), many traces are also to be found in *The Collector of Treasures*. For discussions of this, see Marquard (1978/79) and MacKenzie (1989a, 1989b).

of the community. The story opens with the author's description of the life of Galethebege, a simple yet profound woman caught between her sincere Christian convictions and Setswana custom. An authorial voice relates only the last days and death of Galethebege, and an oral storyteller, here a character in the narrative, the old man Modise, is employed to tell the story of Galethebege's life:

> "I am of a mind to think that Galethebege was praying for forgiveness for her sins this morning," he said slowly. "It must have been a sin to her to marry Ralokae. He was an unbeliever to the day of his death ..."
>
> A gust of astonished laughter shook his family out of the solemn mood of mourning that had fallen upon them and they all turned eagerly towards their grandfather, sensing that he had a story to tell. (8)

In a classic storytelling setting, with the "flickering firelight" lighting up their faces, the old man tells his family the story. The central issue is the conflict between European Christianity and Setswana custom. Galethebege wishes to get married in church. Her husband-to-be, Ralokae, is a firm traditionalist and rejects mission Christianity:

> The God might be all right, he explained, but there was something wrong with the people who had brought the word of the Gospel to the land. Their love was enslaving black people and he could not stand it [...] They had brought a new order of things into the land and they made the people cry for love. One never had to cry for love in the customary way of life. Respect was just there for people all the time. That was why he rejected all things foreign. (9–10)

Galethebege appeals to the missionary for his blessing on the marriage, and the author wryly observes, "as though a compromise of tenderness could be made between two traditions opposed to each other" (10–11). His reply, "'heaven is closed to the unbeliever'" (11), devastates her. She and her family and friends all leave the church. Like all good storytellers, Modise ends on a note which leaves the issue to be silently re-evaluated by the listeners:

> The old man leaned forward and stirred the dying fire with a partially burnt-out log of wood. His listeners sighed the way people do when they have heard a particularly good story. As they stared at the fire they found themselves debating the matter in their minds, as their elders had done some forty or fifty years ago. (12)

There are several aspects of this story that are relevant to a discussion of oral tradition and written literature. In the first place, it should be noted that the story arises from an interview which appears in a chapter of *Serowe: Village of the Rain Wind* that deals with religion in the village. The bare bones of the story are all there: Segametse Mpulambusi tells the story about her grandmother's conflict with, and withdrawal from, the London Missionary Society church – and it is possibly the context of the interview that prompted the author to introduce the device of the storyteller.

It is clear, therefore, that Head wants to present all the familiar components of an African storytelling ethos: the campfire setting, the wise old narrator, a known and intimate audience, an ending that provokes re-evaluation and comment. The reader is introduced to the texture of village life by being drawn to the campfire, as it were, by the storyteller's compelling technique (the storyteller here being both the character, Modise, and the authorial voice).

"Heaven is not Closed," in other words, is an example of how the collection as a whole endeavours to evoke the life of a Botswanan village for the reader by reconstructing the way the village explains itself. The narrative tale, the primary method by which oral cultures deal with the flow of life (Ong 1982: 140), is therefore the genre adopted by Bessie Head. The stories are the kind that the villagers tell each other. They are contained by a larger narrative framework (explicitly at work in "Heaven is not Closed") which contextualizes the tales for the reader and transcribes the oral tale into the written short story.

The author does, however, break into the narrative of "Heaven is not Closed." She employs the device of the storyteller to evoke the flavour of village life in a tangible way, but does not restrict herself to what would conceivably be told by a person of Modise's age and context. By evoking the traditional oral storyteller within the text of a modern short story, the narrative structure works in a double-edged way to give a sense of what it describes. The story conveys its meaning, in other words, in two ways: by what is said, and by how it is said.

The other stories in the collection move steadily into the modern period, addressing issues that arise in the context of a clash between old and new: the new faith-healing religions, independence and a new kind of society, witchcraft and religious conflict, and the confrontation between modern and traditional forms of government. None of them adopts an oral style in the manner of "Heaven is not Closed," but there are various other features which indicate Head's concern to engage with the oral culture of Serowe.

For example, there are vestiges of traditional oral culture in an altered, hybrid form. The traditional storyteller would frequently develop a story around a moral, a saying, or a proverb. The story itself is fluid and context-sensitive but it holds the moral within itself as a kernel of truth, a lodestar. In *The Collector of Treasures*, four proverbs are quoted: "the children of a real woman do not get lean or die" (30); "the children of a real woman cannot fall into the fire" (31); "you can't kill someone who is not your relative" (47); and "Jealousy starts from the eye" (66). These traditional sayings are preceded by such phrases as: the saying goes, the saying is still there, our old people used to say, the forefathers said – which is an authorial technique designed to bestow authority on the saying itself and also to claim kinship for the stories with tales told by a traditional storyteller.

Indeed, Head shows considerable interest in the figure of the story-teller, who has obvious roots in the village life of which she was a part. Her social history *Serowe: Village of the Rain Wind* abounds in descriptions of the wise old men whom other villagers proudly refer to as "our traditional historians." The best example in *The Collector of Treasures* of Head's interest in the storyteller is the title-story. Although this does not employ an oral narrative style, it does possess several features illustrating Head's broader conception of the role of the 'storyteller.'

The story arose in what Head called "village newspaper" fashion from an encounter she had with a relative of the man who was killed by his estranged wife (Head 1981: 2). As with "Heaven is not Closed," she leaves the received story-line intact. When she retells the story, however, she supplies an analysis of the social breakdown occurring in modern Batswana society and the kinds of problems to which this gives rise.

The story describes the desperate plight of Dikeledi, a mother of three, whose husband abandons her and years later returns to reduce her life to misery. All the traditional constraints and prejudices against women operate against Dikeledi and threaten the happiness that she has resourcefully gained for herself and her children. She sees no way out of the trap: she kills her husband by cutting off his genitals and is jailed for life.

Her tragedy is not unique. In prison she shares a cell with four other women who have killed their husbands. There is a distinct sense that society is punishing the victims, not the offenders. But the story doesn't end there. Together the victims try to reconstruct a life for themselves in prison through mutual understanding and a sense of common purpose.

The offering of positive examples, of alternative visions, is something that Bessie Head considers essential to the storyteller's project. In a 1983 interview, she made the following remarks apropos the dilemma of women in Serowe: "I think this is going to be very much to the fore-front – the situation of black women. The fact that there are often not happy relationships between men and women, that black women have long operated at a disadvantage. Now you as the storyteller are going to shape the future" (Head 1989: 14).

Her sense that a storyteller "shapes the future" is a recognition that the storyteller can intervene in the real world, that stories need not remain forever in the abstract realm of a 'literary canon.' The storyteller of Walter Benjamin's conception orders and controls the world that surrounds him and his audience. He says: "The storyteller takes what he tells from experience – his own or that reported by others. And he in turn makes it the experience of those who are listening to his tale" (Benjamin 1973: 87).

In the last story in the collection, "Hunting," Head describes the relationship between a man and his wife, and their dealings with the rest of the village. At the end of each day, Thato would recount the day's events to her husband:

> She had the capacity to live with the conflicts of life in a way he had not. Like all women, she was involved in village gossip and disputes. She knew everything, but the richness of her communication lay in her gift to sift and sort out all the calamities of everyday life with the unerring heart of a good storyteller. (108–109)

Thato tells stories. Using the storyteller's craft of sifting and sorting, she describes events she has seen or about which she has heard. Other villagers would also construct such narratives. Taken all together, these stories constitute what John Berger calls the "village's portrait of itself":

"the function of this *gossip* which, in fact, is close, oral, daily history, is to allow the village to define itself" (Berger 1979: 9). It is this source that Head has tapped in producing *The Collector of Treasures*. She attempts to transpose oral sources into literature, to reshape the spoken to suit the new medium of the written, the guiding intention being to explain a village in its own terms.

The above examples illustrate the fact that Head's engagement with the oral milieu of Serowe influences more than the subject-matter and themes of her stories. In various ways she attempts to reflect the texture of this oral milieu in the narrative style of her stories. However, her stories do not conform to the definition of oral-style story formulated in the introduction to this study. With one exception, none of them attempts textually to represent the contours of oral speech, and all are narrated in the third person.

Mtutuzeli Matshoba

Perhaps the closest one comes to an oral-style narrative mode of presentation in the contemporary South African short story is in the stories of Mtutuzeli Matshoba. Published initially as individual stories in *Staffrider*, *Call Me Not a Man* (1979) gathers together a collection of narratives all of which are narrated in the first person. This narrator, moreover, adopts a tone and style strongly reminiscent of an oral storyteller.

This aspect of Matshoba's stories has not gone unnoticed. Michael Vaughan (1981a, 1981b) has had occasion to comment on Matshoba's storytelling style, and Jenny Williams (1991) has subjected this aspect of Matshoba's writing to an extended analysis.

Much of Vaughan's earlier paper (1981a) deals with Matshoba as an exponent of "populist realism" and the challenge this posed to the South African literary establishment of the 1970s and early 1980s. This aspect of Vaughan's polemic is not strictly relevant to the concerns of my study. However, in the course of analyzing how Matshoba's stories differ from those valued by the liberal literary establishment, Vaughan discusses Matshoba's adoption of an oral storytelling style.

Vaughan identifies three motifs in Matshoba's stories that establish his kinship with an oral storyteller. The first of these is the motif of the *journey* and, accordingly, the notion of "the protagonist as the traveller" (1981a: 19); by virtue of this enforced condition of constant travel between dormitory township and urban place of work, the traveller is also the *storyteller*. The traveller becomes "a philosopher of the people," a storyteller, absorbing the exemplary lessons of experience for the greater benefit of communal selfconsciousness. Another dimension of the traveller, Vaughan goes on, "is that of the *co-ordinator* or the *map-maker*":

> The traveller who looks out of the train window at the passing land-scape achieves a momentary sense of alienation from local environ-ments: he looks with a fresh consciousness at these places, distanced, questioning, in search of the underlying principles of a broad connec-tive history. (23–24)

Another facet of Matshoba's collection is "its concern with the expres-sion of an *exemplary range* of situations and experiences" (24):

> The stories move from the city to the country, from the township to the homeland, from the security of family and home to the needs of political struggle, from the heart to the mind. The idea is that the mind of the reader should not become absorbed in a privileged type of situ-ation and experience, but should recognize the need to get to grips with the diversity-in-unity of the predicament and the interests of the people as a whole, the fragmented people. (24–25)

The second motif Vaughan identifies is that of *conversation*. Whereas liberal fiction, he argues, "privileges individualist modalities of experience," Matshoba "gives prominence to the motif of conversation because this is the medium of collective encounters" (25).

The last motif is that of *counsel*: the traveller "must complement the role of the map-maker with the role of the friend, the neighbour, the counsellor who is also the all-but-identical victim" (25–26). The motif of counsel, Vaughan concludes, "can be seen as that which underlies all the other motifs. The art of storytelling is valued as a medium of counsel" (26).

Vaughan identifies these motifs in Matshoba's writing with the purpose of pointing out how they constitute a challenge to liberal aesthetics. In the second of his essays of this period, he explores the question of whether a writer using such motifs "can become the story-teller" (1981b: 45). Here he notes the contradiction that exists between "producing for a *public*, and assuming a relation of participatory immediacy with a *community* (that is, adopting the role of the story-teller)" (45), but then explores the tension in Matshoba between his identification with the oppressed classes in South Africa and his neglect in his stories of the structural causes of this oppression. Again, Vaughan's concerns are more with the ideological tensions or contradictions in Matshoba's fiction than with the question of literary style of presentation, the issue closer to the concerns of the present study.

Jenny Williams's thesis takes up these matters in greater detail and also focuses more squarely on the issue of Matshoba's closeness to African oral modes of narrative. Arguing that his stories "challenge [...] traditional Western expectations concerning the modern (written) short story" (1991: 13), she observes that they are, "despite their contemporary interests," to be "more closely identified with Walter Benjamin's view of pre-technological, oral art" (15):

> In addressing the themes of bureaucracy, the injustice inflicted by black 'sellouts' on fellow blacks, white oppression of blacks, and miscegenation, Matshoba does not satisfy Poe's dictum of "unity of impression," and the defining characteristic of his stories is certainly not that of a tight, climactic and linear structure. Most are not really short (one being fifty-one pages in length) and nearly all start *in medias res*, a technique which Walter Ong identifies as "not a consciously continued ploy but the original, natural, inevitable way to proceed for an oral poet approaching a lengthy narrative" (1982: 44). The stories also contain flashbacks, admonitions to the reader, and a series of episodes, all these being devices which are typical of 'oral literature.' (16)

Williams thus locates Matshoba's distinctiveness in the hybrid nature of his stories – their infusion with "oral residue." Examples she cites include the story "A Son of the Second Generation," in which "an exemplary situation allows the narrator to philosophize on the dramatic events and to moralize to his readers" (23). The narrator in this story, she argues, "recounts a tale he has overheard on a commuter train, using a narrative strategy that is common in oral tales" (23–24). This strategy is that of narrating as a personal witness to the events described. The narrative point of view soon switches to the third person, so that the drama involving the principal two characters can be conveyed, but there are also interpolations in the first person, which take the form of moralizing asides – "But I do not see what can be immoral ..."; "To me a so-called 'Coloured' human being is a brother" (1979: 91).

In the lengthy story "A Pilgrimage to the Isle of Makana," Matshoba uses a series of flashbacks to establish background for his story. Citing Ong, Williams argues that this is further evidence of "oral residue," as the "oral poet does not have recourse to the revision made possible by the 'rational' analytic arrangements of written composition" (30). Likewise, the motif of the journey also establishes Matshoba's link with oral tradition and "the typical hero's quest in ancient tales" (31).

Other examples Williams cites are the didactic tendency in Matshoba's stories, their use of characters as 'types' rather than unique individuals and of situations as exemplary rather than exceptional. She ends with a plea for a more sympathetic interpretation of Matshoba's stories on the basis of their "hybridity":

> In all the stories of the cycle, Matshoba reveals shifts in structuring processes suggesting difficult, even imperfect transitions from orality to literacy. Crucially, he is able to analyze abstract concepts while retaining an understanding of older, empathetic ways of conceptualising experiences. The formal manifestations might at first seem awkward to Western-trained readers of fiction; I have tried to argue, however, for the impact of stories which explore a period of growth and change, not only in the writer but in his society. (59)

Much of Williams's argument is cogent and legitimate. It restores some critical balance to the somewhat skewed, 'Western' reception of his work, and it does partly address issues central to this study: Matshoba's use of devices drawn from an oral cultural milieu.

To what extent, though, can the devices Matshoba uses be said to constitute an 'oral style' in the sense used in the present study? Despite his extensive use of a first-person narrator, and the fact that this narrator often assumes the style of the oral storyteller, Matshoba's stories do not conform to the definition I have furnished of an 'oral style.' They do not employ an internal narrator (a fictionalized storyteller figure) and are therefore not, narratologically speaking, of the same structure as the stories examined in the main part of this study. It might be contended that the definition 'oral-style' story should then be expanded to include work of Matshoba's sort. Adopting such a course is, of course, theoretically possible; after all, I have identified certain devices as the central, constitutive features of the kind of story I have elected to examine, and could well have argued for others.

However, my underlying premise is that there is a continuity to be discerned in the style of story I have designated 'oral-style,' and this continuity does not extend to the works touched on in this chapter. As I indicated at the outset, there is a significant difference between first-person narratives (African-traditional or otherwise) and oral-style narratives. None of the stories examined in this chapter (with the exception of Head's story) employs a fictional narrator, none attempts to engage the contours of the spoken word as a narrative mode, hence none involves the kind of interplay between teller and reporter of tale that I have identified as a feature of the advanced oral-style story.

Njabulo Ndebele

Ndebele's stories, as I have remarked, move even further away from an oral style. He may be concerned to locate his stories in a distinctive African cultural milieu and use certain icons unique to this milieu, but the style in which the stories are presented owes much to the traditions of Western narrative realism.

The first story of the collection *Fools and Other Stories* (1983), "The Test," sees the protagonist taking up a schoolboy challenge to run home shirtless in the rain. "The Prophetess" describes a young boy's anxiety in his efforts to procure "holy water" from the local medicine woman for his mother and to get it home safely while running the gauntlet of local street kids. In "The Music of the Violin" a young boy struggles to fend off the values and life-style that his overbearing middle-class parents attempt to impose on him.

The longer title-story "Fools" depicts an intense and troubled relationship that develops between a disgraced school teacher and a young, idealistic activist who represents the potential for new life and a new society. It is the most overtly political of the stories, yet the political content is embedded in a complex story-line that includes troubled relationships, drunkenness, misunderstandings, and personal defeats.

In the story "Uncle" can be discerned much of what Ndebele espouses in his theoretical reflections. Like the three shorter pieces, the story also centres on the consciousness of a young boy. The boy's father has died, and he is the only child. He has a close, warm relationship with his mother, who is a nurse by profession and a churchgoer with strong principles and a sense of dignity. Into this protected environment arrives the proverbial black sheep of the family, the mother's younger brother, a man in his late twenties but rich in experience of life. His arrival is the catalyst for a number of events that have a profound effect on the impressionable young boy. "Uncle" sows the seeds of social consciousness in his young nephew's mind, providing him with a personal history imbued with traditional African cultural values.

The character "Uncle" in effect redraws the white man's map of South Africa and charges it with the significance that rises out of a uniquely African perspective. His young nephew will begin to experience himself, his family and his people (the black majority at large) as "makers of culture" (Ndebele 1984: 48) – in other words, as people capable of appropriating the white man's landscape for their own social and political ends.

Ndebele's stories can thus be seen as an attempt to put into practice what he postulates in theory. Most of his most influential postulates are contained in his "Turkish Tales, and Some Thoughts on South African Fiction" (1984). Rejecting protest fiction as an impoverishment of South African writing, Ndebele calls for "storytelling" in the place of "case-making," praising writers who "give African readers the opportunity to experience themselves as makers of culture" (1984: 48). He uses the example of the figure of the oral storyteller on the buses or trains, who tells stories of a largely "apolitical" nature, as tacit support for his own style of "rediscovering the ordinary."

Also implicit in this approach would be the location of the dynamic of this fiction in an authentic black community, employing discourses typical of black township communities. In this regard, Ndebele evokes the sense of the writer's accountability to the majority African population, even if, as he acknowledges, the writing itself usually ends up in the hands of a white liberal readership. This accountability, moreover, would arise not out of some abstract intellectual commitment but, rather, out of a concrete engagement with the forms of culture whose dynamic is expressed in the fiction.

These pronouncements in the abstract are not, however, necessarily borne out by Ndebele's own fictional practice. They exemplify, rather, "some ambiguities or 'silences' in the criticism":

> Although the stories are well crafted, so that they establish their subject matter in effective fictional terms, the skill with which they are composed seems to owe little to the "timeless tradition of storytelling" to which Ndebele refers in his article. (Vaughan 1990: 190)

Arguing that oral culture "enters into the subject matter of the stories, then, rather than into the principles of their narrative composition," Michael Vaughan concludes that Ndebele is "a skilful composer of stories in a *Western, realist tradition* of fiction-writing" (190–91).

Ndebele's stories thus move fairly far away from an oral style in their composition, and his contribution to the issue of "the writer becoming the storyteller" is largely confined to his criticism.

— Ω —

This brief overview of the influence of orality on the postwar South African short story demonstrates that there are two (largely separate) traditions of 'oral-style' stories to be discerned in the larger corpus of South African short fiction. One – the focus of this study – centres on a fictional narrator, and uses the device or convention of the frame narrative. The other – briefly surveyed in this chapter – attempts to conflate the categories of author and oral storyteller, forgoing the device of the fictional narrator altogether. So, while oral culture is frequently *thematized* in post-1970 black short fiction, actual communal narrators rarely appear, and little attempt is made to represent oral performance or register in the written form.

As was pointed out above, there is no real continuity between the two traditions, and two separate theses would have to be advanced to take account of their origins and development. I have chosen to focus principally on the kind of story I have designated the oral-style story, the chief defining characteristic of which is the use of a fictional narrator. With the (perhaps sole) exception of Bessie Head's "Heaven is not Closed," this style of story disappears from South African literature after Bosman. The reasons for this disappearance and the implications thereof are the substance of my final chapter.

——————— ✌ ✆ ———————

Conclusion

❧ ————————————

"WHERE THERE IS NO ADEQUATE FORM for the unmediated expression of an author's thoughts," argues Bahktin in *Problems of Dostoevsky's Poetics*, "he must resort to refracting them in someone else's discourse. Sometimes the artistic tasks themselves are such that they can be realized only by means of double-voiced discourse" (1984: 192).

Bakhtin makes these remarks in the course of a comparison (alluded to in the introduction to this study) between the different uses of *skaz* by Turgenev and Leskov. "Turgenev's *skaz*," says Bakhtin, "signifies autonomously; there is one voice in it and this voice directly expresses the intention of the author" (191). Leskov, on the other hand, "resorted to a narrator largely for the sake of a socially foreign discourse and socially foreign worldview, and only secondarily for the sake of oral *skaz*" (192). Turgenev's *skaz*, according to Bakhtin, is therefore of the "simple" kind, and "monologic" or "single-voiced" in nature; whereas Leskov's is "parodistic," and "dialogic" or "double-voiced."

Bakhtin's distinction between two fundamentally different kinds of fictional strategies in stories that use the voice of a narrator as a narrative mode is (as we saw at various points in this study) particularly useful in an analysis of the internal shift in the South African oral-style story. Put simply, the distinction enables us to see how, technically speaking, the oral-style story can take two different forms – one simple and single-voiced, the other more complex and multi-voiced.

— Ω —

I wish to conclude with a brief overview of the fate of the oral-style story. Demographic patterns in South Africa in the period covered by this study (the mid-1800s to the mid-1900s) reflect a movement of people from the outlying rural areas to the cities. This has affected not only the indigenous populations, but the white settler communities as well. The result is a marginalization of the circumstances that sustained the frontier-fireside tale of the Drayson, Scully, FitzPatrick variety. Later on, Pauline Smith's Little Karoo and, after that, Bosman's Groot Marico also disappeared as fertile ground for the development of oral traditions among the descendants of the early Dutch settlers.

This movement of people has been reflected in the literature of South Africa from the first part of the century until fairly recently. An entire body of literature, known as the 'Jim-comes-to-Jo'burg' genre, has emerged to give artistic expression to the human dimensions of this demographic shift: from Douglas Blackburn's *Leaven: A Black and White Story* in 1908, to W.C. Scully's *Daniel Vananda* and William Plomer's *Ula Masondo* of the 1920s, to Peter Abrahams's *Mine Boy* and Alan Paton's *Cry, the Beloved Country* of the 1940s to works like Mbulelo Mzamane's *Mzala* of the contemporary period.[1]

The net result of this great movement of people has been a re-appraisal of the aesthetic priorities of South African fiction. While two of the most important pioneering works in South African literature – *Cry, the Beloved Country* and *Mine Boy* – grew out of this period, it must soon have become evident to writers in South Africa that they could write about this phenomenon for only so long before the city wholly assumed moral and aesthetic priority. The city, after all, provides the locus for all significant economic, social and political developments, and the excesses of the Nationalist government from the 1950s onwards have made the focus on these areas a moral imperative for the writer of serious fiction.

In South Africa, the tale (the oral-style story), which usually took an anecdotal form and made overt use of the voice of a narrator, has turned inwards on the consciousness of a central protagonist, and the narrative voice is located either in this central consciousness or is other-

---

[1] Stephen Gray's "Third World Meets First World: The Theme of 'Jim Comes to Jo'burg' in South African English Fiction" (1985) is a very useful guide to the development of this genre.

wise vested in an omniscient third-person narrator. This generalization is not, of course, true in all cases. As we saw in the previous chapter, black South African writers from the 1970s onwards have often re-deployed elements of oral culture in their written work, and this frequently involves the evocation of the author as a storyteller figure. However, the fact that there has been a gradual transition from 'tale' to 'modern short story' is undeniable and, with some strategic exceptions, this tendency is unlikely to reverse itself.

Ernest Pereira's comments in this regard (quoted in my intro-duction) are worth repeating. The reason that the postwar generation has produced "no [...] fictional narrators or settings worthy of their talents," he argues, "is indicative of a significant socio-economic change: what could be seen as the challenging *diversity* of South African society has become mere *fragmentation*, whereby communities – and even families – are divided and driven apart" (1986b: 106).

As was observed earlier, this process is reflected in Bosman's oeuvre: from stories in which a single narrator is used to articulate the ethos and values of his community, there is a shift to stories in which a collection of discordant voices is heard. Typically, the arguments are petty and pointless: it is as if Jurie Steyn, Gysbert van Tonder and the others sense that they are becoming increasingly marginalized and their voices accordingly are less representative of the values of their community, raised instead merely to score points off each other in a seemingly endless and inconclusive series of debates.

The South African oral-style story, once dominant, now falters, loses its purchase on postwar, apartheid South African realities, and degen-erates into the assemblage of discordant voices heard in Jurie Steyn's voorkamer. It is as if the wisdom and humanism embodied by the kind of tale that is told to an audience, its self-affirming qualities, were decisively displaced by the brute inhumanity of the large-scale social engineering that began to take place in the 1950s.

A similar social shift is traced in Walter Benjamin's influential essay "The Storyteller: Reflections on the Works of Nikolai Leskov" (1973 [1936]). The backdrop to Benjamin's reflections on Leskov's stories is the historical demise of the era of storytelling. This, he argues, is a phenomenon caused by the emergence of a new world-order, some of the components of which are the growth of cities, the depopulation of the countryside and the dispersion of the peasantry, the rise of the middle class, industrialization, the introduction of mechanized production and the decline of the craftsman as a social class, the development of the printing press and the new premium placed on information or 'news' in the modern sense, the decline in the communicability of experience brought on by the brute inhumanity of the modern war machine, and the new emphasis on the importance of time.

This broad social shift would also be accompanied by fundamental changes in moral and social epistemology. In the modern era, people think differently – sceptically, agnostically. The 'centre' has disappeared, and with it a narrative mode which presupposes a culture of tacit agreement. Hence, as Benjamin argues, the art of storytelling is dying. This, he says, is due in large measure to the world having grown "poorer in communicable experience" since World War I (1973: 84). The continuity of life and the value placed on human experience, he says, had been broken by the brutal events of the war, and life could no longer be understood or related in the same terms.

Benjamin also addresses the issue of the "practical interests" of the storyteller. Every "real story," he asserts, openly or covertly contains something useful. This may consist in a moral, or in some useful practical advice, or in a proverb or maxim. The storyteller, in other words, "has counsel" for his readers. But the communicability of experience is on the decline, and wisdom, essential to the art of storytelling, is dying out. The reason Benjamin gives for this phenomenon is interesting: narrative, he argues, has been removed from the realm of living speech by what he calls "the secular productive forces of history" (87).

In this connection, it is interesting to note the sequence of John Berger's trilogy of works on the life of a French village.[2] The first volume in Berger's trilogy is a collection of stories about French peasant life entitled *Pig Earth* (1979). This volume also contains a historical overview of the rise and fall of the peasant class and a theoretical analysis of the peasant's world-view. What Berger points to in these introductory and concluding essays is the essentially contrary views of time, and sense of continuity, that exist in the rural peasant community, on the one hand, and urban society on the other. A peasant culture is, in

---

[2] The works which make up this trilogy were first published separately and then republished as a single volume entitled *Into Their Labours* (Berger 1992).

Berger's terms, a "culture of survival," tied closely to the cyclical rhythms of the seasons, whereas urban society embraces a "culture of progress" – that is, a linear view of history and a belief in progress.

Peasant culture also contains all the elements conducive to the story-telling milieu: repetitive manual work (the hands busy, but the ears free to listen), a different perception of time, an environment in which local gossip and legend find a home – a predominantly oral culture, in other words. Interestingly, and this is my point here, Berger attempts to insert his narratives into this oral culture by transcribing into written form the stories which do the village rounds – by trying, in other words, to describe the villagers in the ways in which they choose to describe themselves.

The next volume in his trilogy, *Once in Europa* (1989), modifies this oral storytelling form to accommodate the intrusion of elements from the industrialized city. However, the form still contains traces of the village milieu. The last volume of the trilogy, *Lilac and Flag: An Old Wives' Tale of a City* (1990), takes its title from the two characters it describes and is the story of the couple's passage from the countryside to the city. The focus has shifted from the broader community, and the discourse that is germane to its character, to two individuals. The movement from country to city is also reflected on the level of narrative – in *how* Berger decides to tell the story. He moves from sparsely told stories redolent of oral origins, through longer stories (*Once in Europa*) which focus on love affairs and the modernizing of the village, to the extended complexity of the novel in *Lilac and Flag*, involving a plurality of voices, a touch of magical realism, and dense, poetic language. (In another sense, this sequence is a movement from speech to writing.)[3]

The sequence of Berger's trilogy illustrates Benjamin's contention that in the modern era narrative has been removed from the realm of living speech by "the secular productive forces of history." In Berger's work, demographic movements and social change (impelled by Benjamin's "secular productive forces of history") are reflected at the level of narrative structure and form. The way in which they are written, in other words, reflects the broad historical movement of modern French society from rural setting to the city, from speech to writing.

---

[3] Guy Mannes–Abbott's review (1991) of Berger's trilogy makes this point.

Such a shift in narrative mode is suggestive of the broad movement of the South African short story from oral tale to modern short story. As was pointed out above, rural themes and narrative styles congruent with a rural milieu have given way to a preoccupation with urban life and methods of presenting this in narrative. As Ernest Pereira argues, "the South African short story of today is dominated by the products of man's inhumanity to man: anguish, alienation and anger" (1986b: 106). And he alludes to the "predominance of the realist mode – and voice of protest" (106) that characterizes the work of contemporary writers like Gordimer, Cope, Matthews, Matshoba, Roberts, Wilhelm, Dangor and others. Concluding his essay on the fictional narrator in South African literature, Pereira remarks: "Whether the kind of representative voice whose history I have traced in this essay can find significant expression in contemporary fiction remains to be seen" (114).

This study has shown that a large and significant corpus of South African short stories adopts an oral style. This style, it was argued, dominated the South African short story from the mid-1800s to the mid-1900s. That the Vrouw Grobelaar, Oom Mias, Schalk Lourens and the others were 'representative voices' in this period is attested to by the ability of these storytellers to express the themes and concerns of late nineteenth- and early twentieth-century South African life. That their voices are no longer 'representative' is clear from their virtual disappearance from South African literature.

The recent South African short story is heterogeneous and diversified. The social realism so prominent in the 1970s and 1980s has given way mainly to metafictional experimentation in a variety of forms. Predictably, this development involves a further movement away from forms of story-writing which draw on oral culture. The voices heard in the excellent stories of Ivan Vladislavic (1989), for example, are those of alienated city-dwellers, cut off not only from forms of community embedded in the oral tale, but even from the communality of neighbours across the fence.

One of the more significant developments in terms of the concerns of this study is the emergence of the 'urban legend.' Constraints of space allow me to do no more than allude to this recent development, which is represented largely by three collections assembled by Arthur Goldstuck, *The Rabbit in the Thorn Tree* (1991), *The Leopard in the Luggage:*

Urban Legends from Southern Africa (1993), and *Ink in the Porridge: Urban Legends of the South African Elections* (1994). The urban legend is the kind of tale that does the rounds in an oral style – that is, something passed on by word of mouth – but it differs from the oral tale in that the setting is invariably an urban one (hence, of course, the name given to these tales), and this brings into play a whole set of different textures and dynamics.

The emergence of the urban legend, which can be viewed as the modern relative of the fireside tale, testifies to the resilience of the form of narrative that is transmitted from person to person by word of mouth. However, it would be facile to gloss over the substantive differences between a tale told by Scully or FitzPatrick in the late nineteenth century and those garnered by Goldstuck a century later; clearly, a lot more research would have to be done before the precise relationship between the two forms can be determined.

Works Cited

❧ ————————————

Primary Sources

ANON. 1848. "My Uncle's Tale," *Cape of Good Hope Literary Magazine* 2.6: 112–18.

BERGER, John. 1979. *Pig Earth*. London: Writers and Readers.

——. 1989. *Once in Europa*. London: Granta.

——. 1990. *Lilac and Flag: An Old Wives' Tale of a City*. London: Granta.

——. 1992. *Into Their Labours: Pig Earth, Once in Europa, Lilac and Flag: A Trilogy*. London: Granta.

BLIGNAUT, Aegidius Jean. 1980. *Dead End Road*. Johannesburg: Ad. Donker.

BOSMAN, Herman Charles. 1949. *Mafeking Road* (1947). Johannesburg: C.N.A.

——. 1963. *Unto Dust*. Cape Town: Human & Rousseau.

——. 1971a. *Jurie Steyn's Post Office*. Cape Town: Human & Rousseau.

——. 1971b. *A Bekkersdal Marathon*. Cape Town: Human & Rousseau.

——. 1979. *Almost Forgotten Stories*, ed. Valerie Rosenberg. Cape Town: Timmins.

——. 1980. *Selected Stories*, ed. Stephen Gray. Cape Town: Human & Rousseau.

——. 1987. *Ramoutsa Road*, ed. Valerie Rosenberg. Johannesburg: Ad. Donker.

BOYLE, Frederick. 1876. *The Savage Life: A Second Series of Camp Notes*. London: Chapman & Hall.

——. 1884. *On the Borderland*. London: Chapman & Hall.

BROWNLEE, Frank. 1937. *Corporal Wanzi: Stories*. London: Allen & Unwin.

BRYDEN, H.A. 1896. *Tales of South Africa*. London: Archibald Constable.

——. 1900. *From Veldt Camp Fires: Stories of Southern Africa*. London: Hurst & Blackett.

CAREY–HOBSON, M.A. 1886. *South African Stories*. London: Religious Tract Society.

CORNELL, Fred C. 1915. *A Rip van Winkle of the Kalahari and Other Tales of South-West Africa*. Cape Town: T. Maskew Miller; London: T. Fisher Unwin.

DE FENTON, Marguerite. [Marguerite Mostyn Cleaver.] 1885. *Tales Written in Ladybrand*. Bloemfontein: C. Borckenhagen.

DEVITT, Napier. 1928. *The Blue Lizard, and Other Stories of Native Life in South Africa*. Pretoria: Van Schaik.

DHLOMO, H.I.E. 1985a. *Cetshwayo* (c.1937), H.I.E. Dhlomo: *Collected Works*, ed. Nick Visser & Tim Couzens. Johannesburg: Ravan.

——. 1985b. "Ndongeni" (1942), H.I.E. Dhlomo: *Collected Works*, ed. Nick Visser & Tim Couzens. Johannesburg: Ravan.

DHLOMO, R.R.R. 1975. Stories (1929, 1930), *English in Africa* 2.1: 13–70.

DRAYSON, A.W. 1858. *Sporting Scenes amongst the Kaffirs of South Africa.* London: Routledge.

——. 1862. *Tales at the Outspan, or Adventures in the Wild Regions of Southern Africa.* London: Saunders, Otley.

——. 1879. *Among the Zulus; the Adventures of Hans Sterk, South African Hunter and Pioneer.* London: Griffith & Farran.

——. 1889. *The Diamond Hunters of South Africa.* London: Griffith & Farran.

FITZPATRICK, J. Percy. 1897. *The Outspan: Tales from South Africa.* London: William Heinemann.

GIBBON, Perceval. 1904. *Souls in Bondage.* Edinburgh & London: Blackwood.

——. 1905. *The Vrouw Grobelaar's Leading Cases.* London: Blackwood.

——. 1911. *Margaret Harding.* London: Methuen.

GLANVILLE, Ernest. 1896. *Kloof Yarns.* London: Chatto & Windus.

——. 1897. *Tales from the Veld.* London: Chatto & Windus.

GOLDSTUCK, Arthur. 1991. *The Rabbit in the Thorn Tree.* Harmondsworth: Penguin.

——. 1993. *The Leopard in the Luggage: Urban Legends from Southern Africa.* Harmondsworth: Penguin.

——. 1994. *Ink in the Porridge: Urban Legends of the South African Elections.* Harmondsworth: Penguin.

HEAD, Bessie. 1977. *The Collector of Treasures and Other Botswana Village Tales.* London: Heinemann.

——. 1981. *Serowe: Village of the Rain Wind.* London: Heinemann.

HODGES, R. 1860. *The Settler in South Africa and Other Tales.* London: Basil Montagu Pickering.

INGRAM, J. Forsyth. 1893. *The Story of a Gold Concession, and Other African Tales and Legends.* Pietermaritzburg: W.H. Griffin.

JORDAN, A.C. 1973. *Tales from Southern Africa.* Berkeley and Los Angeles: U of California P.

KIPLING, Rudyard. 1928. *Plain Tales from the Hills* (1888). London: Macmillan.

——. 1895. *Soldiers Three; The Story of the Gadsbys; In Black and White.* London: Macmillan.

——. 1904. *Mrs. Bathurst: Traffics and Discoveries.* London: Macmillan, 339–65.

KLERCK, George. 1929. *At the Foot of the Koppie.* Cape Town: Maskew Miller.

MATSHOBA, Mtutuzeli. 1979. *Call Me Not a Man.* Johannesburg: Ravan.

METELERKAMP, Sanni. 1914. *Outa Karel's Stories: South African Folk-lore Tales.* London: Macmillan.

MPHAHLELE, Ezekiel. 1967. *Mrs Plum: In Corner B.* Nairobi: East African Publishing House.

NDEBELE, Njabulo S. 1983. *Fools and Other Stories*. Johannesburg: Ravan.

NOYES, Herbert. 1910. *Jan of the Thirstland: Being for the Most Part Reflections of the Vrouw van Renan of Renanshoek*. Durban: Robinson.

PARSONS, Anthony. 1932. *Bush Gypsies*. London: Grayson & Grayson.

PEREIRA, Ernest, & Michael CHAPMAN, ed. 1989. *African Poems of Thomas Pringle*. Durban: Killie Campbell African Library; Pietermaritzburg: Natal UP.

PLAATJE, Sol T. 1978. *Mhudi* (1930). London: Heinemann.

POE, Edgar Allan. 1953. "The Tell-Tale Heart" (1845), in Poe, *Tales of Mystery and Imagination* (London: Oxford UP): 336–42.

PRANCE, C.R. 1937. *Tante Rebella's Saga: A Backvelder's Scrap-book*. London: Witherby.

RASPE, R.E. 1901. *The Surprising Travels and Adventures of Baron Munchausen* (1785). London: Wells, Gardner, Darton.

SCHREINER, Olive. 1891. *Dreams*. London: T. Fisher Unwin.

——. 1893. *Dream Life and Real Life*. London: T. Fisher Unwin.

SCULLY, W.C. 1895. *Kafir Stories*. London: T. Fisher Unwin.

——. 1897. *The White Hecatomb and Other Stories*. London: Methuen.

——. 1907. *By Veldt and Kopje*. London: T. Fisher Unwin.

——. 1913. *Further Reminiscences of a South African Pioneer*. London: T. Fisher Unwin.

——. 1984. *Transkei Stories*, ed. Jean Marquard. Cape Town: Philip.

SIBSON, Francis. 1926. *A Breeze from the Backveld*. London: Noel Douglas.

SLATER, Francis Carey. 1908. *The Sunburnt South*. London: Digby, Long.

——. 1925. *The Shining River*. London: Longmans, Green.

——. 1931. *The Secret Veld*. London: Nash & Grayson.

SMITH, Pauline. 1925. *The Little Karoo*. London: Jonathan Cape.

——. 1926. *The Beadle*. London: Jonathan Cape.

——. 1935. *Platkops Children*. London: Jonathan Cape.

——. 1993. *Horse Thieves; The Cart: The Unknown Pauline Smith*, ed. Ernest Pereira (Pietermaritzburg: U of Natal P): 24–28; 31–41.

TOWNSHEND, Philip. 1928. *Tales from Ficksrand and Other Places*. Bloemfontein: A.C. White.

VAN DEN HEEVER, Toon. 1948. *Gerwe uit die Erfpag van Skoppensboer*. Johannesburg: Afrikaanse Pers Boekhandel.

VAN PLAAKS, H. [C.A. Fairbridge]. 1848. "Dirk van Splinter, a Legend of the Devil's Peak," *The Cape of Good Hope Literary Magazine* 2.5: 65–79.

VLADISLAVIC, Ivan. 1989. *Missing Persons: Stories*. Cape Town: Philip.

WARD, Harriet. 1850. "Emma, the Sailor Girl," *Bentley's Miscellany* 28 (October): 384–92.

WERNER, Alice. 1932. *African Stories*. London: Watts.

WESTRUP, William. 1937. *Old McBein*. London: Michael Joseph.

Secondary Sources

ABRAHAMS, Lionel. 1971. Compiler's Foreword to *Jurie Steyn's Post Office*, by Herman Charles Bosman. Cape Town: Human & Rousseau.

——. 1980. Introduction to *Dead End Road*, by Aegidius Jean Blignaut. Johannesburg: Ad. Donker.

——. 1988. Foreword to Herman Charles Bosman, *The Collected Works*. Johannesburg: Southern.

AMIS, Kingsley. 1975. *Rudyard Kipling and His World*. London: Thames & Hudson.

ANON. 1907. Review of *The Vrouw Grobelaar's Leading Cases*, *African Monthly* 1.4: 517.

BAKHTIN, Mikhail. 1984. *Problems of Dostoevsky's Poetics* (1929), ed. & tr. Caryl Emerson. Minneapolis: U of Minnesota P.

BANFIELD, Anne. 1982. *Unspeakable Sentences: Narration and Representation in the Language of Fiction*. London: Routledge & Kegan Paul.

BENJAMIN, Walter. 1973. "The Storyteller: Reflections on the Works of Nikolai Leskov" (1936), in *Illuminations*, tr. Harry Zohn, ed. Hannah Arendt (tr. 1969; Glasgow: Collins/Fontana): 83–109.

BENNETT, Tony. 1979. *Formalism and Marxism*. London: Methuen.

BLIGNAUT, Aegidius Jean. 1981. *My Friend Herman Charles Bosman*. Johannesburg: Perskor.

BOSMAN, Herman Charles. 1925. "The Canterbury Tales," *Uniwersiteit van die Witwatersrand Studenteblad* (March): 22.

——. 1936. "The Art of W.W. Jacobs," *South African Opinion* (12 December): 12–15.

——. 1971a. "Stephen Leacock" (1944), in *A Cask of Jerepigo* (Cape Town: Human & Rousseau): 244–45.

——. 1971b. "Humour and Wit" (1946), in *A Cask of Jerepigo* (Cape Town: Human & Rousseau): 239–43.

——. 1980. "Edgar Allan Poe" (1948), *English in Africa* 7.2: 34–36.

——. 1986a. "Aspects of South African Literature" (1948), in *Herman Charles Bosman*, ed. Stephen Gray (Johannesburg: McGraw–Hill): 93–96.

——. 1986b. "The South African Short Story Writer" (1948), in *Herman Charles Bosman*, ed. Stephen Gray (Johannesburg: McGraw–Hill): 96–99.

BOSMAN, H.C., & C. BREDELL, ed. 1952. *Veld-trails and Pavements: An Anthology of South African Short Stories* (1949). Johannesburg: A.P.B.

CONSTANCE, Geraldine. 1992. "From 'Manichean Allegory' to the Beginnings of Enlightenment: A Study of the Three 'South African' Novels of Perceval Gibbon" (M.A. thesis, University of Natal).

CORNWELL, Gareth. 1983. "FitzPatrick's *The Outspan*: Deconstructing the Fiction of Race," *English in Africa* 10.1: 15–28.

COUZENS, Tim. 1978. Introduction to *Mhudi*, by Sol T. Plaatje. London: Heinemann.

DICKSON, Vivienne Mawson. 1975. "The Fiction of Herman Charles Bosman: A Critical Examination" (PhD dissertation, University of Texas at Austin).

DOYLE, John Robert. 1971. *Francis Carey Slater*. TWAS. New York: Twayne.

EICHENBAUM, Boris. 1994. "O. Henry and the Theory of the Short Story" (1926), in *The New Short Story Theories*, ed. Charles E. May (Athens: Ohio UP): 86–91.

GOLDBLATT, David. 1986. "Bosman's Bosveld Revisited" (1965), in *Herman Charles Bosman*, ed. Stephen Gray (Johannesburg: McGraw–Hill): 53–54.

GRAY, Stephen. 1976. *Sources of the First Black South African Novel in English*. Pasadena: California Institute of Technology.

——. 1977. "Bosman's Marico Allegory: A Study in Topicality," *English Studies in Africa* 20.2: 79–94.

——. 1979. *Southern African Literature: An Introduction*. Cape Town: David Philip.

——. ed. 1980. Introduction to *Selected Stories*, by Herman Charles Bosman. Cape Town: Human & Rousseau.

——. 1985. "Third World Meets First World: The Theme of 'Jim comes to Jo'burg' in South African English Fiction," *Kunapipi* 7.1: 61–80.

——. ed. 1986. Chronology, introduction and bibliography, *Herman Charles Bosman*. Johannesburg: McGraw–Hill.

HEAD, Bessie. 1981. Interview with Anne Bolsover, *Arts and Africa*; BBC World Service (17 June), Transcript 392G: 1–2.

——. 1989. Interview (1983) with Michelle Adler et al., *Between the Lines: Interviews with Bessie Head, Sheila Roberts, Ellen Kuzwayo, Miriam Tlali*. Grahamstown: National English Literary Museum, 5–30.

JORDAN, Z. Pallo. 1973. Foreword to *Tales from Southern Africa*, by A.C. Jordan (Berkeley: U of California P.): ix–xxiii.

LANG, Andrew. 1971. "Mr Kipling's Stories" (1891), in *Kipling: The Critical Heritage*, ed. Roger Lancelyn Green (London: Routledge & Kegan Paul): 70–75.

MACHEREY, Pierre. 1978. *A Theory of Literary Production* (1966), tr. Geoffrey Wall. London: Routledge.

MACKENZIE, Craig. 1989a. "Short Stories in the Making: The Case of Bessie Head," *English in Africa* 16.1: 17–28.

——. 1989b. *Bessie Head: An Introduction*. Grahamstown: National English Literary Museum.

MANNES–ABBOTT, Guy. 1991. "No Return," *New Statesman and Society* (1 February): 36.

MARQUARD, Jean. 1978. "Introduction" to *A Century of South African Short Stories* (Johannesburg: Ad. Donker): 11–40.

——. 1978–79. "Bessie Head: Exile and Community in Southern Africa," *London Magazine* 18.9–10: 48–61.

——. 1984a. "A Neglected Pioneer in South African Literature: W.C. Scully" (PhD dissertation, University of Witwatersrand).

——. 1984b. Introduction to *Transkei Stories*, by W.C. Scully (Cape Town: David Philip): i–xxvi.

MAUGHAN BROWN, David. 1984. "On the Reading of Readings of Texts," *Social Dynamics* 10.1: 26–37.

NATHAN, Manfred. 1925. *South African Literature: A General Survey*. Cape Town: Juta.

NDEBELE, Njabulo S. 1984. "Turkish Tales, and Some Thoughts on South African Fiction," *Staffrider* 6.1: 24–25, 42–48.

ONG, Walter J. 1982. *Orality and Literacy: The Technologizing of the Word*. London: Methuen.

PEREIRA, Ernest. 1986a. "Short Stories," in *Companion to South African English Literature*, comp. David Adey et al. (Johannesburg: Ad. Donker): 181–82.

——. 1986b. "Tall Tellers of Tales: Some Fictional Narrators and their Function in the South African Short Story in English," in *Herman Charles Bosman*, ed. Stephen Gray (Johannesburg: McGraw–Hill): 103–15.

RANDALL, Peter. 1987. "Foreword" to *The Outspan: Tales of South Africa*, by J. Percy FitzPatrick. Johannesburg: Lowry.

ROSENBERG, Valerie. 1976. *Sunflower to the Sun*. Cape Town: Human & Rousseau.

——. ed. 1987. Introduction and notes to *Ramoutsa Road*, by Herman Charles Bosman. Johannesburg: Ad. Donker.

SACHS, Joseph. 1951. "The Short Stories of Gordimer, Lessing and Bosman," *Trek* 15.11: 15–16.

SCHEUB, Harold. 1973. "Introduction" to *Tales from Southern Africa*, by A.C. Jordan (Berkeley: U of California P.): 1–13.

——. 1981. "Pauline Smith and the Oral Tradition: The Koenraad Tales," *English in Africa* 8.1: 1–11. (Article followed by reprints of Smith's "Horse Thieves" and "The Cart": 13–23.)

SCHOPEN, Irmgard. 1986. "The Literary Criticism of Edgar Allan Poe and Herman Charles Bosman," in *Herman Charles Bosman*, ed. Stephen Gray (Johannesburg: McGraw–Hill): 115–25.

SIEBERT, Gillian. 1977. "'Stardust' and 'Red Earth': A Study of the Development of H.C. Bosman's Short Stories in the Light of Prevalent Images" (MA thesis, Rand Afrikaans University).

——. 1986. "'A More Sophisticated Bosman': Review of *Jurie Steyn's Post Office* and *A Bekkersdal Marathon*" (1972), in *Herman Charles Bosman*, ed. Stephen Gray (Johannesburg: McGraw–Hill): 72–74.

SMITH, Malvern van Wyk. 1990. *Grounds of Contest: A Survey of South African English Literature*. Cape Town: Juta.

STONE, Wilfred, Nancy PACKER & Robert HOOPES. 1976. *The Short Story: An Introduction*. New York: McGraw–Hill.

TITLESTAD, Irmgard. 1987. "From Amontillado to *Jerepigo*: Herman Charles Bosman's Use of Edgar Allan Poe as a Source and Influence," (MA thesis, Rand Afrikaans University).

TRUMP, Martin. 1986. "The Short Fiction of Herman Charles Bosman," in *Herman Charles Bosman*, ed. Stephen Gray (Johannesburg: McGraw–Hill): 164–78.

VAIL, Leroy, & Landeg WHITE. 1991. *Power and the Praise Poem: Southern African Voices in History*. Charlottesville: UP of Virginia.

VAUGHAN, Michael. 1981a. "Literature and Politics: Currents in South African Writing in the Seventies" (unpublished seminar paper, 37pp.).

——. 1981b. "The Stories of Mtutuzeli Matshoba," *Staffrider* 4.3: 45–47.

——. 1988. "The Writer as Storyteller?" (seminar paper presented at the African Studies Institute, University of the Witwatersrand, 7 March, 29 pp.).

——. 1990. "Storytelling and Politics in Fiction," in *Rendering Things Visible*, ed. Martin Trump (Johannesburg: Ravan): 186–204.

WEBSTER, Mary Morison. 1973. "The Short Story," in *English and South Africa*, ed. A. Lennox-Short (Cape Town: NASOU): 74–78.

WILLIAMS, Jenny. 1991. "Decolonising the Mind: The Challenge of Mtutuzeli Matshoba's Texts" (MA thesis, University of Natal).

WYLIE, Dan. 1995. "Shaka and the Myths of Paradise," *English in Africa* 22.1: 19–47.

Index